W9-CUZ-716

DATE DUE

DEMCO 38-297

A "Capacity for Outrage"

Judge J. Skelly Wright

A "Capacity for Outrage"

The Judicial Odyssey
of J. Skelly Wright

ARTHUR SELWYN MILLER

Foreword by
Judge Frank M. Johnson, Jr.

Contributions in American Studies, Number 74

Greenwood Press
Westport, Connecticut • London, England

KF
373
.W73
M54
1984

Library of Congress Cataloging in Publication Data

Miller, Arthur Selwyn, 1917-
   A "capacity for outrage."

   (Contributions in American studies, ISSN 0084-9227 ;
no. 74)
   Bibliography: p.
   Includes index.
   1. Wright, J. Skelly. 2. Judges—United States—
Biography.   I. Title.   II. Series.
KF373.W73M54   1984   347.73'2034 [B]   83-22761
ISBN 0-313-23304-7 (lib. bdg.)   347.30714 [B]

Library of Congress Catalog Card Number: 83-22761
ISBN: 0-313-23304-7
ISSN: 0084-9227

First published in 1984

Greenwood Press
A division of Congressional Information Service, Inc.
88 Post Road West, Westport, Connecticut 06881

Printed in the United States of America

10 9 8 7 6 5 4 3 2 1

10162678

5. 1. 85 AC

Justice, and only justice, you shall follow.
—Deuteronomy 16:20

The chief end of the law is to respect the dignity of human life.
—J. Skelly Wright (1980)

The judiciary is different from the political process. It is in the nature of courts that they cannot close their doors to individuals seeking justice. . . . The judicial process forces a judge to take the short run into account. The consequences of his decision are thrust before his eyes, and so he must bend principles in order to produce a result he can live with.
—J. Skelly Wright (1973)

Contents

Foreword

JUDGE FRANK M. JOHNSON, JR.*

It is indeed a pleasure to have the opportunity to write about Skelly Wright as a person and as a judge to serve as a foreword to Professor Arthur Miller's biography of Judge Wright.

My first impressions of Skelly Wright were made in New Orleans during the May, 1956, Judicial Conference of the old Court of Appeals for the Fifth Circuit. I was a recently appointed district judge for the Middle District of Alabama, and at that time Skelly Wright had been a district judge for the Eastern District of Louisiana for almost seven years. Volume 223 of the *Federal Reporter, 2d Series*, had just been published, and Judge John R. Brown, later to serve as the Chief Judge of the Fifth Circuit and now in senior status, was, as I, attending his first circuit conference.

The second *Brown v. Board of Education* decision by the Supreme Court (1955) that placed the burden on federal district judges to implement the earlier *Brown* decision declaring that racial discrimination in public education is unconstitutional had just been decided. In retrospect, it is probably just as well that none of us members of the federal judiciary for the southern states had the prescience of the tremendous legal, social, and emotional problems with which we were to be confronted during the 1960s and early 1970s.

Now the circuit conferences for the Fifth Circuit are attended by several hundred judges, delegates, and guests. In some instances more than one hotel is required to house the attendees. In 1956 only circuit judges, district judges, and lawyer delegates attended—less than fifty in all. The conference was held in one of the Fifth Circuit courtrooms in New Orleans and there was more than ample space.

Skelly Wright was a program participant at this, my first, conference. He discussed some procedural problems encountered by a federal trial judge and his proposed solutions to those problems. I do not remember the details of the discussion made by this young 45-year-old, but experienced, federal

---

*Judge, United States Court of Appeals, Eleventh Judicial Circuit, Montgomery, Alabama.

trial judge, but I do have a vivid recollection of a technical mastery of the Federal Rules of Procedure. He talked, as I was later to learn was customary, with his reading glasses pushed up into his hair, and with no notes. While I was not aware of his keen analytical mind until our later assocation made it evident, I was immediately impressed with his dedication and sincerity—traits that his long judicial career have not dulled or tarnished.

Skelly Wright was not troubled with *Brown* as much as some district judges. He, along with Circuit Judge Richard T. Rives and District Judge Herbert Christenberry, successfully handled one of the hardest cases spawned by *Brown*—*Bush v. Orleans Parish School Board*. In doing so, the pattern was set for effective implementation of *Brown* in Louisiana.

As Professor Miller recounts in detail, after leaving the district court in 1962 Skelly Wright, as a Court of Appeals judge for the District of Columbia Circuit, has dealt with a full range of knotty constitutional and other public law problems. He has, furthermore, left his mark etched deeply and indelibly in our law of judicial review of administrative decisions. His basic and most consistent approach is that administrative discretion at all levels of government was created by law, and there is no reason why the law, through judicial review, should be unable to control it. Judge Wright's philosophy, sometimes written and sometimes unwritten, in his decisions that review the acts of our many governmental agencies is that, while deference is to be accorded to an agency's exercise of its discretionary authority, that deference will not justify a judicial stamp of approval on action outside the law. And the final determination as to what action is outside and is within the law is for the courts.

Skelly Wright's tenure as a federal judge—some of his critics say that he has been enclosed in an ivory tower—has spanned over a third of a century. During this time he has never for one moment lost sight of the fact that a judge's highest calling is to ensure in his every decision that the implementation and enforcement of the laws of this country must be to upgrade and civilize the manner in which these laws are enforced. He is one of our federal judges who has served and continues to serve as a beacon of hope and as a great source of law that protects individual rights and property. Skelly Wright has contributed enormously to making it possible for the people of America to have faith in their courts and in their laws. While many lay citizens do not understand intricate, complicated jurisdictional problems or technical legal procedures, they, because of the Skelly Wrights on our courts, repose with confident security, with a knowledge that under the laws of this country there is a limit that oppression cannot transgress, that no governmental entity or individual can punish them without being reviewed by a judgment of a duly constituted court impartially applying the laws of our land. They can also repose in confidence with the belief that for any wrong there is a legal remedy under the Constitution and laws of the United States, guaranteed by the judges who sit upon the courts of the United States. Yet, after serving over 30 years as a member of the federal judiciary, the last 21 on one of the highest courts of the land, Skelly Wright has retained his healthy perspective. He realizes that federal judges will be appointed and that they will someday pass away. One generation rapidly succeeds another, but, whoever comes and whoever goes, the law of the United States remains supreme. He has greatly contributed to its strength and tradition.

Judge Wright will long be recognized as the role model of how members of our judiciary can and should speak truth to power, to require disinterested fairness in the face of hysteria and to insist on equality when others demand expediency. While Skelly Wright's receding hairline will not now accommodate those reading glasses, his enthusiasm, dedication, and technical mastery of the law have not dimmed or diminished one whit. He will justly be remembered in this country's judicial history as the epitome of what a good judge should be.

Skelly Wright uses as his pole star, and often quotes, these stirring words from the Supreme Court's opinion in *West Virginia Board of Education v. Barnette* (1943):

The very purpose of a Bill of Rights was to withdraw certain subjects from the vicissitudes of political controversy, to place them beyond the reach of majorities and officials and to establish them as legal principles to be applied by the courts. One's right to life, liberty, and property, to free speech, a free press, freedom of worship and assembly and other fundamental rights may not be submitted to vote; they depend on the outcome of no elections.

I do not know if he has done so consciously but I do know that, in his judicial performance, he has consistently lived by Abraham Lincoln's creed: "I do the very best I know how; the very best I can; and I mean to keep doing so until the end. If the end brings me out all right, what is said against me won't amount to anything. If the end brings me out wrong, ten angels swearing I was right would make no difference." Our nation is far richer for having had Skelly Wright as a federal judge for well over 30 years.

Preface

This book is a personalized view of the judicial career of Judge J. Skelly Wright. It is not an orthodox biography. Rather, it attempts to place the career of Judge Wright in the context of the development of law, principally constitutional law, during the past three to four decades. Most chapters deal with substantive areas of law. Each begins with an explication of the specific larger problem and then goes on to evaluate how Wright has dealt with it. An opening chapter sets forth the approach I took in writing the book; and the final chapter evaluates Judge Wright's career in general terms.

I emphasize that this volume is in no way an authorized biography. Judge Wright was quite specific about that, writing to me in July, 1981: "As you apparently have perceived, I would not be a participant in an 'authorized' biography." He knew that it was being written and, with characteristic courtesy, made himself available for lengthy interviews. I have quoted liberally, with his permission, from these interviews. The biography is a companion volume to a collection of some of the more important of his nonjudicial writings, published simultaneously under the title *On Courts and Democracy: Selected Nonjudicial Writings of J. Skelly Wright.*

This, then, is a book that discusses the career of Judge Wright as I have seen him, both from afar (as when his name first came to my attention in the 1950s) and from close at hand (as when I first made his acquaintance in Washington, D.C., in the 1960s). Throughout the text may be found reactions that I—a professor of constitutional law—have to what Wright has wrought. Some are critical but the overall evaluation is favorable. On beginning the book, I told him that I was not going to paint a portrait of "Saint Skelly," nor was I undertaking a hatchet job. He (and I) would have it no other way.

Furthermore, this is more an impressionistic view of Judge Wright's career than an exhaustive delineation of everything he has done on the bench. Wright is at once a complex personality and an almost transparently open individual. I have not tried to write a psychobiography. My knowledge about him comes from reading his judicial and nonjudicial writings and from long conversations with him. My respect for him is deep and abiding. He has been able to overcome an indifferent education and a family background that was strictly non-Establishment; and through hard work and persistence, he has become one of the shining stars of the federal judiciary. Wright, in my judgment, should have been named to the Supreme Court by President John F. Kennedy. Kennedy instead chose Byron White (who is still on the Court) and Arthur Goldberg (who served only a brief period). Neither one has that special quality that characterizes J. Skelly Wright. Had Wright been nominated to the seat that went to Goldberg, he would still be on the Supreme Court—and that Court would show a much different face today. The country is the poorer for Kennedy not naming him. Not that Judge Wright has not been able, as an appeals judge on what at times is called an "inferior"—in the sense of lower—court, to make his weight felt. He has indeed been influential. It probably is accurate to maintain that he is the best known of all federal judges, except, of course, those on the Supreme Court.

***

This book could not have been written without the help of several people. I single out some for special mention: Judge Wright himself, of course, and his secretary, Martha Scallon. Professor Stephen Halpern of the State University of New York at Buffalo was of great help through his careful reading of several chapters. Professor Gerald Caplan of the National Law Center at George Washington University provided crucial insights into criminal law matters that are the subject of Chapter 8. Jeffrey Bowman not only read the entire manuscript but provided me with indispensable research assistance. To all, I am sincerely grateful. My gratitude goes particularly to my wife, Dagmar, who caught many of my egregious errors in syntax and composition, and who also created an environment in which the work could proceed with minimum interruption. Whatever errors of omission or commission that remain in the biography are entirely my responsibility.

—Arthur Selwyn Miller

Key West, Florida
August 1983

A "Capacity for Outrage"

1

Introduction: Setting the Pattern

I try to do what's right.

—J. Skelly Wright (1983)[1]

I

I declare an interest.

I have known, and liked, Judge Skelly Wright for many years. He is a judge who is "more than usually courageous and independent of immediate public opinion, and one with a stronger than usual sense of substance over form."[2] In a profession little known for either courage or independence and among several hundred judges who, in general, tend to be fearful of innovation, Wright is one of a handful who have dared to stand tall in the furtherance of decency and human dignity. Not that he employs those terms in his judicial opinions; his is the language of the legal craftsman. Save for a tendency to be overly lengthy and too heavily footnoted, his opinions differ little in *appearance* from those of other judges. Where he diverges, at times quite widely, is in the *results* reached and in the reasons employed to explain those results. Wright's passion for human dignity is to be derived from *what* he decides more than how he explains his decisions. One may disagree, as many do, with some of those results, but no one can question that they were carefully arrived at and explained in the form and language with which lawyers are familiar. Judge Wright believes in *justice*—that overworked and seldom defined concept—although it is obvious that his conception of what justice requires in particular circumstances differs from that of many of his judicial colleagues as well as many in the professoriate. That makes him perhaps the quintessential "pragmatic instrumentalist" of the modern era.

This book is an intellectual biography of James Skelly Wright, as seen through his work as a federal judge—on the District Court in New Orleans and the Court of Appeals in Washington, D.C.—and his nonjudicial writings. (An accompanying volume collects some of the more important of these articles.)[3] His 20-plus years tenure on "the second most important court in the nation"[4] is reason enough for a biography. Wright has been involved in most, perhaps all, of the important constitutional issues of the day. Add his several stormy years in New Orleans, when he had the difficult and path-breaking task of integrating public schools in a state that had historically kept black Americans in a rigid caste system, and there is more reason for such a study. President John F. Kennedy once called him "one of the great judges of America"—and that he has been and still is. Even though he is in his seventies, and thus eligible to take senior status, he still retains his position as a full-time judge. More, Chief Justice Warren Burger has named him to be Chief Judge of the Emergency Court of Appeals. Wright still works a full day, keeping three law clerks and a secretary busy.

This volume begins, not with Skelly Wright's decisions as a judge, but with him in his first case as a lawyer before the Supreme Court. That case, *Louisiana ex rel. Francis v. Resweber* (1947),[5] has been consigned for some inexplicable reason to the dustbin of history—wrongfully so, for its facts pose many of the truly significant questions about the role of judges in a society that trumpets it is democratic. The *Francis* case is the focus of Chapter 2; it is used as a means of discussing Judge Wright's judicial philosophy and comparing it to Justices of the Supreme Court (principally Felix Frankfurter).

Each subsequent chapter develops a different subject matter, with a case or cases in which Wright has participated being used to illustrate larger points. Of necessity, the exposition often is comparative. How does Judge Wright differ from other judges and the orthodox thinking about not only law, but also the nature or type of society that law helps to regulate? Is it possible to evaluate the impact his rulings have had, both on the development of law and on society? Those questions pose deeper ones. What is the role of law, however and by whomever promulgated, in effecting social change? Are there limits to effective legal (judicial) action? Not that Wright has been overtly concerned with these profound and controversial questions. His is not a philosophic mind; rather, it is one of "pragmatic idealism." He is far more interested in doing "what's right" in individual cases than in larger jurisprudential problems. Wright has an abiding sense of injustice. He knows intuitively the difference between right and wrong and seeks within the constraints of a judge on a lower federal court (who must deal with others on a multimember tribunal) to correct those wrongs. His perception of the rightness of societal or governmental decisions may not always be correct (by whatever hierarchy of values one might posit); but as his colleague Judge David Bazelon has said, central to his decisions is "compassion and a sensitivity to the plight of the oppressed."[6]

Judge Wright is considered to be the foremost judicial "activist" of modern times—damned by those who dislike his decisions, criticized by others who may approve of those results but dislike his activism, derided by some who see him as an unguided judicial missile deciding by fiat rather than law, but applauded by those who salute his basic honesty, decency, and integrity. Activism is the propensity of judges to substitute their views, often on constitutional questions, for those of legislative and executive officers (state and federal). Wright, in fact, is less activist than his critics assert—and perhaps even less than he himself believes—and that is so even though he has not hesitated to create law when he thought the circumstances warranted it. Indeed, as Judge Abraham D. Sofaer (one of his former law clerks) said of him, he has a "capacity for outrage."[7] He has seen some of the great injustices of his time and has striven, within the law, to rectify them. He knows full well that law is fluid, that judges have choices to make, and that in constitutional (and probably all) matters there is always room for law-creation. Quite forthrightly, he freely states: "If I want to do something, I can find a way to do it."[8] (Other judges, and many in the professoriate, are not so candid.) The essential point, nonetheless, is that Wright has always operated *as a lawyer*. As such, it is fair to say that he exemplifies both the merits and the shortcomings of the legal profession,.

In no way is this an authorized biography. Judge Wright knew that it was being written and made himself available for interviews. In addition, his collected papers, particularly those from his tenure as a district judge in New Orleans, were perused. No part of this book was ever shown to him, let alone reviewed by him, before publication. Not once did he suggest what should be written. If the overall product is favorable to Wright, as it is, that fact should be attributed not to any preconceived ideas on my part, but to an evaluation of a man's public life that is as objective as possible. Complete objectivity or impartiality is, of course, a chimera; nevertheless, I have tried to exercise what Justice Felix Frankfurter once called an "invincible disinterestedness"[9] in my appraisal of a man who fully deserved appointment to the Supreme Court of the United States.

Nor is this a psychobiography. Even so, it is impossible not to wonder why and how Skelly Wright came to some of his views. How much, for example, did his participation in *Willie Francis's Case* (see Chapter 2) have on his sense of compassion and sensitivity for the oppressed and disadvantaged? Almost 40 years after Francis was executed, Wright obviously is still bothered about the Supreme Court's decision as well as his own performance as Francis's lawyer.

The principal goal was to set Skelly Wright's judicial career into the larger context of the movements in law and the judicial process of the past 40 years—a period of almost unparalleled fecundity in constitutional law, a period of enormously rapid social change. He emerges as one of a very few whose head may be seen rising above the ruck of the federal judiciary. Professor Philip Kurland, no admirer of Judge Wright, once observed that, "for the most part, judges are narrow-minded lawyers with little background for making social judgments."[10] That is generally accurate. The point about Wright, however, is that he has been able to transcend his background and thus has been able to make significant social judgments, rulings that have the effect of being a "conscience for a sovereign people."[11]

More than one person, on learning this book was being written, asked: "Why write a biography of Skelly Wright?" The answer is easy: He is one of the most important judges of this century. Americans, as Abraham Lincoln once observed, have a "reverence for law"—a mental attitude that is transferred in some way to lawyers when they become judges. The United States is the most legalistic of all nations, which means that judges occupy a special place in society. By any criterion, furthermore, Wright has been as controversial as any modern judge, and much more so than most. He has been the target of severe criticism and ridicule; at the same time, he has the respect and admiration of many. A fair reading of the pages that follow surely will demonstrate to any reasonable-minded person that Skelly Wright deserves a biography that will bring him and his career to the attention of an audience larger than professional lawyers. In some respects, he exemplifies a latter-day Horatio Alger hero—a man who with intelligence, hard work, and integrity, coupled with the luck to know the right people at the right time, has been catapulted from an obscure family in Louisiana to the pinnacle of his profession.

Americans today are engaged in a great debate over the nature of the "good" society. Not since 55 men sat in Philadelphia in the hot summer of 1787, supposedly merely to revise the Articles of Confederation (instead they produced the Constitution), has there been such widespread contention over what American government should do and how it should be structured. (The Civil War is an exception to that generalization; it was a war that settled in blood what law could not—that the United States is truly a united state, a union not a confederacy.) The Constitution—the document of 1787 and its 26 amendments—still endures; it is the oldest written fundamental law in the world. (In fact, the American Constitution is as much—and probably more—unwritten as it is written.) Judges, despite the contrary myth that they are, or should be, "interpreters" and not "makers" of law (and, thus, of changing the Constitution), are deeply immersed in the debate over the direction of American society. This has long been known, albeit stoutly resisted at times. A century and a half ago, Alexis de Tocqueville wrote in his classic *Democracy in America* that most political questions in the United States ended up before courts, having been judicialized, and thus left to lawyer-judges to decide. Many, though not all, of those questions still do. That means that as officers of a theoretically independent but actually political branch of government, judges cannot escape the task of contributing to the debate. Increasing numbers of Americans, to the dismay of some (including Chief Justice Warren Burger), look to courts for surcease from ills, actual or supposed, that the political order cannot or will not remedy. Whether judges deal with the enduring questions of providing current meaning to ancient constitutional precepts or with the ostensibly more mundane issues of private law (such as contracts and torts and property) or with federal or state statutes, they are unavoidably part of the national policy-making process. Put perhaps too bluntly, but not inaccurately, they are political officers in black robes—part of the governing coalition of the nation.

Judge Wright once wrote of the Supreme Court that the ultimate test of the Justices' work (and thus of his, since his court deals with the same questions as does the Supreme Court) should be "goodness"[12]—which he did not define. (Asked what he meant by the term, he replied: I meant it in its "philosophical sense."[13]) In asserting that goodness is the goal of judicial action, he strayed far from the public position of other judges who maintain that their task is, as Justice Oliver Wendell Holmes once said, "to play the game according to the rules."[14] What those "rules" were Holmes did not say. Indeed, there is no generally accepted model of how judges should operate, the "rules" being much more fluid than Holmes intimated. Moreover, appellate judges, such as Skelly Wright and Supreme Court Justices, routinely are confronted with the Principle of Doctrinal Polarity—the idea that the litigants, employing the adversary process, present to judges two inconsistent rules of law of approximately equal persuasiveness. Thus it is accurate to say that Holmes's "rules" are uncertain on two scores: on how judges should operate, and on the doctrines or rules that lawyers bring to them. That means that *the* truly important question to ask about judicial decisions is: *Cui bono*? Who in fact benefits from them? It is true that Judge Wright has consistently asked, tacitly or overtly, that question in the more than 1,000 decisions he has made.

Prescription of what judges should do is, of course, quite different from *description*. That Judge Wright adheres to a personal conception of justice already has been suggested. Nowhere, however, has he attempted any systematic or comprehensive definition of the word. If for no other reason than that it is familiar, justice is a more useful term to employ than goodness; and insofar as the written record permits, what follows shows what Wright means by the term. In so doing, the idea of *social justice* will be used as a concept that is employed to assess the distribution in a society of benefits that come from that society's major institutions. Social justice concerns such matters as wealth distribution, protection of personal rights through the judicial process, and allocation of benefits. Social justice, whether realized or not, is the very stuff that judges routinely confront and what the Constitution is all about—the Constitution, that is, in its express provisions and silences, and in its informal and operative (or living) sense. In what ensues, a distinction will be made between the *formal* and the *operative* Constitutions, drawing upon Woodrow Wilson's observation that the Constitution in operation "is manifestly a very different thing from the Constitution of the books."[15]

Conceptual analysis alone is inadequate to understand the concept of social justice. Reference must perforce be made to the relevant history and sociology and political economy of the United States. Social justice is not a mere legal concept; it concerns human affairs, of which law is only one relatively small part. But being small does not mean that it is insignificant. Quite the contrary. To give the concept greater specificity, Dr. David Miller's "three conflicting principles of justice" are relevant: "to each according to his *rights*; to each according to his *deserts*; to each according to his *needs*."[16] Dovetailing that classification to "rights" and "needs," a representative sampling of J. Skelly Wright's published opinions and articles reveals that his concern for human *needs* oft-times is at odds with what others, on and off the bench, view as *rights* justice. The "deserts" segment of Dr. Miller's social justice triad has been dropped because in large part what a person *deserves* can be subsumed under the rubric of what that person *needs*.

It was, and is, Skelly Wright's fate to sit as a judge on important courts at a time when American society (indeed, global society) is rapidly changing, when well-nigh unparalleled strains were and are being leveled against constitutional mechanisms and institutions, and when the very notion of constitutionalism as it has been received and understood is under severe and sustained attack. How he dealt with social change in the context of a legal system that reflects society, but that most lawyers think is separate and apart from the warp and woof of society and, indeed, from the state itself, is a basic theme of this volume. Wright has a conception of the good society, but it is one that he seldom articulates—and never fully. One must search the interstices of his writings to discern the rudiments of a philosophy, and even then it remains a shore dimly seen. He is not an ideologue, unless one can say that his overriding concern for equality and human dignity make him one. As for his image of society, it seems to be a direct descendant of the Progressive Age in which he was born.

It is not possible to avoid making normative evaluations. Hence, although I have tried to be objective, conclusions about the usefulness or the validity of what Judge Wright has done have been drawn. There is a myth of neutrality in legal research and writing, just as there is in judging. As Professor Philip Rhinelander observed: "There is no such thing as totally unbiased knowing. . . . The ideal model of an empty mind passively contemplating pure data presented to pure awareness" must be rejected. Therefore, he went on, "we must direct our primary attention to the assumptions and patterns of analysis that we bring to all our acts of knowing and judging."[17] If that be so, as surely it is, then students of law and judging, as well as practitioners and those lawyers who become judges, should face and articulate their valuations. The remainder of this chapter outlines some of the "assumptions and patterns of analysis" brought to this study of the judicial odyssey of J. Skelly Wright.

II

All public officials in the Western world, including the United States, have had to deal in recent decades with situations far different from the previous 300 years. We seem to be approaching the end of an epoch of comparative ecological and economic abundance, comparative, that is, to Western Europe prior to the sixteenth century. Americans have always enjoyed being a "people of plenty." Humankind today is in the midst of what Arnold Toynbee called a "time of troubles"—a transition to what is still an unknown future. Familiar societal institutions are being transformed, some with bewildering rapidity. For example, representative democracy and its economic counterpart, private-enterprise capitalism, are under severe continuing strains. No one quite knows what will evolve; what is known is that social change, because of scientific and technological developments, will continue to be extremely rapid. These new facts in the American experience are not yet fully assimilated. Lawyers have been particularly slow in adapting to new conditions. Some political scientists and economists are better, but not much.

As a consequence it is becoming increasingly evident that time-honored institutions require re-examination to determine their usefulness and relevance to the modern age and the emergent future. Little is being done, however, although it is true that some private groups in the United States, notably the Committee on the Constitutional System, have begun thinking about the need for major institutional—that is, constitutional—change. What, if anything, will emerge from these efforts cannot be forecast with certainty. The efforts are significant, however, because thoughtful people, many of whom are former high governmental figures, perceive that something is awry in the constitutional order.

Constitutionalism in America has always been seen as normative. It is concerned with placement of legal limitations on government. People and the groups they formed were to be given maximum liberty to act, the theory (seldom articulated) being that through the operation of what Adam Smith called an "invisible hand" the common good would be realized. The rise of mass population, coupled with an insistent drive for egalitarianism by those who had been left behind in the race for material plenty, has created a new social milieu—precisely at the time when the seemingly inexhaustible resources available to Americans began to diminish. The time, accordingly, has come to determine whether the institutions wrought by the Founding Fathers in the constitutional convention of 1787 are sufficient to the needs of Americans today. Evidence is mounting that they are not.

Furthermore, we are beginning to perceive that a profound shift in the way that humans view the environment—a paradigm shift—is under way. This means that there are steadily increasing alterations in the perceptions and values that mirror a particular vision of reality. The Constitution was drafted at the height of the Age of the Enlightenment, reflecting the values of John Locke and Adam Smith and the cosmology of Isaac Newton and René Descartes. Locke, the "father" of the Constitution, saw nature as basically benevolent, with the need being to create governmental institutions that would protect and preserve property. Behind Locke was the Newtonian-Cartesian paradigm, which was essentially mechanistic. Principles of balance—the universe was likened to a great clock with interacting parts—were considered to rule. Those principles are reflected in the Constitution's separation of powers in the national government and in the principle of federalism—dividing the powers of governance between the states and the general government. Today, perceptive observers increasingly recognize that those principles of balance must give way to a conception of reality as a process. The cues came first from Charles Darwin and then from Albert Einstein. The Constitution today is best seen as a flow of decisions reflective of the differing circumstances that each generation of Americans face. The meaning is clear: Each generation of Americans must, of necessity, write its own fundamental law as new exigencies confront them that could not have been remotely in the minds of the men who drafted the Constitution of 1787.

We live today, not in a static society as the Framers may have assumed, but in one that is in a state of permanent revolution. The term "revolution" is employed not in the sense of revolt but to characterize changes in the social structure that have become so evident in the past 100 years. If there is one constant in the modern age, it is rapid and continuing social change. Nothing like it was ever experienced before. The modern age is truly unique, mainly because of the impacts of unceasing technological change. Other factors that are new to Americans include the Cold War, as well as a series of "brushfire wars," such as in Korea and Vietnam; the disappearance of many of the fabulous resources of the nation; the immersion of the United States in world affairs in the "global village" of a planet that is shrinking because of advances in communications and transportation; the slowing down of economic growth (with the possible creation of a "steady state" economy); and the loss of beliefs in the ideas of progress and the perfectability of man in this world. Immense strains are, as a consequence, being leveled against familiar institutions. Change, being rampant in society, ultimately means change in politics and economics—in, that is, the political economy of the United States.

Judge Skelly Wright was born at a time when the ancient wisdom—basically, the ideas of the Enlightenment—was still current. His career illustrates how he has tried to incorporate those ideas into relevant legal doctrine. Whether he is cognizant of the paradigm shift that is now in full swing is problematic at best; certainly, he is not so publicly. This does not mean that he should be faulted. Few judges or legal scholars have more than a fleeting knowledge of a turning point in human history. Subconsciously, however, Judge Wright may intuit that mankind is in the midst of a great transformation. In Chapter 2, I argue that he reveals that recognition by adhering, albeit without explicating it, to a basic political principle in many of his decisions—the Principle of Reason-Directed Societal Self-Interest. That principle, I also argue, helps to lend legitimacy to judicial review in a polity that calls itself democratic. Neither law nor legal institutions exist in a social vacuum. They are significant aspects of human endeavor, serving definable purposes and the causes of definable people. Skelly Wright realizes, however incompletely, that law must keep up with societal changes. He knows also that there must be a concern for the human—the humane—element in law if society is to remain a cohesive whole. Judges, of course, make law (rather than merely "interpreting" existing laws). The law that Judge Wright makes frequently helps individual members of society who have not been favored by material plenty.

III

After more than 200 years as a nation-state, with a judiciary that ever increasingly is important in the governing process, there is no settled, widely accepted conception in the United States of how judges *should* operate. Furthermore, because of the pervasive secrecy within the courts, accompanied by a myth structure that erects an impossible standard for judges to attain plus a general failure of the professoriate to analyze in depth what actually goes on in courts, there is little actual knowledge about how judges *do* operate. In briefest terms, all judges are "result-oriented." (So, too, are all commentators on the judiciary.) Apparently one of Justice Felix Frankfurter's neologisms, result-orientation is a term of opprobrium. Frankfurter and his acolytes used it to castigate those Frankfurter considered to be his enemies on the Supreme Court, particularly Chief Justice Earl Warren and Justices Hugo Black and William Douglas. No one quite knows what the term means; it has never been precisely defined. As nearly as can be learned from its frequent use by legal writers, the term refers to judges (and commentators) who believe that attention should be paid to the consequences of judicial decisions, to who the litigants are, and making (or, in the case of commentators, approving) decisions in accordance with the personal characteristics of the litigants—their ethnicity, their poverty, their general status in society. In other words, rather than looking only *retrospectively* to determine what "the law" is (or the rules are) and applying that discovery in a particular case, judges look *prospectively* as well and seek to alter or solidify someone's (at times, some group's) position vis-à-vis government or other persons and groups. Said another way, judges are instrumental in their decision making—or, in Professor Robert Samuel Summers's terminology, they are "pragmatic instrumentalists."[18]

The basic difference between judges (and between commentators) is important on the level of operational reality: They differ in their philosophies, in their personal predilections. In some large, albeit immeasurable, part those differences may well consist of different views of the importance of egalitarianism in American society. The Frankfurterites—the late Professor Alexander Bickel is the leading exemplar—are essentially neo-Burkeans, followers of Edmund Burke, and thus anti-egalitarian. To them, the principle of equality is strictly limited. But to Judge Wright (and certainly to Chief Justice Warren and his Court) equality or egalitarianism was the tune to which they marched for at least three decades.[19]

No useful purpose is served by categorizing judges as "liberal" or "conservative." People of lesser minds apparently cannot think unless they succeed in pinning some shorthand label upon a person and then analyzing what that person says or does in accordance with the label. Human behavior is too complex to be able to label anyone with a single term. The important question to ask about judges, and others, is *which* values do these persons adhere to, values that ineluctably color the positions they take. Judges, especially those on appellate courts, have choices to make. They have discretion in determining and applying the law. The adversary system of litigation cannot, in the final analysis, be otherwise justified. Thus it is that judges, rather than applying *the law*, make choices between *laws*. In all litigation before appellate courts, and probably elsewhere as well, the Principle of Doctrinal Polarity operates. Each litigant, through his attorney, can and does marshal arguments of at least colorable persuasiveness and often of approximately equal merit. Judges must, and do, choose from between these principles; and in so doing, make law. That is always true of the Supreme Court; but is also true of other courts, including Judge Wright's. The choices made depend ultimately upon the major premises a judge brings to the case at bar. Sometimes those premises are articulated; but quite often they are not. Theodore Roosevelt said it well: "The decisions of the courts on economic and social questions depend on their economic and social philosophies."[20]

The question of judicial method and personal values of judges will be a major concern of this volume. The pretense is that judges' opinions should be "reasoned" or "principled"—by which it is apparently meant that they should be logical derivations from pre-existing rules, without regard to who the litigants are or, of more importance, the consequences (the social impacts) of judicial decisions. Thus it is that "a court of law which achieves a desirable result by an inexact use of legal conceptions arouses more criticism from legal scholars than one which achieves an undesirable result in a learned way.''[21] Felicity of language and erudite reasoning, accordingly, become substitutes for just results. That position is intellectually untenable. The values furthered by litigation, including the identity of who wins and loses, are far more important. Judge Wright so believes.

In Chapter 2, Judge Wright's work as an advocate before the Supreme Court will be assessed. His views will be juxtaposed against those of Justice Frankfurter. To anticipate: they have different ideas about judicial propriety. Not that Frankfurter was not result-oriented; or course he was. Rather, it was that his values—the values he chose to further in deciding cases—differ markedly from those of Skelly Wright. Wright was the lawyer (in his first case before the Supreme Court) who lost *Willie Francis's Case*—the case of the bungled execution—because Frankfurter chose to exalt a political theory of federalism over the Constitution's command of according everyone ''due process of law.'' The present point, however, is that it is the consequences, the results of judicial decisions and other political decisions, that are of ultimate importance. No one can escape the intellectual trap of subjectivity. That is expected and tolerated in legislators and presidents; but judges are supposed to be immune from the frailties of the human mind. That they are not immune should be obvious. The odd fact is, that even though this might be admitted, many observers still insist that judges act in accord with the ideal model. They demand the impossible, often on the theory that people generally would lose their reverence for the law and for judges were the always-present subjective element of judging to be widely admitted.

IV

Who, then, is James Skelly Wright?

Two basic points provide initial insight. First, as suggested above, Wright was born into and thus is a product of the prevailing mind-set of the Progressive Age. It was a time when people could still believe in the American Dream, a time when the idea of progress was in full bloom, a time, that is, when a combination of work and integrity coupled with a deep-seated belief that humans, through their own efforts, could create a better life for themselves and their posterity. It was, in sum, a time before the loss of American innocence. Out of that background has come Wright's sense of compassion and a continuing feeling for the plight of the disadvantaged. The pole star of his personal belief system is a commitment to human equality. (In that, one might note, he follows the precepts of the Declaration of Independence rather than those of the Constitution as drafted in 1787—which made no reference to equality or equal protection of the laws.) Second, Skelly Wright's judicial career coincides almost exactly with the civil rights/civil liberties revolution brought about by the Supreme Court headed by Chief Justice Earl Warren. Wright's professional activities are best understood as an extension of and embellishment upon principles initially promulgated by the Warren Court. This point, which will become clearer in the chapter dealing with Judge Wright and the crime problem, is fundamental to an appreciation and understanding of Skelly Wright as judge. Before he became a federal judge in 1949, there was little in his background or activities that would have led anyone to believe that he would embark upon a stormy and controversial tenure on the bench. Indeed, had his rulings been predictable, he would never have been appointed either as a district judge or an appeals judge. His representations of Willie Francis (see Chapter 2) and of Ann Johnson (see Chapter 8) before the Supreme Court highlighted an otherwise uneventful career. The man who was to be denounced in Louisiana as "Judas Scalawag Wright" and "Smelly Wright," and hanged in effigy on many occasions, shifted intellectual gears once he became a judge. A latent sense of decency and compassion surfaced. Beginning in 1950, he anticipated the Warren Court's decision in *Brown v. Board of Education* (1954)[22] by desegregating the Louisiana State University Law School. Accepting the "separate-but-equal" doctrine as authoritative law, Wright's opinion paralleled exactly the Supreme Court's 1950 decision and opinion in *Sweatt v. Painter*[23] concerning the University of Texas Law School. Wright saw that the separate law school for Louisiana blacks was greatly inferior to those at LSU, and ruled that Louisiana had violated the "equal" part of the "separate-but-equal" rule. That decision began his judicial career that was to be remarkably similar to that of the Warren Court (1953-1969) and even to some extent that of the Burger Court (1969 to date).

Wright's vital statistics give no measure at all of the man. He was born on January 14, 1911, in New Orleans, the second of seven children. His family was poor. His education, such as it was, can only be characterized as mediocre. Raised as a Roman Catholic, he attended Loyola University in New Orleans, graduating from its law school in 1934. Lack of money forced him to work during the day and attend night school in law. Unable to find a law-related job in the depths of the Depression, he taught mathematics and English history at Fortier High School.

The young Skelly Wright did have two things going for him: a burning ambition to succeed and a relative, Joseph P. Skelly, who was influential in New Orleans politics. It was the latter's influence that landed him a job as Assistant U.S. Attorney in 1936. Skelly Wright cut his judicial teeth as a prosecutor, beginning in the narcotics section. His driving energy and enormous capacity for hard work—attributes he still has at the age of 72—enabled him to handle 271 cases in 18 months. He was highly successful: There were 268 convictions, most of which, he readily admits, came on pleas of guilty. He remained in the U.S. Attorney's office until

1942, when he entered military service in the Coast Guard. Most of his war-time experience was in London, where he was on the legal staff of Admiral James Stark.

While in London, he "courted" Helen Patton, a young American embassy employee, "among the buzz bombs," and married her on February 1, 1945. They have one son, James Skelly, who is now a practicing lawyer in Washington, D.C. After the war, Wright returned to the U.S. Attorney's office in New Orleans. In the spring of 1946, he moved to Washington, D.C., and started law practice. Most of his practice dealt with maritime and shipping issues. In 1947, he entered into a partnership with John Ingoldsby and Marvin Coles, a relationship that was to last only a few months. Early in 1948, the U.S. Attorney's position in New Orleans became vacant. Showing perspicacity, and knowing that the position would aid him in attracting clients, he made the correct political moves and got the job. Few others, it should be noted, wanted it. Federal Attorneys are political appointments and serve at the pleasure of the president. Few expected Harry Truman to be elected in 1948; when he was, he extended Wright's tenure in the office. Helen, who had remained in Washington because both thought Wright would be in New Orleans only a few months, then joined him with their son, who had been born in 1947.

As U.S. Attorney, Skelly Wright was very much the mainstream prosecutor. He did not hesitate to pursue communists in the labor unions. Believing that communists in unions could seriously harm the United States in the event of a conflict between the U.S. and the U.S.S.R., Wright worked actively to identify them and expel them from the unions. He took a rather simplistic view of national security matters at that time, a position that has been modified somewhat as a judge (as will be shown in Chapter 5). National security is an extraordinarily complex matter, as Wright has recognized in several decisions.

Then in June, 1949, a vacancy occurred on the United States Court of Appeals for the Fifth Circuit. Again, Wright was politically astute, had the right friends, and was in the best position to fill the vacancy. He was a friend of Tom Clark, the Attorney General of the United States, and had supported Truman in 1948 when most Louisiana Democrats bolted the party to support Strom Thurmond's Dixiecrat campaign. So he had little real competition for the position; and Wright's nomination was forwarded by Clark. At the last moment, however, his appointment was blocked by the chief judge of the Fifth Circuit, Joseph Hutcheson, who prevailed on Clark's successor, James McGrath, to withdraw the nomination on the grounds that Wright was too young. The appointment, accordingly, went to District Judge Wayne Borah. But that meant that the district judgeship was open. Wright was nominated for that position, was quickly confirmed, and on October 26, 1949, replaced Borah as a federal trial judge. He was only 38 years old—the youngest federal judge in the nation. His work as a judge will be the focus of subsequent chapters. Suffice it for now to quote from a tribute paid to him by former Justice Arthur J. Goldberg of the Supreme Court:

Judge Wright was one of our most able district judges. He is an outstanding court of appeals judge, universally and justly recognized as a jurist of extraordinary competence. True, every judge is cast in his own mold; but there are, nonetheless, some similarities in judicial outlook among judges past and present. In the case of Skelly Wright, I am reminded of the statement by Lord Mansfield, who, long ago, expressed the credo of any judge worthy of the name and office.

"I will not do what my conscience tells me is wrong to gain the huzzahs of thousands, or the daily praise of all the papers which come from the press. I will not avoid doing what I think is right, though it should draw on me the whole artillery of libels, all that falsehood and malice can invent, or the credulity of a deluded populace can swallow. . . . Once for all let it be understood, that no endeavors of this kind will influence any man who at present sits here." Chief Judge Wright lives by this belief. . . .

Judge Wright knows what history teaches: that judicial timidity is far more likely to be the undoing of the judiciary as an institution than the faithful exercise of judicial responsibility.

It is regrettable that all too often great judges of the Courts of Appeals are not elevated to the Supreme Court. Judge Learned Hand is an example. Skelly Wright is another. But, notwithstanding, Chief Judge Wright has made an enduring contribution to the attainment of the still unrealized goal of equal justice under law.[24]

So he has, as will be shown.

But what of Skelly Wright as a person? He has, as he admits, two all-consuming passions—his wife, Helen, and his work. He is a true workaholic; and Helen has adapted herself to the role of watching over him. Wright has a sharp, incisive mind, a quick mind that enables him to cut through the dross that lawyers bring to him and get to the core of the disputes before the court.

He relies heavily on his law clerks, who are drawn from elite law schools—Harvard, Yale, Columbia, and Stanford mainly. Not having a profound mind, Wright knows what he wants and relies upon his clerks to provide much of the detailed argumentation to support those decisions. Hence, his opinions look scholarly, in the sense that articles in legal periodicals, which are usually larded with mountains of footnotes, are considered to be scholarly. This is a direct consequence of his reliance on clerks, each of whom has been a top editor for a law journal. His nonjudicial writings follow the same pattern: Wright gives the theme and a clerk (or clerks) provides the language. In some respects, this has led him at times to give at least the appearance of inconsistency—mainly because he has rather uncritically accepted language from some legal aide.

Skelly Wright is a quiet and reserved man. He has few close friends but many acquaintances. Of medium height, he was at one time rather stockily built. In recent years, however, he has lost weight and now presents a spare figure that is far from frail. Not a person to have an inflated view of himself, he rides the public bus from his home in Maryland into the District of Columbia, usually getting off several blocks from his office and walking to get exercise. He keeps punctilious hours, arriving at approximately 9:00 A.M. and departing at 5:00 P.M. He often lunches "on the fly," in the cafeteria of the Courthouse. He is highly organized; paper does not pile up on his desk. A kind, even courtly gentleman, Wright is a man who can call his wife "Sugar" (and she him), but behind that courtliness is a tough, sagacious person who knows what he wants as a judge and works mightily to get it.

2

Judge Wright and Social Justice

The ultimate test of the [Supreme Court's] work . . . must be goodness.
—J. Skelly Wright (1971)[1]

I

Skelly Wright became a federal judge at the time that the Supreme Court began an unprecedented protection of individual rights and liberties. As a judge on lower courts, he theoretically did not have as much freedom as Justices on the High Bench to follow the dictates of his conscience and to create new doctrine. Of course, as was suggested in Chapter 1, even Supreme Court Justices are supposed to be bound by the never defined but nonetheless existent limits of their function. They are, in short, supposed to be judges, not legislators; they are to settle the dispute that is before the bench and not promulgate general norms. True it is that they do not often overtly make law *wholesale*; but they do so *retail*, as Justice Byron White observed in 1966 in his dissenting opinion in *Miranda v. Arizona*:

> The Court has not discovered or found the law in making today's decision, nor has it derived it from some irrefutable sources; what it has done is to make new law and new public policy in much the same way that it has in the course of interpreting other great clauses of the Constitution. *This is what the Court historically has done. Indeed, it is what it must do and will continue to do until and unless there is some fundamental change in the constitutional distribution of governmental powers.* (Emphasis added.)[2]

Justice William Brennan reaffirmed that observation in 1980.[3] Supreme Court lawmaking is accomplished in two main ways. First and of greater importance is the propensity of judges and lawyers alike to view particular decisions as statements of general rules (unless, as is sometimes the case, the Justices expressly limit the thrust of a decision). This means that a general principle is inferred from one particular, which is a logical impossibility (but one that does not perturb anyone). Second, at times the Court issues express norms of general applicability; they state, as, for example, the Justices did in the *Miranda* case, a legislative rule for all others similarly situated.

As a district judge in New Orleans in the 1950s, Skelly Wright was one of the "58 lonely men"[4] who were confronted with the forbidding task of translating the Supreme Court's nebulous "with all deliberate speed" command in *Brown v. Board of Education*[5] into operational reality. Almost a century after the Civil War had freed them in the formal law, American blacks began to get protection from a judicial system that had as its motto "equal justice under law." Until the 1950s, black Americans had been kept in a rigid caste system—first in the Constitution itself (which recognized slavery but did not require it), and then in a *de facto* system of peonage that for most of the freed slaves was little better, and at times worse, than their pre–Civil War condition. Not all were in that dismal situation, to be sure, for some managed by one means or another to escape the invisible bonds of America's "untouchables"; but enough—in fact, the great majority—saw the rhetoric of democracy routinely ignored by governmental officers at all levels—local, state, and national—and suffered accordingly.

When Wright was elevated to the Court of Appeals in Washington, D.C., he in theory had more leeway. In fact, all judges have much more discretion than the myth system of the American legal system accords them. The pretense is that it is the will of the law that controls in judicial decisions, but the hard fact is that all too often it is the will of the judge. That is particularly true for appellate judges, but it is also so for trial judges. Both must deal with what was called in Chapter 1 the Principle of Doctrinal Polarity. This chapter is a generalized discussion of how J. Skelly Wright has perceived his task of judging his fellow humans. His approach in large part is opposite to that of the late Justice Frankfurter. For that reason, considerable attention will be paid in this chapter to a long-forgotten case, *Louisiana ex rel. Francis v. Resweber*,[6] the case of the bungled execution, the case where Wright was Francis's lawyer and Frankfurter cast the deciding vote that sent Francis to the electric chair a second (and successful) time.

I will maintain that Wright as judge has been motivated in substantial part by a concept of *Reason-Directed Societal Self-Interest*. This term means, in briefest form, that through the application of *his* reason Judge Wright, by helping disadvantaged individuals, in effect has acted to help further the overall societal good. He has "invited" the "un-poor" and the "un-black" to use *their* reason to see where their true self-interest lies. He tries to bridge the chasm between social justice for an individual *qua* natural person and social justice for the collectivity—the community—in which that individual lives and spends his life. To repeat his 1983 comment: "I try to do what's right." Rightness, the point is, has both an individual and a social content. By attempting to employ the concept of goodness in his decisions,

Wright has, whether or not he consciously realized it, thought not only of the individual litigant, but also of the general good. I do not maintain that Skelly Wright had that goal (the general good) foremost in his mind when making decisions; nor will I suggest that those who sharply criticize him have been cognizant of that goal. What I do say is that Wright is as interested in the good of society as he is in justice for the individual—and that he is able to mesh the two interests in his mind.

In making such an analysis, I shall draw upon the basic idea that all social activities, not excluding government, have certain identifiable functions; and second, that those functions can be divided between *manifest* and *latent*.[7] In other words, judicial decisions have, when their consequences are considered, both manifest (or obvious) and latent (or hidden) beneficiaries. One example will suffice for the moment (further explication will come below): When judges finally began to accord decent treatment to black Americans and thus to fulfill the promise of the formal Constitution, the manifest function of their decisions was to help black Americans become part of the mainstream of national life. Blacks, thus, were the manifest beneficiaries. But at the same time, surely it is accurate to maintain that latent functions (and beneficiaries) existed; those decisions helped to siphon off growing discontent, even rebelliousness, among the 11 percent of Americans who are of African descent. Stated another way, *Brown v. Board of Education* and progeny were not illustrative of a new-found altruism by the dominant white majority. Blacks began to be treated better because it was in the long-term self-interest of whites to do so. This is a hard truth, perhaps an unpleasant truth, but the truth nonetheless. Black Americans began to get protection under the formal (but, as we will note, not necessarily under the operative) Constitution less because it was the morally right thing to do than because it was the necessary thing to do. (One other factor is relevant: Better treatment of blacks coincided almost exactly with America's true "golden age"—the 25-year period following the end of World War II. Of that, more in Chapter 3.)

II

Two matters require discussion before analyzing the Principle of Reason-Directed Societal Self-Interest. First, what is the orthodox conception of the judging function? Second, as has been said, how did the Supreme Court—and principally Justice Frankfurter—act in the *Francis* case? Both of these matters will then be shown in juxtaposition to what Judge Wright has done.

The orthodox view of the proper role of judges derives from William Blackstone, by any criterion the most influential legal writer of early American history. His ideas still have wide currency. In his famous *Commentaries*, Blackstone wrote that a judge is "sworn to determine, not according to his own private judgment, but according to the known laws and customs of the land; not delegated to pronounce a new law, but to maintain and expound the old one.''[8] Only in this way, he asserted, can litigants as well as society generally be assured that the same acts will be treated in the same way and, therefore, that reliance can be placed on law. If the law is to be both a guiding principle in society and the matrix within which the affairs of people can be legitimately conducted, it must be obeyed; and ''to be obeyed or followed, what is decided today must be followed tomorrow.'' That is the so-called declaratory theory of judging; it is based upon the bedrock idea that whatever is, is right—that stability in the legal system is the *summmum bonum*. Law, accordingly, is profoundly conservative; it seeks to retain existing customs and practices. Blackstone's theory also is said to serve a symbolic function—that judges ''are bound by a body of fixed, overriding law, that they apply the law impersonally as well as impartially, that they have no individual choice and have no program of their own to advance.'' Justice, accordingly, is not only done; of equal or perhaps greater importance, it is *seen* to be done. The appearance of justice is said to be of major significance.

Blackstone's theory still abides, but it has long been exploded. No thoughtful person believes it today, although it is important to note that, sadly, the content of most legal education in America is predicated upon the Blackstone model or a close variation of its theme. Law is still being taught using the outmoded Newtonian paradigm of a verbally consistent body of legal principles. Law professors readily admit the faults in Blackstone; but for the most part, they refuse to construct a better model. Some even go so far as to assert that the knowledge of the faulty Blackstonian model should be kept from people generally—on the notion that it is better for people to believe in a myth, since they do not have the moral fiber to handle the harsh truth.[9] And that is so even though Felix Frankfurter, as a professor and before he became a Justice of the Supreme Court, maintained:

We speak of the Court as though it was an abstraction. To be sure, the Court is an institution, but individuals, with all their diversities of endowment, experience, and outlook, determine its actions. The history of the Supreme Court is not the history of an abstraction, but the analysis of individuals acting as a Court who make decisions and lay down doctrines, and of other individuals, their successors, who refine, modify, and sometimes even overrule the decisions of their predecessors, reinterpreting and transmuting their doctrines. *In law also men make a difference.* (Emphasis added.)[10]

So they do. People in positions of power, including judges, are able to apply *their* preferences and predilections in the decisions they make. The myth system of the American judicial process is otherwise, of course, but it will not withstand rigorous scrutiny. Under the ''operational code'' of the process, judges have wide discretion to make law. The myth system is a more or less clearly stated set of rules of behavior that purportedly guide human conduct; and the operational code is what tells people when, by whom, and how certain things may be done outside the myth system. In some respects, it is similar to the difference between the formal and the operative Constitutions.[11]

Once the Blackstone myth had been shattered, a search began for an acceptable substitute. Was there a middle ground, the question became, between slavish adherence to the intellectually untenable declaratory theory and an outright recognition that judges had an open-ended power to read their notions of wise public policy into law? The answer for many—those who constitute the new orthodoxy—lay in accepting Justice Frankfurter's view that his decisions could *not* rest on "my notions of justice," and then going on to assert that judicial propriety consisted in decisions that are "principled" or in accord with "reason." Judges, therefore, should exhibit craftsmanship in their opinions, a notion that seems to mean that they should make them look like those written by Frankfurter or, possibly, the late Justice John M. Harlan II. Most judges, not excluding Skelly Wright, adhere, at least outwardly, to the notion that their decisions should be "principled." Where they diverge, often quite widely, is in the identification and application of *which* principles are relevant in a given case. Choices among principles always exist in constitutional (and other) disputes; and there is no such thing as a principled approach to judicial decision making that requires the same results to be reached by all judges. Justice Oliver Wendell Holmes made what perhaps may be the classic statement, as Judge Learned Hand related:

Remember what Justice Holmes said about "justice." I don't know what you think about him but *on the whole he was the master craftsman of the time*; and he said, "I hate justice," which he didn't quite mean. What he did mean was this. I remember once when I was with him; it was on a Saturday morning when the Court was to confer. It was before he had a motorcar; and we jogged along in an old coupé. When we got to the Capitol, I wanted to provoke a response, so as he walked off I said to him, "Well, sir, good-bye. Do justice." He turned quite sharply and he said, "Come here, come here." I answered, "Oh, I know, I know." He replied, "That is not my job. *My job is to play the game according to the rules.*" (Emphasis added.)[12]

Holmes really could not have believed that statement, at least in its entirety. The episode is a restatement of Blackstone overlaid with the modern "middle" view. Holmes knew quite well that the rules are flexible, that choices must be made among them, and that judges were guided as much by their perceptions of the felt necessities of the times as by the rules. He knew also that the rules, such as they are, were not neutral, that they favored the dominant groups in society, and that they were a means by which the "incomplete hegemony of the ruling class"[13] perpetuated their authority. Holmes did not care for justice as anything more than shoring up the status quo; he believed in judicial self-restraint because he realized that, speaking generally, those of the class whence he came would generally prevail in the political process. "Savage, harsh, and cruel," he was willing as a Supreme Court Justice to aid "the rich and powerful to impose their will on the poor and weak."[14]

In net, the new orthodoxy of judicial propriety ignores the significance of the result in a given case and emphasizes the reasoning used to explain or justify that result. A plethora of books and articles are written in which it is argued, often quite stridently, that a court has reached the correct result but for the wrong reasons. Three examples, by no means atypical, will suffice to illustrate the point. First, Dean John Ely of the Stanford Law School: "If a principled approach to judicial enforcement of the Constitution's open-ended provisions cannot be developed . . . responsible commentators must consider seriously the possibility that courts simply should stay away from them."[15] Next, political scientist Richard Funston: "Opinions based upon reasoned principle . . . are necessary to the very self-preservation of the Supreme Court. Assuming that the institution is worth preserving, Justices must sometimes sacrifice what they conceive to be a desirable result, if they cannot logically justify that result. In other words, procedure may be as important as substance; means more important than ends."[16] These academics, and their intellectual cohorts, are not accurate; neither is law Professor Richard Saphire in the third example: "The notion that a judicial decision should be 'principled'—that is, based upon nonarbitrary distinctions between the case at hand and others similarly situated—has been universally endorsed."[17] That just ain't so, as witness the statement of a person whose job it is to judge, Justice Richard Neely of the West Virginia Supreme Court:

Even law professors who are in the business of making sense out of what courts do and are responsible for showing that courts act according to "legal principles," and not according to what judges had for breakfast, have to twist themselves out of shape to reconcile . . . constant ideological shifts with any notion of a written constitution which is being "interpreted." In fact, almost every theory defending or defaming courts has developed backward from the result sought by the commentator to some rule which dictates that result. This is not reasoning from principles, however, but mere apologizing for or criticizing the exercise of raw power.[18]

In other words, judges and commentators routinely start with the result desired and reason—or search for rules—to buttress that result.

The new orthodoxy is as intellectually barren as the Blackstone theory. Judge Wright knows that, although, as was noted above, he makes his opinions look like orthodox "principled" decisions. He does not believe in a purely procedural approach to the problems of judging (as do Ely, Funston, and Saphire). I will argue below that Wright adheres to Professor William A. Galston's view:

The quest for a purely institutional or procedural solution to the practical problem of obtaining justice is futile. Every community, whether democratic or not, must rely on a rudimentary sense of fairness and equity among its members. This sense is not innate, but must rather be fostered through some system of education. The traditional American penchant for political engineering or institutional tinkering is thus profoundly one-sided; democratic procedures are almost vacuous in the absence of collectively held moral convictions.[19]

Wright believes that judges are a part of that "system of education" Galston mentions; they can help engender "collectively held moral convictions." In Wright's language, courts can be the "conscience of a sovereign people." That, of course, is directly contrary both to the old and the new orthodoxies. An analysis of *Willie Francis's Case* will serve to show the new orthodoxy and its manifest shortcomings. Section II deals at length with that case and with the manner in which Justice Frankfurter operated when considering it, because it is an excellent contrast to the judicial method of Judge Wright.[20]

II

Willie Francis's Case was, as has been said, Skelly Wright's first appearance before the Supreme Court. The case has largely been relegated to an intellectual limbo; it deserves resurrection. The facts are relatively simple: the time is 1946; the place is rural Louisiana. Willie Francis was nervous—understandably so. The slim black teenager was being led from his cell in St. Martinville to a makeshift execution chamber, where the state of Louisiana, in the person of Sheriff E. L. Resweber, was preparing to kill him by "causing to pass through" his body a current of electricity "of sufficient intensity to cause death." His shackled body was strapped in the portable electric chair, and Captain E. Foster, the executioner, threw a switch, sardonically saying "Goodbye, Willie." Willie's body strained against the straps, but although some electricity passed through his body he obviously was not dying. Foster frantically flipped the switch back and forth, but to no avail. Willie merely sizzled. Foster yelled out the window to the operator of a portable generator to give him more juice, only to be told that the machine was operating at full capacity. Willie would later recall: "The electric man . . . could of been puttin' me on the bus for New Orleans the way he said 'goodbye,' and I tried to say goodbye but my tongue got stuck . . . and I felt a burnin' in my head and my left leg and I jumped against the strap. When the straps kept cuttin' me I hoped I was alive, and I asked the electric man to let me breathe. . . . They took the bag off my head."

As would be learned later, the two men who had set up the electric chair were drunk. Neither was a qualified electrician; and one was a convict who claimed to know something about electricity. The execution had been botched. No one quite knew what to do, although Foster snarled that he would try again and if the chair still did not work, he would kill Willie with a rock. Finally Resweber ordered Willie to be taken back to his cell. At that time, what some persist in calling the majesty of the law swung into action. Could Louisiana, having bungled the first attempt, have a second chance? The Louisiana authorities, up to and including the governor, were of one mind: Yes. Neither the Pardon and Parole Board nor the Supreme Court of Louisiana nor the governor altered one iota from that central position: Try again and do it right. Kill Willie Francis. Before they could do so, Willie's father got a lawyer, Bertrand DeBlanc, to contest the second attempt. Willie had been represented by court-appointed counsel at his trial—a trial that by any criterion was a travesty of justice. After failing to sway the Louisiana authorities, DeBlanc contacted a young lawyer fresh out of military service who was beginning law practice in Washington, D.C., and asked him to handle Willie's case before the Supreme Court. That lawyer was James Skelly Wright.

Although he had ample time, he worked hastily. His brief to the Court was indeed that: It was brief. That in itself is not necessarily bad. But what was not very good was the slimness of his argumentation and the general inadequacy of the brief. In 1982, Judge Wright, recalling his effort, would term it "inadequate"[21]—and that it was by any objective standard. His oral argument, however, was characterized as "good" by Justice Harold Burton.

The Justices heard Willie's case, and considered some subsequent petitions for rehearing and for habeas corpus, agonized over their decision, and by the slimmest of margins—5 to 4—gave Louisiana a second chance. This attempt succeeded; Willie Francis was killed on May 9, 1947. His debt to society, if that it was, was paid. Skelly Wright (and DeBlanc) could have done a better job (indeed, Wright conceded as much in 1982), but even so, he probably would not have saved Willie; Justice Frankfurter, the crucial fifth vote in a $4 + 1 = 5$ to 4 decision, exalted his personal political theory of federalism and what he thought was the proper function of federal courts vis-à-vis state governments over his *own* view of what "due process of law" requires; and Justice Hugo Black was more interested in establishing his view that the Bill of Rights bound the states than in Willie's ordeal. The case and his part in it has weighed heavily on Wright's mind—and still does. In July, 1982, he tried unsuccessfully to elicit from Frankfurter's then law clerk details about what took place within the Court.[22] As for Frankfurter, his concurrence with the Court majority, rather than being a triumph of judgment over feeling, is, when coupled with his subsequent secret efforts to get executive clemency for Willie, an example of intellectual dishonesty.

By no means were Skelly Wright's efforts as a lawyer much below the norm for advocacy before the Supreme Court. Certainly, his futile attempts to save Willie are not typical of his other work as a lawyer, both in private practice and as a United States Attorney. (In his second appearance before the Supreme Court, we will see in the chapter dealing with his views on the crime problem that he won—again by a 5 to 4 margin.) The level of advocacy before the Supreme Court is generally depressingly low. Probably Wright would have lost without regard to the quality of his work. The Justices, after a preliminary changing of minds, seemed to be adamant in their positions. No amount of argument, of whatever quality, likely could have swayed the five who sealed Willie's fate.

The *Francis* case is highlighted for several reasons. First, as has been said, it has been ignored by most who write about American constitutional law, particularly those who worship at the shrine of Felix Frankfurter; second, because it poses in stark form the dilemmas that judges face when novel factual situations come before them, disputes that could not have remotely been in the minds of the men who wrote the Constitution; third, because some of the internal dynamics of a tribunal that has always had a fetish for secrecy are now available in the collected papers of the then Justices; and finally, because the case provides a vehicle both for assessing a young Skelly Wright as a lawyer and also for evaluating various theories of judging. It will become evident that the storied rule of law is in fact the rule of men, often at least, and very fallible men at that.

Willie Francis's background can be briefly summarized. Little is known about his life before his arrest and conviction. One of fourteen children born into a family that lived in dismal poverty—his father, a laborer, earned an average of $9 per week—Willie's education, such as it was, came in a segregated school that was separate but, despite the Supreme Court's bland assumption in *Plessy v. Ferguson*, far from equal. He lived in a caste society, bound by the invisible but nonetheless tight constraints that white Americans have always placed around blacks. Being poor and black and in rural Louisiana in the 1940s was about as low as one could be in the social pecking order of a nation that trumpets it is a constitutional democracy, "dedicated," as Lincoln said (surely it was with tongue in cheek), "to the proposition that all men are created equal." That Willie was functionally illiterate, or almost so, cannot be doubted. He could read and write a little, but not much. He, however, apparently was basically an intelligent and sensitive youth, who attended church regularly and was able to read the Bible.

As for his literacy, consider whether this statement, said to have been scratched on the wall of his cell (allegedly by Willie), indicates the caliber of his education: "I kill Andrew Thomas and today he is lying in a grave and I am not a killer but I wonder where I am going to be lying and in what kind of grave I don't know." The statement was not signed. Whether Willie Francis actually wrote that "confession" will never be known. Sheriff Gilbert Ozenne of Iberia Parish claimed that he saw it, but his account cannot be verified because he is now dead. No one other than Ozenne is known to have seen the scrawl. If Willie had in fact written it, it would be some sort of confession (but not admissible as such in court).

Had it not been for the bungled execution, Willie Francis would have lived and died unheralded and unsung, a mere statistic in the dreary record of white man's justice in darkest Louisiana. Why was the first attempt botched? The answer is easy. He did not die because of wanton recklessness and carelessness by the executioners, conduct that by almost any standard approached the edge of an intentional act. That much *is* known today—and that much *was* known when the Supreme Court finally slammed the door on Skelly Wright's frantic efforts. It is worth mention that Willie himself agreed that further legal proceedings on his behalf should be halted. Saying he was ready to die, he asked Bertrand DeBlanc to stop trying. Whether DeBlanc should have tried to dissuade him is one of the unanswered questions in the *Francis* case. Willie was a minor; without much doubt, his father could have filed a suit for habeas corpus in federal district court—where Willie would have been given another chance. Wright had filed such a suit in the Supreme Court, which dismissed it "without prejudice" to filing in the lower court. Certainly the effort should have been made by DeBlanc.

Before the Supreme Court, Skelly Wright argued that a second execution attempt would constitute both double jeopardy and cruel and unusual punishment. Conceding that those provisions in the Bill of Rights bound the federal government only, he maintained that the Fourteenth Amendment's due process of law clause "incorporated" them ("no state shall deprive any person of life, liberty, or property without due process of law"). The first argument was specious; by no criterion was Willie being tried twice for the same crime. Wright acknowledged the point: "The State of Louisiana had a right to execute the man [*sic*] but this right has been forfeited by subjecting [him] to the torture, both mental and physical, of being prepared for death, of being placed in the electric chair, of having electricity applied to his body." Willie was not a man; he was a teenager, fifteen years old at the time of the murder.

Three opinions were published by the Supreme Court—one by Justice Stanley Reed for the plurality in favor of giving Louisiana another chance, one by Justice Harold Burton for the four-man minority, and one by Justice Frankfurter. Each saw the facts of this heretofore "unprovided" case differently, insofar as judicial technique was concerned. Reed quickly dismissed the double jeopardy argument and then went on to reject the cruel and unusual punishment plea, holding that since Louisiana had adoped electrocution for a humane purpose, its will should not be thwarted because, in its desire to reduce pain and suffering in most cases, it may have inadvertently increased suffering in one particular individual. Stating that "this case is without precedent in any court," Reed found that "the state officials carried out their duties in a careful and humane manner." That simply was not true. He further reasoned that although the first attempt caused "mental anguish and physical pain," it was the result of an "unforeseeable accident" and therefore not intentional. That, too, is highly dubious. Reed maintained that Willie's suffering was no greater than the hardship a prisoner might experience from a fire in his cell block—hardly an apposite analogy. Thus, Reed can be said to have followed the technique of applying known law by analogy—except for one crucial factor: There was *no* law relevant to Willie's case. Reed had to create it, all the while tacitly denying he was doing so.

Frankfurter, asserting that "great tolerance toward a state's conduct is demanded by this Court," approved a second attempt to execute because he believed that the due process clause was not violated; Louisiana had met "civilized standards." He did not proffer reasons for the "great tolerance" a state should have; nor did he reveal where he located those "civilized standards." He further wrote that "a state may be found to deny a person due process by treating even one guilty of crime in a manner that violates standards of decency more or less universally accepted though not when it treats him by a mode about which opinion is fairly divided." What that means is completely mysterious: What, for example, is "more or less," and what does "universally accepted" mean? Which universe did he have in mind?

Frankfurter agreed with Reed that since the first attempt had failed because of an "innocent misadventure," a second would not violate those "universally accepted" "standards of decency" and, thus, would not be "repugnant to the conscience of mankind." That a collectivity called "mankind" could not, by any criterion, have a unified conscience did not enter his mind. How Frankfurter, furthermore, determined that conscience was left unanswered. Although he asserted a "personal revulsion" at both a second attempt to execute and Louisiana's "insistence on its pound of flesh," he maintained that if he voted to overturn the Louisiana decision he would be enforcing his "private view rather than the consensus of society's opinion." That means, although he did not say so, that Frankfurter was accusing the dissenters of enforcing *their* private views; it also means that he believed he knew something that they did not—how to determine a societal consensus. Frankfurter suggested that Willie's hopes must lie in "executive clemency" from Louisiana's governor. In that, he displayed a willful ignorance about the ways in which state politicians act, as well as ignorance of Louisiana law. The governor at that time had no independent power to pardon or commute sentences.

Justice Burton, in dissent, maintained that a second attempt, "under circumstances unique in judicial history," would be impermissible cruel and unusual punishment. He disagreed with Reed's application of a state intent test: "The intent of the executioner cannot lessen the torture or excuse the result. It was the statutory duty of the state officials to make sure that there was no failure." Echoing Skelly Wright's argument, Burton asked: "How many deliberate and intentional reapplications of electric current does it take to produce cruel, unusual and unconstitutional punishment?" He also implied that there were serious mental effects attendant to a second trip to the electric chair. (Many have recognized the mental suffering of prisoners awaiting execution. They undergo a "fate of ever-increasing fear and distress," so intense that "the onset of insanity while awaiting execution of a death sentence is not a rare phenomenon.")

What should one conclude about the three *Francis* opinions? The answer is clear, at least for that case: Supreme Court Justices make up the law as they go along, in accordance with their personal philosophies. The validity of that conclusion may be discerned when the collected papers of several of the then Justices are scrutinized. The narrative is worth recounting if for no other reason than it sheds light on the question of whether the rule of law—of, that is, the demand for principled decisions—is possible.

On November 23, 1946, five days after oral argument, the Court met to consider the merits of *Willie Francis's Case*. The discussion began with Chief Justice Frederick M. Vinson. According to notes taken by Justice William Douglas, Vinson discussed Wright's double jeopardy argument and indicated that "it was clear to him [that] it [the Louisiana Supreme Court] should be affirmed." Justice Frankfurter began by noting that it was "not an easy case." He had voted to grant review because, as he later wrote, it seemed "too serious a question for this Court to think too unimportant even to consider—particularly when one takes account of the really trivial cases that we do take." After briefly discussing double jeopardy, Frankfurter took up the cruel and unusual punishment argument and remarked that for the state to have a second chance was not so offensive "as to make him puke." He derived that earthy "test" of unconstitutionality from Justice Oliver Wendell Holmes. (Its very use in Supreme Court conference, a secret meeting, is proof positive, if indeed proof is necessary, of the subjective nature of the judging process.) Frankfurter voted to affirm the Louisiana Supreme Court and was followed by Douglas, who, surprisingly, also voted to affirm. (Douglas had voted to deny review in the case.) Justice Frank Murphy voted to reverse, and Justice Robert Jackson voted to affirm. Justice Wiley Rutledge then voted to reverse, as did Justice Burton (who had originally objected to granting review).

As is the practice in the Supreme Court, when the Chief Justice votes with the majority, he assigns the case to someone (or keeps it himself) for an opinion to be written for the Court. Vinson assigned Willie's case to Reed on November 25, 1946. On December 11, 1946, Reed first circulated a draft opinion; it spawned a number of concurring and dissenting opinions. Black and Jackson drafted separate concurrences, as did Frankfurter. Early on, dissents by Murphy, Rutledge, and Burton were written. Only Vinson and

Douglas did not write an opinion. In the next month, the seven separate opinions were reduced to the Reed plurality opinion, the Frankfurter concurrence, and the Burton dissent.

Reed wrote five different draft opinions. The first was to prove to be quite similar, in both length and content, to the fifth—with one major exception—on the question of whether the fourteenth amendment's due process clause "incorporated" the eighth amendment's cruel and unusual proscription. In his early drafts, Reed relied solely on the due process clause. Black changed Reed's mind. He circulated a draft concurrence in which he argued that Louisiana was bound by the eighth amendment. Even so, he did not think that a second attempt would be cruel and unusual punishment: "I cannot agree," he wrote, "that any provision of the Constitution authorizes us to rule that any accidental failure fairly to carry out a valid sentence of death on the first attempt bars execution of that sentence."

Reflecting Black's concerns and perhaps to keep his vote, Reed removed the offending language from his opinion and inserted the following:

To determine whether or not the execution of the petitioner may fairly take place after the experience through which he passed, we shall examine the circumstances under the assumption, but not without so deciding, that violation of the Fifth and Eighth Amendments, as to double jeopardy and cruel and unusual punishment, would be violative of the due process clause of the Fourteenth Amendment.

That same day, January 11, 1947, Black scrawled "I agree. H.L.B. Jan. 11-47" on his copy of Reed's draft, and dropped his concurring opinion.

This is no mere technicality, as Justice Frankfurter was quick to point out. After receiving Reed's final draft, he prepared a Memorandum for the Conference dated January 11, 1947, in which he began by noting that "in order that there be an opinion [for the Court] in addition to expressing my own views," he had voted with the Reed plurality. This, he went on, was no longer possible: "The reason I cannot do so . . . is that I do not think we should decide the case even on the assumption that the Fifth Amendment as to double jeopardy is the measure of due process in the Fourteenth Amendment." Further: "it makes for nothing but confusion in the consideration of constitutional cases under the Due Process Clause to cite cases that construed the scope of the double jeopardy provision of the Fifth Amendment." Therefore, he concluded, "I respectfully cannot join in Reed's opinion."

Reed, however, was able to convince Justice Jackson to drop his draft concurrence. On December 20, 1946, Jackson circulated a concurring opinion that is noteworthy because it opened with a strong denunciation of the death penalty:

If I am at liberty, in the name of due process to vote my personal sense of "decency," I not only would refuse to send Willie Francis to the electric chair, but I would not have sent him there in the first place. If my will were law, it would never permit execution of any death sentence. This is not because I am sentimental about criminals, but I have doubts as to the moral right of society to extinguish human life, and even greater doubts about the wisdom of doing so. . . . A completely civilized society will abandon killing as a treatment for crime.

Like Frankfurter, Jackson believed that judges should suppress that type of personal feeling because "judges are servants, not masters, of society and it is society's law that should govern judges." That can hardly be accurate: It begs the question. It is "society's law" that was the very issue before the Court; the question was whether that law comported with the Constitution. Society's law was to be weighed against the command of the fundamental law. Like Black, "unable to cite any constitutional backing for my prejudice against executing Francis" and finding that "I cannot believe that the Founding Fathers ever intended to nationalize decency," Jackson concluded that he "must vote to leave the case to Louisiana's own law and sense of decency." That Jackson thought Louisiana officials would act with decency is beyond comprehension. Surely he knew that a black youth accused and convicted of murdering a white man in rural Louisiana, in 1947, had little chance of being treated decently. He wanted it both ways—to be seen as a "lawyer's lawyer" by the profession and to be perceived as compassionate by his peers on the Supreme Court. That was intellectual dishonesty.

Justice Rutledge saw through Jackson's disingenuous effort, writing in an undated memorandum: "I consider it to be more than absurd for the prosecutor at Nuremberg to say that he doesn't approve of capital punishment. If he didn't approve, he should never had taken the job. The remarks at the bottom of page 1 about 'the duty of prosecutors' add to rather than detract from the absurdity." The latter reference is to a comment in Jackson's withdrawn concurrence that "so long as society adheres to its policy of death penalties, it is for us in individual cases to apply the policy of the law, as it is the duty of prosecutors, whatever their personal conviction, to advocate it."

The unpublished dissents of Murphy and Rutledge clearly rejected the judicial approach of Jackson and Frankfurter that a judge could divorce his personal views from decision making. Murphy wrote that "to me, it is inhuman and barbarous to subject any person to the torture of two or more trips to the electric chair in the hope that one of them will result in the taking of the person's life." He felt that in the unique circumstances of the *Francis* case, "We have nothing to guide us in defining what is cruel and unusual apart from our own consciences. . . . Our decision must necessarily be based upon our mosaic beliefs, our experiences, our backgrounds and the degree of our faith in the dignity of the human personality." Further: "The mental anguish which characterizes preparation for execution must be repeated, an anguish that can be fully appreciated only by one who has experienced it." That anguish of a second attempt was what makes "the total punishment cruel and unusual." Murphy particularly noted that "it is not without significance that this cruel and unusual punishment is about to be inflicted upon a helpless and inarticulate member of a minority group." Murphy's views had the virtue of intellectual honesty.

Rutledge's unpublished opinion stressed Willie Francis's mental torture and dealt with the idea of negligence by the executioners that Reed had relied upon. He rejected the distinction between an "unforeseeable accident" and intentional torture. The "subjective motivation" of Louisiana's officials in the first attempt was of no significance in determining whether they had acted cruelly and unusually. "I do not think the element of torture is removed," Rutledge wrote, "because the state acts carelessly rather than deliberately." He believed that "torture, for the victim, is not a matter of the executioner's state of mind. It may be inflicted as much by carelessness and bungling or taking a chance as by design." He concluded that "Willie Frances cannot be electrocuted again without undergoing the death pangs he already has suffered and which now I think the state has no right to reinflict." That the Louisiana officials did act "carelessly," and even worse, cannot be doubted.

The four dissenters soon coalesced around the Burton opinion. On December 20, 1946, Douglas reversed his vote and became the first to join Burton. Burton recorded in his diary that on that date he "conferred with Justice Douglas and got his consent to my dissent in #142 as modified by his suggestion." Shortly thereafter, Murphy and Rutledge dropped their dissents and joined Burton. In a December 31 note to Burton, Rutledge revealed the narrowness and uncertainty which at that point still surrounded the Court's consideration: "Please allow me to join in your opinion. It's a good job, right, and I hope will induce the change in the additional necessary vote." That additional vote likely was Frankfurter, who remained the "swing" Justice. Although he voted with the then majority at conference, his strong verbal opposition to capital punishment is evident in letters between him and Burton. For example, on December 13, Frankfurter revealed grave misgivings regarding his vote, indicating that he had read Burton's dissent and "reflected upon it with sympathy." "I have to hold on to myself not to reach your result," Frankfurter wrote. "I am prevented from doing so only by the disciplined thinking of a lifetime regarding the duty of this Court in putting limitations upon the power of a State, when the question is merely the power of the State under the limitations imposed by the Due Process Clause." That seems to mean that Frankfurter thought the four dissenters were engaging in undisciplined thinking. He then went on to quote with approval Justice Oliver Wendell Holmes, who "used to express [the relationship between the Supreme Court and the states] by saying that he would not strike down state action unless the action of the state made him 'puke'."

Frankfurter concluded in more circumspect language: "I cannot say that [a second execution attempt] so shocks the accepted prevailing standards of fairness and justice not to allow the State to electrocute after an innocent, abortive first attempt," Frankfurter wrote Burton, "that we, as this Court, must enforce that standard by invocation of the Due Process Clause." Frankfurter failed to disclose how he ascertained "the accepted prevailing standards of fairness and justice"—thus making his conclusion purely one of his personal views. He went on: "After struggling with myself—for I do think Governor of Louisiana ought not to let Francis go through the ordeal again—I cannot say that reasonable men could not in calm conscience believe that a state has such power. . . . And when I have that much doubt, I must, according to my own view of the Court's duty, give the benefit of the doubt and let the State action prevail." Curiously, Frankfurter ended the letter by complimenting Burton for listening to his conscience (and thus apparently ignoring *his* duty to the Court): "It is one of the most cheering experiences since I have been on this Court to have you, who felt so strongly against taking the case at all, come out in favor of reversal as a result of your own conscientious reflections." Frankfurter did not vouchsafe any reason why a state should have the "benefit of the doubt." The most that can be gleaned from his opinion is that abstract principles of federalism outweighed the facts of the bungled execution. That, in sum, exalted a political theory over a teenager's life, a teenager who at no time was given a fair shake of the legal dice by Louisiana.

Burton responded to Frankfurter in a note dated December 26, in which he argued that the Louisiana statute, as written, did not permit a second execution:

Every sentence of death imposed by this State shall be by electrocution; that is, causing to pass through the body of the person convicted a current of sufficient intensity to cause death, and the application and continuance of such current through the body of the person convicted until such person is dead.

Burton maintained that the statute did not provide for electrocution by repeated applications at intervals of several days. Thus, Burton was telling Frankfurter that by his (Frankfurter's) own conception of due process, he could vote to save Willie without failing to pay the deference deemed due to Louisiana.

Frankfurter, however, was adamant. He responded with a "Dear Harold" letter in which he continued to maintain that "whatever scope the State court gave to a state law is binding upon us even though the State court gave it a scope which we think it should not have given or failed to give it a scope which we think it should be given. All this is purely a State question beyond our purview." For Frankfurter, the question was "whether, under the circumstances in which the State court found no violation of state law, there is a transgression of the Due Process Clause."

He answered in this way: "I cannot bring myself to believe that if I were to hold that there was, I would not be enforcing my own private view rather than the allowable consensus of opinion of the community which, for purposes of due process, expresses the Constitution." That, however, is precisely what he did do—enforce his own private view. He concluded his letter to Burton with these words: "I am sorry I cannot go with you, but I am weeping no tears that you are expressing a dissent."

As with Jackson, Frankfurter wanted it both ways. He knew his was the deciding vote, yet he relied on something he did not and could not know—the "consensus of opinion in the community"—to send Willie to his death. Societal or community consensus is merely a convenient counterpane under which a judge can hide his personal predilections. Frankfurter did not indicate which community or society he had in mind—the United States as a whole, the State of Louisiana, or St. Martinville. In like manner, he failed to say how such a consensus was determined. By no means would he have accepted a public opinion poll as a means of determining that consensus. Indeed, had a poll been taken, Willie Francis would probably have escaped the electric chair. In the week following the first attempt, the governor of Louisiana was "deluged with an unprecedented flood of mail. . . . Thousands of letters, telegrams and postcards poured in from all parts of the United States urging clemency for Willie Francis."

As with the other great generalities of the Constitution, due process is not susceptible of precise definition. The Constitution has throughout American history always been relative to circumstances—as seen through the eyes of the Justices. In the 1930s, Justice Benjamin Nathan Cardozo established this test for due process in criminal law matters: A state may act unless its action "offends some principle of justice so rooted in the tradition and conscience of our people as to be ranked as fundamental." That is the test that Reed said he applied in the *Francis* case. Quite obviously, however, it is no test at all; it is not an external standard of judgment but a means of allowing maximum subjectivity in judges. Frankfurter's variation on the Cardozo theme is no better. Both are invitations to Justices to legislate their personal preferences into law, to enact the products of what Chief Justice Earl Warren once called their "own consciences." As early as 1948, one commentator saw through the frailty of the Frankfurter approach:

Tentatively, it can be argued that Frankfurter's objective standard is a way of expressing two things: his own set of values for his society and his own conception of the safe limits of his function. Some things he believes in strongly enough to use his power to protect them. Others he may believe in but not strongly enough to risk the charge of abuse of power.

That is about what the call for "principled" decisions—what I above labeled as the "middle way" of judicial decision making—means. Modern

technology has yet to produce a device that judges can use to determine
what traditions are rooted in the collective conscience of the people.

After the Supreme Court's decision in the *Francis* case was announced,
Frankfurter took extraordinary, secret means to try to get executive
clemency for Willie. He wrote a lawyer in Louisiana, an old friend, and
asked him to intercede. To no avail. The Louisiana officials unanimously
sent Willie to his death. How possibly could the politically astute
Frankfurter have seriously thought that his extrajudicial effort would
succeed? Surely he knew that Louisiana was a racist society, at least so far
as its political leaders were concerned. His attempt to save Willie by secret
means was a pitiful try at salving his own conscience for not voting with
Justice Burton. Frankfurter knew that Willie had been denied due
process—*by Frankfurter's own test*. He knew that the executioners were
drunk, so drunk as to be careless, so drunk as to fail to wire the chair
properly (one wire from the generator went into the ground, not the chair).

Although there is no way of knowing for certain, Skelly Wright as a judge
would probably have voted with Burton. In his words: "The judicial
process forces a judge to take the short run into account. The consequences
of his decision are thrust before his eyes, and so he must bend principles in
order to produce a result he can live with." And further: "The judiciary is
different from the political process. It is in the nature of courts that they
cannot close their doors to individuals seeking justice." The difference
between Wright and Frankfurter may be simply stated. Both are activists,
but Wright is forthrightly so, whereas Frankfurter tried to cloak his
activism behind a theory of judicial self-restraint. Both are result-oriented;
they differ in the results that Frankfurter reached and Wright reaches.

III

Willie Francis is long since dead.[23] His bones lie moldering in some
forgotten grave. In one sense, however, he still lives: His case posed many
of the questions that plague constitutional commentary today. And Willie is
no Lazarus; he will not be resurrected. His ordeal has been discussed at
some length, however (and at greater length elsewhere),[24] simply because it
enables one to contrast different judicial methods. In the final analysis, his
case presents the perennial problem of what to do with the "unprovided"
situation, the dispute that is novel and far from the contemplation of those
who drafted the Constitution. Those who drafted the Constitution of 1787,
the Bill of Rights in 1791, and the Civil War amendments (thirteenth,
fourteenth, and fifteenth), purposely employed language of high-level
abstraction. The litigable parts of the document are in fact invitations for
later generations of Americans to write their own fundamental laws. That is
precisely what has happened. Only a few antiquarians still cling to the long-
exploded belief that value choices of the Founding Fathers can be

determined either by reading the Constitution or by trying to ascertain the intentions of the Framers. Any constitution, whether written or unwritten, is always in a state of becoming. Not static or frozen, the American Constitution is a river rather than a lake, a river, moreover, that has no predestined course and that knows few specific, unalterable banks.

The Constitution has some absolutes that are never litigated. For example, there shall be two houses of Congress; each state shall have two senators; and there shall be one Supreme Court. Some seeming absolutes, as in the first amendment's provision that "Congress shall make no law . . ." are in fact more cautionary admonitions than interdictory commands. In addition, as Arthur Bentley noted in 1908, "The American method of electing the president is one thing in the written constitution, and another in the actual constitution."[25] Massive changes have occurred—in the living or operative constitution—in the divisions of powers established by the Constitution: the federal-state relationship and the ways in which powers are separated in the national government. It is, accordingly, fair to say that the true Constitution—Bentley's "actual" Constitution, or the living or operative Constitution—is tied to the document of 1787, and its amendments, only in symbolic or metaphorical ways. The pretense is otherwise, to be sure, but it is just that—a pretense, not a fact. And that is so even though Judge Wright has written that the most important societal value choices were made by the Founding Fathers.[26] Once the lofty abstractions of the Document are applied in specific, factual situations—as, for example, in *Willie Francis's Case*—it becomes clear beyond doubt that those ancient value choices ineluctably derive their meanings from current circumstances. It is only by a transparent, indeed an indefensible, fiction that present-day decisions can be said to be logical derivations from the ancient text.

Judicial review provides the classic example. The Supreme Court seized power to give ultimate meaning to the Constitution—"seized" because judicial review is not mentioned in the document. But that Court cannot do it all; it decides "on the merits" only about 150 of some 5,000 cases that are filed each year. This means that state supreme courts, and, more important, the U.S. courts of appeals, are usually final. Of the latter set of courts, by far the most important is that on which Judge Skelly Wright sits—the Court of Appeals for the District of Columbia Circuit.

No one should wonder that nebulous constitutional provisions have meant different things at different times in American history. Constitutional law is *a posteriori* rather than *a priori*. Justice Hans Linde of the Oregon Supreme Court has stated the popular wisdom, which is a corollary to the "middle" way alluded to above, when he asserted that "a constitution must prescribe legitimate processes, not legitimate outcomes, if . . . it is to serve many generations through changing times."[27] Linde was not quite correct: His position is based on the assumption, by no means self-evident and probably at odds with social reality, that deliberation about means to achieve political ends is sufficient to the need, because, as Yves Simon once put it, the problem of social ends has been settled.[28] It is, however, precisely because the problem of those ends has *not* been settled that many constitutional questions arise. One example will suffice: White Americans, speaking generally, have never been able to accept on either the plane of equality of opportunity or of condition the 11 percent of the citizenry who are of African descent.

It is exactly here that Judge Wright's philosophy of judging comes into sharp focus. He is concerned not only with correct procedures, but with the human goals that those procedures are supposed to achieve. To him, law is far from being a homeless, wandering ghost; it is a species of human action established for human purposes and administered by identifiable human beings. That he perceives some of those purposes differently from others surely does not mean that he is wrong or perversely wrong-headed. "The heart has its reasons," Pascal told us, "that reason itself does not know." So it is with Skelly Wright. It has been previously suggested that Wright as judge sees federal courts as a means of fostering fairness and equity in society because they are important teachers in a "system of education." The problem, as Justice Frankfurter once remarked, is to balance "sociological wisdom" with "logical unfolding" in making constitutional decisions.[29] The primary emphasis has to be—and, indeed, it is—on "sociological wisdom," for there is no possible way that the precepts of the numinous document that is the Constitution can be logically unfolded. Wright is quite aware of that, although he has never publicly stated it so bluntly.

In analyzing Judge Wright's judicial method, I do not deal with all of the 1,000-plus decisions he has rendered, but mainly with the "unprovided" cases—those that present new problems to the constitutional order. The facts of these cases can be wrenched into precedent only by Procrustean means. It is on these frontiers of decision making that Wright's work can best be evaluated.

I have previously called Wright a pragmatic instrumentalist, by which was meant that he makes decisions on an *ad hoc* basis with an eye to the consequences of his actions. Despite his assertion, noted above, that "constitutional choices are in fact different from ordinary decisions. . . . The most important value choices have already been made by the Framers of the Constitution,"[30] Wright knows, with Judge Learned Hand, that those constitutional words "are empty vessels into which [a judge] can pour nearly anything he will."[31] Wright harbors no illusions, as apparently Justice Frankfurter did in the *Francis* case, about the surpassing merit of state and local governments. Weaned in the seamy politics of Louisiana in the 1930s and 1940s, he saw at close hand the indignities heaped upon the poor and the disadvantaged. He, therefore, is not at all likely to exalt an abstract political theory over considerations of social justice, as did Frankfurter in *Francis*; nor is he likely to believe that white elected officials would extend a hand of mercy to the sorely troubled Willie Francis.

The work of the Supreme Court in *Willie Francis's Case* has been examined. Suggested above is the idea that Judge Wright has generally followed the Principle of Reason-Directed Societal Self-Interest when making decisions; the remainder of this chapter is mainly devoted to what is meant by that term. It is best seen when cast against the background of the concept of social justice. Wright has wrestled with the difficult problems of reconciling the conflicting imperatives of social justice.

Social justice, as has been adumbrated, is basically distributive. It is concerned with the ways in which benefits are distributed in a given society through its major institutions—how, that is, wealth is allocated, personal rights are protected, and other positive benefits are divided among the populace. Dr. David Miller maintains that the "most valuable general definition of justice is that which brings out its distributive character most plainly: justice is *suum cuique*: to each his due."[32] Further: "The just state of affairs is that in which each individual has exactly those benefits and burdens which are due to him by virtue of his personal characteristics and circumstances." Implicit in that definition is the idea that "equals should be treated equally."[33]

How, then, can it be determined what a person's "due" actually means? Dr. Miller carefully distinguishes "conservative" from "ideal" justice:

For, from one point of view, we are disposed to think that the *customary* distribution of rights, goods, and privileges, as well as the burdens and pains, is natural and just, and that this ought to be maintained by law, as it usually is: while, from another point of view, we seem to recognize an ideal system of rules of distribution ought to exist, but perhaps have never yet existed, and we consider laws to be just in proportion as they confirm to this ideal. (Emphasis in original.)[34]

Similarly, D. D. Raphael contrasts "conservative" and "prosthetic" justice, the former having the object of preserving "an existing order of rights and possessions, or to restore it when any breaches have been made," the latter aiming at "modifying the *status quo*."[35] As Willie Francis's lawyer and as judge, Skelly Wright has had to balance the idea of justice as rights against his instinctive belief in justice in an ideal or prosthetic sense. The Constitution of 1787 is basically one of rights, but in the sense of "vested" rather than "civil" rights. Rights as an aspects of social justice may be summed up in the phrase "to each according to his rights"; or in David Miller's words, rights

generally derive from publicly acknowledged rules, established practices, or past transactions: they do not depend upon a person's current behavior or other individual qualities. For this reason it is appropriate to describe this conception of justice as 'conservative.' *It is concerned with the continuity of a social order over time*, and with ensuring that men's expectations of one another are not disappointed. (Emphasis added.)[36]

Social justice as rights requires that judges protect the "is" in society. Judges generally do so, and that includes Skelly Wright. The task of the judiciary in any modern industrial society is to be a part of the governmental order and thereby both underpin the stability of the system as well as protect the system from attempts to change it. No one becomes a judge in the United States who is not either a member of that nebulous but nonetheless existent group called the Establishment or has views contrary to that group. The legal profession is rights-oriented, as Professor Edward S. Corwin used the term when he maintained that vested rights was the basic doctrine of American constitutional law.[37] Those rights revolve mainly around the concept of property, the protection of which, John Locke maintained, is the first duty of government. Litigation is spawned when those rights come into conflict with human needs. The tension between those two fundamental concepts has been reconciled, so far as reconciliation is possible, by Judge Wright in the application of the Principle of Reason-Directed Societal Self-Interest.

Rights do not exhaust the concept of social justice; needs must also be considered. James C. Davies has maintained, accurately in my judgment, that no one can expect humans to participate in politics (which is what constitutions are all about) until certain basic human needs are fulfilled.[38] Human needs theory is not only a means of explaining certain political behavior but also a basis for judging politics and political institutions. Indeed, one can validly argue that reasonably adequate satisfaction of human needs is the ultimate purpose of politics—and of constitutions. Judge Wright has long focused on human needs in making decisions. The essential point, however, is that, in so doing, he has also protected vested rights. What he has done is to perceive the problem of satisfaction of human needs as basic to social stability. In David Miller's words, he is concerned "with the continuity of a social order over time." Stability and continuity are conservative virtues that, paradoxically, are furthered by the liberal, activist decisions of Skelly Wright. Put another way, Wright is fully aware of the fact that people today live in a time of extraordinarily rapid social change; and he bends his efforts to help preserve the fundamental values of an open society. He knows that as society changes, so too must law; but there are certain basics that are immutable (to him) and that should be protected.

What, then, are human needs? Only an adumbration is possible at this time. Perhaps the best known is Abraham Maslow's hierarchy: "physiological, safety, love, esteem, and self-actualization."[39] That formulation need not be accepted, although, as Professor Christian Bay has observed, it should be used at least until a more useful alternative model is provided.[40] Professor William Galston has asserted that the concept of need has a "threefold classification: natural need, social need, and luxury."[41] Natural needs are "the means required to secure, not only existence, but also the development of existence." Developmental needs include adequate nurturance, adequate education, institutions that permit the exercise of a wide range of capacities, and friendships and social relations. To David Miller: "Harm, for any given individual, is whatever interferes directly or indirectly with the activities essential to his plan of life; and correspondingly, his needs must be understood to comprise whatever is necessary to allow these activities to be carried out.[42]

Obviously, the concept of human needs as a philosophical and jurisprudential construct is complex and controversial. It calls for reorientation of orthodox thinking about law and legal institutions. To analyze the judicial process generally and Judge Wright's work specifically, employing a dichotomous model of rights and needs, is to tread upon legal *terra incognita*. When one deals with language that is part of a constitutive act, when one deals, that is, with "the" Constitution of the United States, much more than purely legal phenomena must be considered. H. J. McCloskey has written:

Needs are things which ought, where possible, to be available, not withheld, prevented, and indeed, to be supplied where necessary; . . . *where needs cannot be met, society or the world ought to be reordered so that they are capable of being met, or obtained by the person with the need, provided that greater goods are not thereby jeopardized*; . . . talk of human needs and needs of particular persons involves reference to natures, the perfection, development, nonimpairment of which are good. (Emphasis added.)[43]

To an indeterminate extent, Judge Wright is interested in reordering society to lend help to those in need. He perceives this goal both as a moral imperative and as a means by which the fundamental values of constitutionalism can be preserved. That intellectual dualism, one overt and the other tacit, comes together in the Principle of Reason-Directed Societal Self-Interest.

Consider, in this regard, Judge Wright's views on equality; they are well known. In 1980, he stated flatly that he was an "uncompromising 'activist' " in the "area of equal rights for disadvantaged minorities."[44] And so he is.

Since the beginnings, Americans have—under their myth system—struggled to fulfill the commitment to equality contained in the Declaration of Independence. Not that the myth comported with bleak reality: It did not, as indentured servants, slaves, Indians, and women, among others, knew and know all too well. The Declaration's commitment to equality was dropped in the Constitution of 1787. Not until 1868, when, after the sanguinary Civil War, the fourteenth amendment was added, did "equal protection" become an express constitutional command. The hard fact, even then, was that paper promises quickly proved to be ephemeral for many Americans. Blacks, as J. R. Pole has remarked, did not have "the consolations of equality or the practice of protection."[45] The Supreme Court did not enforce the equal protection clause. In *Hall v. DeCuir* (1878), for example, the Court struck down a Louisiana statute requiring similar accommodations for all travelers and expressly forbidding discrimination on the basis of color.[46] "Equality is not identity," intoned Justice Nathan Clifford for the Court, in what was to become a famous aphorism—and thereby helped to commit the freed slaves to a *de facto* caste system, a system that was further constitutionalized in 1896 when the Court determined, through an intuition known only to it, that equal protection meant "separate but equal." Says Pole: " . . . white racial prejudice was profound and resilient, as the history of Reconstruction shows. The Court chose to settle [the problem of racial antagonism] not in accordance with its authority under the Fourteenth Amendment . . . but in accordance with the actual distribution of social and political power in Southern states."[47] In so doing, the Justices were major contributors to the development of a boiling reservoir of social discontent.

Skelly Wright is quite aware of the *de facto* caste system in America. He grew up in it and, indeed, accepted it with little or no question until he was a mature man. He changed, as will be shown in the next chapter, during the decade of his thirties. Perhaps his participation in *Willie Francis's Case* was one of the primary motivating factors. Since he has been a judge—for well over thirty years—he has tried as best he could to help alleviate some of the worst features of the caste system (and to aid members of other disadvantaged groups). My suggestion, to repeat, is that he does that both because he perceives it as a moral imperative of the Constitution and because he realizes, probably subconsciously, that the interests of all segments of society are closely intertwined and that, in the last analysis, social harmony depends upon the reasonable satisfaction of the desires (the human needs) of those who live in the lowest social strata.

During Wright's time on the bench, equality has become a major theme of governmental policy. The lead came from federal judges and, of them, principally the Justices of the Supreme Court. But Skelly Wright's career parallels that of the Warren Court; and he has done as much as any, and more than most, to further the cause of equality, of "equal justice under law." Few scholars have asked why the judicial explosion in civil rights and liberties, both revolving around the equality theme, came when it did. In 1927, Justice Holmes sneered that equal protection was "the usual last resort" of constitutional arguments,[48] and summarily dismissed a woman's plea that she should not be sterilized involuntarily by the state of Virginia. Within a generation, that judicial attitude had changed. The question is why. I do not propose to give an answer here, but will set forth two factors that seem significant (and are thus worth further study). First, in the post-World War II period, the United States entered its true Golden Age, a time when the economic pie was getting larger. It therefore became possible to carve slices out of that pie for theretofore "have-nots"—without diminishing the material well-being of the "haves."[49] (That Golden Age is now over, and with it there has come the end of the Second Reconstruction.) Second, the civil rights/civil liberties decisions—the movement toward at least formal equality—were a means of siphoning off discontent from the disadvantaged. Blacks, for example, were extended gains under the formal Constitution (but, as will be seen, few have benefited under the living or operative Constitution). In other words, the equality decisions may be seen as part of the development of a permissive society, one which keeps the bulk of the populace in relative docility. One other factor is worth noting (and study): Blacks and others among the "underclass" were forced to fight and die in World War II, Korea, and Vietnam. The hypothesis is that governmental programs promoting equality are a part of the trade-off, the payment, that was made for that sacrifice.[50]

During America's short-lived Golden Age, Skelly Wright paralleled the Warren Court in intuiting that the person, particularly a member of a disadvantaged group, was a freestanding individual struggling to retain or to gain a measure of personal identity in an increasingly bureaucratized society. Knowing that one's personhood or identity comes only from being able to stand tall in the community, Wright sought to enhance the status of some on the lower rungs of a *de facto* class society, both because they deserved it as persons and because of larger community interests. "Justice," David Miller remarks, "as respect for established rights, without regard to how those rights are distributed among persons, is intelligible when it is seen as the principle which restrains men from destructive greed."[51] It is intelligible, that is, when those who are favored by fortune have the good sense—the common sense, that most uncommon of all the senses—to perceive that it is in *their* interest to help the less favored.[52] It is on this basis that Skelly Wright as jurist can and should be evaluated. He seeks to help Americans answer George Orwell's question about Great Britain: "Whether the British ruling class are wicked or merely stupid is one of the most difficult questions of our time, and at certain moments a very important question."[53]

Skelly Wright as judge realizes the importance of satisfying human needs in order to attain and retain the collective values of stability and vested rights. Not that he has outwardly or even consciously been motivated by the Principle of Reason-Directed Societal Self-Interest; but his decisions, taken together, are an invitation to those Americans who are highest in the social pecking order to use *their* reason to perceive that *their* self-interest lies in reasonably satisfying—within environmental constraints, of course—the needs of those less favored. Wright has not spelled out this principle in so many words; rather, he has followed his instincts—of hardheaded compassion, of knowing what is decent in the circumstances, and of translating those instincts for helping what Mencken called the "great unwashed" into an implicit signal to those who rule to make minimal adjustments so that all will benefit. He uses *his* reason to determine, as best he can, where the self-interest of society—of all affected by his decisions—lies.

The Principle of Reason-Directed Societal Self-Interest by no means is a new technique of governance. Alexis de Tocqueville noted 150 years ago that the United States had an ingrained drive toward equality: "Equality," he wrote, "every day gives every man a multitude of little delights. The charms of equality are felt every hour and are within everyone's reach: the noblest hearts are not insensitive to them and the commonest souls delight in them. The passion to which equality gives birth must thus be at once energetic and general."[54] So it must, although America's ruling class has not been quick to perceive the point. De Tocqueville knew that: "I am of the opinion, on the whole, that the manufacturing aristocracy which is growing up under our eyes is one of the harshest which ever existed in the world."[55] Not until the Progressive movement of the early twentieth century—out of which Skelly Wright emerged—came into fruition in President Franklin D. Roosevelt's New Deal was there even a grudging concession by the "manufacturing aristocracy" (America's ruling class) that it was in their interests to help the poor and the disadvantaged. The New Deal was a social safety valve, bleeding off discontent from among those who were being denied any real chance of fulfillment of the American Dream. It was a means by which the system of corporate capitalism could be saved at minimum cost. Discontent was siphoned off by a series of programs aimed at alleviating the worst aspects of poverty. Even so, "the central dedication of the Franklin Roosevelt administration was to business recovery rather than to social reform."[56] That many "economic royalists"—FDR's label—did not see the New Deal that way suggests that, in Orwell's terms, they were certainly "stupid" (and perhaps "wicked" as well).

The New Deal did not solve the Great Depression; the Second World War did, at least for a time. And a new safety valve was found in a form of economic plenty—not from new lands and newly discovered resources, but because the United States, as has been noted, entered its true Golden Age. New Deal programs continued in effect after the war and were even increased—more and more people were seen to have "entitlements" from government—for the period of American hegemony was seemingly to last indefinitely. Even the first Republican administration after the war knew that help for the disadvantaged had to continue. After all, the war had largely been fought with conscripts—in the name of democratic principles. As in Great Britain, it was as least tacitly perceived by those who wield actual power to see to it that as many as possible benefited from what appeared to be an ever-growing economic cornucopia. As Professor C. B. Macpherson has observed, the Welfare State came because of "the sheer need of governments to allay working-class discontents that were dangerous to the stability of the state. It was Bismarck, the conservative Chancellor of Imperial Germany, and no great democrat, who pioneered the welfare state in the 1880s, for just this purpose."[57]

Simultaneously, as was adumbrated above, another safety valve came into existence: the spate of civil rights/civil liberties decisions coming from the Supreme Court, other federal courts, and some state courts. For the first time in American history, the rights of ordinary Americans and even of the disadvantaged received judicial (constitutional) protection. Led by the courts, all of government became committed to the principle of at least formal equality. It was a major constitutional revolution. Skelly Wright has been deeply immersed in that movement since the time when he represented Willie Francis, and particularly since he became a judge.

The constitutional revolution had many faces, not all of which were judicially sponsored or governmentally approved. A profound social, rather than merely legal, change, it was characterized by the implicit promises of the Declaration of Independence. Furthermore, it was a cultural change, one in which a permissive society came into being. Life-styles were altered. A drug culture blossomed; alcohol consumption escalated; abortions became routine; the most flagrant pornography was no longer outlawed; freedom of expression received the highest degree of protection under the formal Constitution in American history; the poor and disadvantaged dared to hope that they, too, could sup at the groaning tables of opulence that was the American economy—all these, and more, have created a society in which the citizenry enjoys increased rights (at least in the formal Constitution) *against* the state and at the same time receives greater benefits—entitlements—*from* the state. That was something new under the constitutional sun.

All political and social phenomena have identifiable functions. In *The Pathology of Politics*, Professor Carl Friedrich argued that such dysfunctional—some would say aberrational—matters as violence, betrayal, corruption, secrecy, and propaganda all serve definite functions, "notably that of facilitating the adaptation of a system or regime to changing conditions occurring either in the system or the social structure, or in the outside environment."[58] Judicial decisions are political epiphenomena; and courts are instruments of politics, both in their lawmaking proclivities and in the fact that they often are the targets of interest groups. The judiciary's main function is to produce decisions that are not only system-maintaining, but also system-developing. A political function, Friedrich maintains, "is the correspondence between a political process or institution and the needs or requirements of a political order." Any political order requires both stability and a process of orderly change. The great and continuing task of federal judges is to facilitate both elements. They buttress the existing constitutional order—the "system"—and by successive interpretations they enable change to occur. That change, it is important to note, is within rather severely constricted boundaries; federal judges. may have participated in a constitutional revolution, but they emphatically are not wild-eyed revolutionaries. They make haste slowly; their changes in law are incremental rather than fundamental.

So it is with J. Skelly Wright. I have previously called attention to the distinction between *manifest* and *latent* functions of societal institutions. Simply put, manifest functions are the obvious ones, the outward ones. They are important by themselves, but must be considered in conjunction with latent functions—those that do not immediately meet the eye but may be of far greater significance. Using that classification, what may be said about Judge Wright's hundreds of decisions since 1949? The answer is clear. Their manifest function, quite often at least, was to help bring discrete minorities into the mainstream of American life, to protect the individual in his personhood against arbitrary governmental actions. Subsequent chapters will discuss how that goal is reflected in a range of decisions involving the status of black Americans, environmental hazards, the position of those caught in the toils of criminal law enforcement, national security, and freedom of expression. At the same time, it is fair to say that the latent function of many of Wright's decisions was and is to protect the system and those who profit most from it. He has helped to siphon off hydraulic pressures of social discontent but has done so at least possible cost to those who control and rule. Skelly Wright is, first and foremost, a member of the Establishment, but one who sees more clearly than others that there must be some play in the constitutional (and thus, the social) joints if the system is to endure.

I do not, of course, maintain that all of Wright's decisions can be so categorized; nor do I say that he either stated or even realized what in fact he was doing. What I do say is that he knows intuitively that some sort of social trade-off must be forthcoming, so that those of lesser status can enjoy some of the fruits of America's bounty—and, thus not unduly rock the existing social structure. And I do not contend that those in positions of power will either read or, of more importance, heed the implicit warning that Skelly Wright and other judges are issuing. The contrary might well be true.

Since judges, including J. Skelly Wright, are invariably taken from the Establishment, how is it that some of them can see farther and see truly what others cannot (or will not)? Their heredities and biographies do not seem to differ in any essential way. Can this be called the X factor? Some, as with Skelly Wright, have X; whereas others, indeed most, do not. If one takes Wright's decisions as a whole, what does one perceive? The judge *engagé*—and perhaps even *enragé*. A man committed to decency, to be worked out through legal processes. A legal craftsman who has been able to overcome a mediocre education. A man with a penchant for excellence. A natural politician, both as United States Attorney and as judge. A person who is able to cut through legal technicalities and see the human factor in the disputes brought before him. The X factor, therefore, is an ability to both see and empathize with the human beings who are caught, one way or another, in the webs of society's inequities in the administration of the law; and to realize that law and legal process are, in first and last analysis, instruments to further human ends rather than being ends in themselves. Skelly Wright as judge is not enmeshed in the ideological swamp of legalism, as are so many lawyers and lawyer-judges. He sees the *needs* as well as the *rights* involved in specific cases, and strikes balances between them. Of course he is result-oriented; but so, too, are all judges—including Justice Frankfurter, who liked to pretend that he was not. Wright has no magic formula to determine "goodness"—or, indeed, to make more than an informed, albeit intuitive, guess as to where the balance between needs and rights should be struck. If he says that needs, as I have defined them, should at times override rights—again, as I have defined them—it is because of two primary factors: an abiding compassion and an instinctive grasp of the overall societal weal. In saying that he is compassionate, I do not mean that his is a weak-kneed sentimentality. Far from it. His compassion is hardheaded.

I do not maintain that all of Judge Wright's work fits into the category of Reason-Directed Societal Self-Interest. What I do say is that important decisional categories can be so analyzed. That will become evident in Chapter 3, dealing with race relations, where Wright's commitment to equality may be seen in its starkest form. A final caveat is necessary: Based on a speech delivered in 1979, Wright has been considered by some to have receded from his advanced position as a judicial activist. I doubt that this is true, but some of what he said then is worth quoting:

To put the question baldly: should judges be meddling less in the running of the country?

There is no easy answer. The more the Congress by its laws and the Executive by regulations intrude into the lives of the citizenry and the operations of the business community, the more the judicial branch is asked to intervene to safeguard property or liberty. Moreover, the courts themselves are often accused of imposing their own unwanted restrictions on the operation of government. For my part, I believe the judges *should* retrench from the disposition to act as final arbiters of the public good. We should, I think, be more reluctant than we have been to fault other agencies of government and, also, more hesitant about filling the void when, in our judgment, the elected branches of government should have acted and failed. But I make one important exception: the area of equal rights for disadvantaged minorities. As to that, I remain an uncompromising "activist." (Emphasis in original.)[59]

This is not the language of a perfervid judicial activist. Does it signal a change in his judicial philosophy, rather like what seemed to happen to Justice Hugo Black toward the end of his career? The answer, on the whole record, is no.

3

Judge Wright and the "American Dilemma"

The American Negro is a totally American responsibility. Three hundred years ago he was brought to this country by our forefathers and sold into slavery. One hundred years ago we fought a war that would set him free. For these last one hundred years we have lived and professed the hypocrisy that he was free. The time has now come when we must face up to that responsibility. Let us erase this blemish—let us remove this injustice—from the face of America. Let us make the Negro free.

—J. Skelly Wright (1965)[1]

I

Except for the eighteenth century, when the institution of slavery was written into the Constitution and protected, white Americans have had a great uneasiness about black Americans. The Founding Fathers had no doubt and no uneasiness about involuntary servitude; after all, many were themselves slave owners. At best, the Framers were able to forget their own enslavement of blacks while simultaneously conjuring up fancied British efforts to subject them (whites) to slavery. Said Thomas Jefferson in 1774: The British have undertaken "a deliberate systematical plan of reducing us to slavery."[2] Not that the British were above that—after all, a few decades later they complacently watched many Irish die from starvation—but the refusal to admit what anyone could see was an early example of the hypocrisy that Skelly Wright observed in 1965. In effect, he echoed Samuel Johnson's sarcastic question: "How is it that the loudest yelps for liberty come from the drivers of slaves?"[3] The men who in the Declaration of Independence could flatly assert that "all men are created equal" really did not believe that hortatory slogan, for they were the same men who began the systematic genocide of native Americans (Indians) and who saw no discrepancy in owning and selling men (and women and children) much the same as farm animals—even white slaves, as Fawn Brodie has recounted: "When the celebrated republican savant and refugee, the Comte de Volney, visited Monticello in June 1796, he noted in his journal astonishment at seeing slave children as white as himself. *'Mais je fus étonné de voir appeler noirs et traiter comme tels des enfants aussi blanc que moi.'* " Volney was appalled by Jefferson's treatment of his slaves—the *"deminudité miserable et hideuse"* condition of the great libertarian's fieldworkers.[4]

Jefferson, of course, was not atypical; others among the group that Alexander Hamilton called the "rich and the well-born" (in the constitutional convention)[5] saw no impropriety in owning, working, and selling humans. Indeed, this group—those who wrote the Constitution—feared the mass of the people and designed the new charter of government in ways to insulate government from what Hamilton called the "unsteadiness" of the people. Their political power was derived from wealth and position. "They were located at or near the seats of government and they were in direct contact with legislatures and government officers. They influenced and often dominated the local newspapers which voiced the ideas and interests of commerce and identified them with the good of the whole people, the state, and the nation. The published writing of the leaders of the period are almost without exception those of merchants, of their lawyers, or of politicians sympathetic to them."[6] In sum, the Framers feared what John Adams called a "democratical despotism" and took pains to ensure that the levers of political power would not be democratically exercised.

Throughout American history, white Americans have never come to terms with the brutal treatment of Africans and their descendants—whether as slaves or in the post-Civil War *de facto* caste system of peonage or even when the formal emancipation of blacks began when the Supreme Court decided *Brown v. Board of Education* in 1954. (That decision, as will be shown, has changed many lives, including that of Judge Wright.) Whites have pretended that all people are equal, all the while knowing that large inequalities existed and were protected by law. Blacks were not the only victims; but since they were locked into legal servitude, they were the most obvious. "The equal legal and moral status of free individuals was America's reason for independent existence. Yet only at comparatively rare—and then generally stormy—intervals has the idea of equality dominated American debates on major questions of policy. . . . The discrepancy between the public commitment and the public concern to translate commitment into policy can hardly be explained on the comfortable ground of an achievement that had at any time left little room for advance."[7] There has always been a wide gap between pretense and reality in America's belief in "equal justice under law"—the slogan deeply carved in the facade of the Supreme Court's building in Washington. And there can be little doubt that white Americans prefer a *de facto* class (caste) system, in which blacks are relegated to a permanent underclass—out of which few can or will escape. Skelly Wright knows this very well; it is the "hypocrisy" about which he wrote in 1965. It still exists.[8]

Black Americans today have formal equality under the law. But the living or operative Constitution speaks otherwise: They have neither equality of opportunity nor equality of esteem. I, of course, am speaking in general terms, not about a few individuals such as Marian Anderson, Leontyne Price, Ralph Bunche, William T. Coleman, William Raspberry, Martin Luther King, Jr., Andrew Young, Thurgood Marshall, and others who have been able by one means or another to reach the pinnacle of their professions. Blacks *en masse*—there are more than 20 million—are still second-class citizens in a nation that stoutly but inaccurately maintains that it is a democracy and is not ridden by class or undue privilege. Having formal equality under the Constitution will remain a meaningless "commitment" of the American people until such time as the formal law is meshed with the living or operative law. The basic hypocrisy of the Founding Fathers still abides. In this chapter, how Judge Skelly Wright has dealt with what Gunnar Myrdal aptly called "an American dilemma" is discussed, with the principal focus upon his work as a district judge in Louisiana and an appeals judge in Washington. I do not, of course, suggest that the abrasive and unresolved problem of race—of *skin color*—exhausts the constitutional concept of equality. Far from it. Since, however, this is a book about Skelly Wright as a judge, racial matters are emphasized because they have far and away been the principal preoccupation of his equality decisions. Furthermore, inasmuch as Wright's work as judge has paralleled that of the Supreme Court, and at times has preceded it, some attention will perforce be paid to the High Bench's equality decisions as well. For example, Wright's views on *de facto* racial segregation may well have had influence on Supreme Court decisions. Judge Carl McGowan, one of Wright's colleagues (now retired) in Washington, made the general point in 1969:

It is . . . no detraction from the Supreme Court's achievement in the school segregation cases to conclude that its path was made easier, its range of alternatives enlarged, by decisions taken earlier in the life of the republic with respect to the organization of national judicial power. The same can be said of many other advancements and alterations in legal doctrine summoned into being by the Supreme Court's expansive reading of familiar constitutional phrases. . . . Without the availability of the local federal courts, it is difficult to believe that this audacious venture by the Supreme Court into the political thickets would have appeared feasible in the first place.[9]

In other words, the federal judiciary is a system, a continuing system; and Judge Wright's decisions in racial segregation cases should be perceived as a segment of interactions between the Supreme Court and lower federal courts.

II

The Constitution of 1787 did not contain an express commitment to equality (or "equal protection of the laws"). That idea was lost somewhere between the Declaration of Independence in 1776 and 1787, as was "the pursuit of happiness" as a governmental goal. And none came into the document until 1868, when the fourteenth amendment was rammed through the states and duly ratified. Even then, the amendment dealt only with the actions of the several states, not with the federal government (". . . no state . . . shall deny to any person within its jurisdiction the equal protection of the laws"). That cryptic phrase has spawned numerous lawsuits, particularly in recent years. It is shot with ambiguity. What, for example, does the term "state"—or, as it is usually put, "state action"—mean? To what extent does state involvement in nominally private activity, such as corporations, bring those groups within the reach of the amendment? What, precisely, does "equal" mean? And what are the "laws"?[10]

This is not the place to undertake a thoroughgoing examination of the concept of equality in the Constitution.[11] A few general statements must suffice. First, at times the Supreme Court "incorporates" the equal protection clause into the fifth amendment's due process clause, so as to make the equality principle applicable to the national government. The leading judicial statement is *Bolling v. Sharpe*, a 1954 decision dealing with racial segregation in the District of Columbia public schools.[12] Second, the amendment reaches all types of official action—legislative, executive, and judicial. Third, at times but far from usually, "state action" under the Constitution has been applied to private groups (usually in cases concerning issues other than equal protection). Fourth, since Supreme Court decisions in particular cases are routinely considered to promulgate general rules, an edict of the Court in equal protection (and other) cases can and does have an impact far beyond the immediate litigants. Finally, "equal" is not defined literally or absolutely. It is not a legal leveling device, designed and interpreted to bring all Americans into roughly the same status. Under the formal Constitution (of the books), equality of *opportunity* appears to be protected—but not equality of *esteem* or of *condition*. Under the actual (or living) Constitution, even the protection of equality of opportunity is honored more in the breach than in the observance. Governments can and do classify persons routinely; the test of classificatory actions is usually for the Supreme Court to inquire into whether they were "rational." Did they meet a test of reasonableness as intuited by federal judges? That means that judges act as psychologists in black robes, but without benefit of training in the esoterica of psychology or even of what rationality means. The Supreme Court operates as a little lunacy committee, making *ad hoc* determinations as to whether other governmental officers were making "rational" decisions. At relatively rare times, classifications or distinctions made by government are subjected to what, in legal jargon, is called "strict scrutiny"—those dealing with "fundamental" rights (fundamental, as determined by the Supreme Court)—which means that some classifications are of an inherently "suspect" nature. Hence, they require much more factual and other justifications to be sustained. Race is such a suspect classification. Obviously, that use of such nebulous formulae results in considerable, at times absolute, discretion in judges. As was said in Chapter 2 about judges determining a societal consensus or conscience, modern technology has not produced a device by which reasonableness can be measured. It is not an external standard of judgment; rather, it is a way that judges and others can pretend that law rules, while simultaneously allowing the subjective determinations of men (and women) to control. Judge Wright knows that, and acts accordingly.

Two other points merit present attention. First, the ways that laws are administered can be held to violate equal protection. A statute or ordinance that is nondiscriminatory "on its face" can, by unequal administration, be constitutionally invalid. That requires, of course, inquiry into what governmental officers actually do, as distinguished from what the formal laws state that they are supposed to do. Second, the Supreme Court in recent years has discovered, through an intuition known only to the Justices, that equal protection requires a subjective intention to discriminate unfairly. The mere fact of difference in treatment is not enough. That places an onerous burden upon those who contest official classifications: they must prove a state of mind. If, however, as the saying goes, "the devil himself knows not the mind of man," how possibly can the motivation of legislators and administrators be shown in any convincing way? The point here is that the Supreme Court has recently begun to recede from its commitment to equality, as seen, for example, in *Brown v. Board of Education* and progeny.

There is, in sum, an eroding commitment to racial (and other) equality on the part of the Supreme Court. Skelly Wright, and a few other judges on federal and state courts, continue to try to further civil rights and liberties, but their efforts are slowly being chipped away by a Court dominated by Justice William Rehnquist. True enough, *Brown v. Board of Education* has not been overruled—and there is no likelihood that it will be—but the Nixon Court is managing to limit its reach. Put another way, the Justices are refusing to mesh the explicit command of the formal Constitution with that of the living or operative Constitution. The United States is not reverting to the *status quo ante*. The odious formula of "separate-but-equal" that the Supreme Court enunciated in 1896 (in *Plessy v. Ferguson*) is not the formal law. In fact, however, black Americans—most of them—are both separate *and* unequal. We have not come full cycle, but if present trends continue—and they show few signs of diminishing—the United States will indeed become, as the Kerner Commission commented in 1968, "two societies, one black, one white—separate and unequal."[13]

"What white Americans have never fully understood—but what the Negro can never forget—is that white society is deeply implicated in the ghetto. White institutions created it, white institutions maintain it, and white society condones it."[14] There is an "insidious and pervasive white sense of the inferiority of black men."[15] It is the nation's shame, its deepest failure, its greatest challenge. Consider the role of the Supreme Court in legitimizing this shame and failure (we come later to the Court's brave meeting of the challenge). In *Plessy v. Ferguson* (1896),[16] the Court invented the "separate-but-equal" doctrine as a sufficient way to satisfy the command of the Constitution's equal protection clause. Said Justice Henry Brown for the Court: If blacks thought that racial discrimination was invidious and constitutionally improper, it was only because of their own beliefs and not because of anything Louisiana had done (in making it unlawful for blacks to sit in railroad cars reserved for whites). The lone dissenter, Justice John M. Harlan I, saw through the charade in a famous passage:

The white race deems itself to be the dominant race in this country. And so it is, in prestige, in achievements, in education, in wealth, and in power. So, I doubt not, it will continue to be for all time, if it remains true to its great heritage and holds fast to the principles of constitutional liberty. But in view of the Constitution, in the eye of the law, there is in this country no superior, dominant, ruling class of citizens. *There is no caste here. Our Constitution is color-blind and neither knows nor tolerates classes among citizens.* In respect of civil rights, all citizens are equal before the law. The humblest is the peer of the most powerful. The law regards man as man, and takes no account of his surroundings or color when his civil rights as guaranteed by the supreme law of the land are involved. (Emphasis added.)

Much of Harlan's statement is really not correct. True, the *formal* law is "color-blind," and castes are not decreed by law. But when one delves below the formality of the Constitution, of the statutes enacted pursuant to it, and of the judicial decisions construing both, one soon perceives that classes—and, indeed, a *de facto* caste system—*do* exist—and always have throughout American history. The "humblest" is by no means "the peer of the most powerful," yesterday and today. The point is generally valid—for the poor and disadvantaged of whatever ethnic origin. Blacks, however, are the most prominent of the underclass, and the ones with the longest history of indecent treatment by whites.

That became utterly clear only three years after *Plessy* was decided, when the Court determined that a board of education could close a black high school for economic reasons, even though black students were not admitted to the white high school.[17] In a 1980 law journal article, Skelly Wright stated in pungent terms his views of what the Supreme Court had done:

> Color-blind theory has proven to be the main tribute inequality pays to the principle of equality in our national life. At the nation's founding, the assertion that "all men are created equal" was used to justify establishment of a regime in which enslavement of the black population was given constitutional sanction. In 1857 the Supreme Court managed to harmonize the principle of equality with the continued existence of slavery by simply declaring that black persons are not citizens. In 1896 the Supreme Court placed its imprimatur on a ghastly system of apartheid, but in doing so, felt it necessary to declare the policy "separate but equal." It is a tribute to the American ideal of equality that the High Court was driven to *lie* rather than admit what it was doing. (Emphasis in original.)[18]

And lie the Justices did, as did most others in positions of authority. The "ideal of equality" Wright mentions has never been more than that—an ideal, often far from the spotted actuality.

Plessy v. Ferguson signaled the end of the First Reconstruction, embedding into the Constitution a concept of *de facto* peonage and second-class citizenship for Americans of African descent. It was to take decades before the Second Reconstruction began. Starting in 1938, albeit haltingly, when the Court repeated the *Plessy* doctrine but held that Missouri had to provide a law school for black students, and moving slowly until the late 1940s, "separate but equal" was finally repudiated in 1954. The case was *Brown v. Board of Education*, and with it *Bolling v. Sharpe*. Formal constitutional law has not been the same since, and neither has the Supreme Court. "*Brown v. Board of Education* was the beginning,"[19] both of official attempts to put black Americans into the mainstream of the nation's life and of a new posture for the Supreme Court. (I have dealt with the latter development elsewhere, and will not repeat myself here.[20])

The promise of *Brown* has not been realized. The Second Reconstruction, though not formally dead, is dying, killed by whites who dominate the politico-legal system and who simply will not accept blacks as a group into the mainstream of society. A few, yes, but not *en masse*. Most blacks exist in what seems to be a permanent underclass. Skelly Wright's judicial career illustrates the rise and fall of the Second Reconstruction. There are two principal episodes: (1) *The rise*: Wright's tenure as a federal district judge in New Orleans when he had the responsibility of implementing the Supreme Court's decree in the *Brown* case; schools were to be racially integrated "with all deliberate speed." This period shows how Wright dealt with *de jure* segregation (that required by law). (2) *The fall*: Wright's work in Washington as an appeals judge, where he was confronted with *de facto* segregation (not mandated by law but by housing patterns). In what follows, attention will also be paid to so-called affirmative action programs, which have been developed to help remedy the continued social and economic deprivation of blacks and other minorities. Wright has not dealt with this issue as a judge, but has made his views known in law journal articles. In addition, some mention will be made of "black nationalism"—the desire, ever more insistent, of many blacks to maintain a separate identity as a group. Many blacks today wish not to be fully integrated into white society but, rather, to exist as a separate nation within a nation. They still want equality of treatment, however, a fact which creates a high potential for social tension and conflict. Oddly, these black leaders call for "separate but equal," although not in the sense of the odious *Plessy v. Ferguson* formulation. Judge Wright has yet to confront this emergent question.

III

I begin with the *de facto* segregaton issue because it best shows the interaction of the Justices of the Supreme Court and lower court judges and because Skelly Wright's views on that type of segregation may well have had an influence beyond an important decision he rendered in 1967. By that decision, *Hobson v. Hansen*,[21] he has been accused of "ruining" the schools in Washington, D.C.[22] *Hobson* was not one decision, but a series lasting from 1967 to 1973. It shows in microcosm the difficulties of judges acting as social planners. Judicial review historically was naysaying: It told officers in other branches of government that they had exceeded their proper bounds (set by the Constitution, statutes, or the common law). It constrained action, rather than commanded it. *Hobson* typifies judges as commanders—affirmatively requiring action. *Hobson* is such a case. But it is more than an example of a judge trying, and succeeding at best only imperfectly, to rectify traditional social inequities; its facts display the pervasive refusal of white Americans to accept blacks in anything more than a token way. Finally, *Hobson* illustrates the limits of law, however and by whomever promulgated, as a principle of social order.[23]

The Supreme Court's numerous decisions in *Brown v. Board of Education* and progeny swept away *de jure* racial separateness. That separate public institutions could not be equal was the essential message of both those decisions and Congress's enactment of such statutes as the Civil Rights Acts of 1964 and the Voting Rights Act of 1965. Both statutes were aftermaths of the Court's initial breakthrough. A nationalization of consciousness and of conscience, without precedent in American history, gripped the nation: The Second Reconstruction was born, a lusty infant that seemed to have the portent of changing society itself. But that was not to be. *Brown* and progeny did not alter fundamental economic and social structures. Nor did those pronouncements effect a psychological change in the minds of most whites. So blacks have remained, throughout the land, crammed into nauseous ghettos that are mandated not by law, but by dint of both circumstance and the ability of whites generally to isolate themselves in their own privileged enclaves. In recent years, the Supreme Court, in a series of decisions, has aided whites in their wish to be separate. For example, in *City of Mobile v. Bolden* (1980)[24] the Court held that the city's at-large voting system for electing city commissioners was valid over an argument that the votes of blacks were unconstitutionally diluted. Professor Aviam Soifer has summed up the implications:

It is as if in 1980 black citizens no longer constitute a discrete and insular minority. A black citizen's constitutional claim will not prevail unless he can demonstrate precise intentional discrimination against himself as an individual or some specific and intentional discriminatory treatment of blacks. Otherwise, the promise of the fourteenth and fifteenth amendments, and the civil rights revolution, has either been satisfied or is properly left to the politicians. As we enter the 1980s, it is presumed that we all compete fairly. When no bad guys can be connected to evil discriminatory deeds, the Court apparently assumed that we all enjoy equal and fair opportunity.[25]

That Soifer was correct in his assessment was verified by the Court itself in 1981. In *City of Memphis v. Greene*[26] the Court sustained blocking a street that led from the ghetto to a white enclave. The Justices held that it was a mere "inconvenience" to blacks and that no discriminatory motive had been proved. Said Justice Thurgood Marshall in dissent: "A group of white citizens has decided to act to keep Negro citizens from traveling through their urban 'utopia,' and the city has placed its seal of approval on the plan." So, too, did the High Court, which in effect declared victory in the battle for civil rights, even though blacks do not—and on the undisputed facts, should not—feel victorious. And it is worth remembering that, as has been noted, outlawry of *de jure* segregation came simultaneously with America's true Golden Age—the period from 1945 to about 1970.

Dual, racially separate schools (and other facilities) were maintained in Washington, D.C., until the 1950s. In 1954, the Supreme Court ended that when it read an equal protection provision into the fifth amendment's due process clause. But the actual changes have been minimal: Racial integration was avoided by whites because of housing patterns. Blacks lived and still live mostly in the northeast and southeast sections of the city, while whites were and are congregated in the northwest and southwest. Students were permitted to choose their own schools, provided they supplied their own transportation. Whites made the greatest use of this option. In 1953, the white population of public schools was 56.9 percent, but by 1965 it was only 10 percent. Today, it is almost nonexistent. *De facto* segregation thus became the rule, with white families sending their children to private schools or moving to the suburbs of Virginia and Maryland.

When the school board established an "ability grouping" or "tracking" system, grouping students according to their ability, the result was further resegregation. The tracking plan, accordingly, drew severe criticism. Charges were made that children were placed in "tracks" because of their race and that, once placed, a child was seldom transferred to other tracks. In addition, teachers were segregated along racial lines. Ghetto schools not only were overcrowded and comparatively underfunded, but also did not have the same quality of education as schools in predominantly white areas. All of this led Julius Hobson, a federal employee, to sue the Board of Education, alleging that black and poor children were denied their constitutional right to equal educational opportunity. The consequence was *Hobson v. Hansen,* heard and decided by appeals Judge Wright sitting as a trial (district) judge because at that time all of Washington's district judges were disqualified. By law, they had appointed the Board of Education. (That law has since been changed.)

The challenge was daunting. *Hobson* was one of those "unprovided" cases; little or no precedent was available. Skelly Wright had to write on a clean slate. He did so. Meeting the challenge head-on, and drawing on a number of racial segregation cases as well as other equal protection cases, Wright distilled the proposition that the equal protection clause was "the cutting edge of our expanding constitutional liberty." The liberty protected by the fifth amendment's due process clause was neatly merged into a concept of equality. Desegregation, mandated by the *Brown* decision, was to become integration, both *de jure* and *de facto.* The right of an individual had been translated into the right of a group. That was an exponential jump in law, the goal of which was to merge blacks into the dominant white community. Individual rights, in matters of race at least, had become status rights—the right of an individual as a member of the group. (Others, most of whom are not faced with the burden of having to make decisions in such contentious matters, have faulted the idea that liberty and equality are, as Wright said, congruent.)[27]

Skelly Wright made a sociologically wise decision in the *Hobson* case, but only so far as black students in Washington were concerned. It would be difficult to convince the whites who fled to other schools that the decision was wise. He conceded that "it is regrettable that in deciding this case this court must act in an area so alien to its expertise. It would be far better for these great social and political problems to be resolved in the political arena. . . . But there are social and political problems which seem at times to defy such resolution. In such situations, under our system, the judiciary must bear a hand and accept its responsibility to assist in the solution when constitutional rights hang in the balance." By focusing on the negative effects that the tracking system had on disadvantaged minorities, Wright determined that their human needs had been violated without a showing of an overriding governmental justification. He thus went beyond the traditional "rational basis" test of the validity of classifications when challenged on equal protection grounds. He wrote:

If the situation were one involving racial imbalance but in some facility other than the public schools, or unequal educational opportunity without any Negro or poverty aspects (e.g., unequal schools all within an economically homogeneous white suburb), it might be pardonable to uphold the practice on a minimal showing of rational basis. But the fusion of these two elements irresistibly calls for additional justification. What supports this call is our horror at inflicting any further injury on the Negro, the degree to which the poor and the Negro must rely on the public schools in rescuing themselves from their depressed cultural and economic condition, and also *our common need of the schools to serve as the public agency for neutralizing and normalizing race relations in this country.* With these interests at stake, the court must ask whether the virtues stemming from the Board of Education's pupil assignment policy . . . are compelling or adequate justification for the considerable evils of de facto segregation which adherence to this policy breeds. (Emphasis added.)

That is an express illustration of Wright's adherence to the Principle of Reason-Directed Societal Self-Interest. Not only were the disadvantaged to be helped by judicial action—in furtherance of the equality concept—he also spoke of "our common need" for the schools to help ameliorate racial tensions. He thereby signaled the avowedly political branches of government to face up to the chore of equalizing in fact the "cultural and economic" conditions of the blacks, both for the good of those in "depressed" situations and for society at large.

Judge Wright rendered what he perceived to be the just result by using what has been called "the high talents of a constitutional *bricoleur.*" *Bricolage,* a French term, is "the art of the do-it-yourself handyman who must solve problems given only limited tools and his own ingenuity."[28] For that, he has been faulted by many whites. In substantial part, the basis for his decision was undercut by the Supreme Court in 1973 when it repudiated the notion that there was a constitutional right to education, while refusing to order equalization of expenditures between school districts in San Antonio, Texas.[29] That decision, however, came several years after *Hobson,* and was one of the earlier examples of the previously-noted Supreme Court retreat from advancing civil rights. Wright anticipated, at least inferentially, the furor that erupted after *Hobson.* He stated in his opinion that "judicial deference" to legislative and administrative judgments ordinarily

is predicated on the confidence courts have that they are just resolutions of conflicting interests. This confidence is often misplaced when the vital interests of the poor and racial minorites are involved. For these groups are not always assured a full and fair hearing through the ordinary political processes, not so much because of outright bias, but because of the abiding danger that the power structure—a term which need carry no disparaging or abusive overtones—may incline to pay little heed to even the deserving interests of a politically voiceless and invisible minority.

Wright's use of the word "deserving" in that quotation clearly indicates that his concept of human needs (which is central to his placement of equality highest in the hierarchy of his constitutional values) includes, however inchoately, some degree of human deserts. It will be recalled that, in Chapter 2, I drew attention to Dr. David Miller's triad of social justice concepts: rights, needs, and deserts. *Hobson* is a case of which Judge Wright came squarely down upon the manifest needs and deserts of the black populace in Washington. The difficulty arises, as has been mentioned, when he meshes equality with liberty. Precisely whose liberty did he have in mind? It can be persuasively argued that the liberty of the white students was being curtailed. That, at least, was the way in which many saw the situation. Furthermore, by employing the term "power structure," Wright knew quite well that he had to convince those who were at the levers of power in Washington that the dreary condition of blacks had to be bettered. He was not at all confident that that could be done.

Be that as it may, it is certain that Wright in 1967 (and later) perceived no feasible alternative, under his views of social justice, in making the decisions in *Hobson*. Are there bases for faulting his rulings? Three may be mentioned. First, there can be no doubt that he made up the law in the case. But this objection falls of its own weight. Judges since the beginnings of time have been acting in similar or at least analogous ways. The history of Anglo-American law is largely one of judges making the laws, all the while proceeding, as has been mentioned, as though they were merely "finding" them. Second, he had previously gone in public record, in a speech delivered at New York University, as being opposed to *de facto* segregation. That meant that he had apparently prejudged the case. This criticism has more substance. By hindsight at least, the speech was ill-advised because it tarnished the requirement for the appearance of impartial justice. Wright has admitted as much, saying in June, 1983, that had there been a timely motion by the defendant, he would have had to recuse himself.[30] There are two answers to the criticism, neither of which is fully satisfactory. On the one hand, many other judges—including, among those presently sitting, Chief Justice Warren Burger and Justices William Rehnquist and Sandra O'Connor of the Supreme Court—have not been reluctant to express their general views about issues of public policy that have eventually come before them. The short answer to this is that, as the cliché goes, two wrongs do not make a right. But knowing that others have done it, publicly and privately, helps to set Wright's speech in perspective. On the other hand, when a person becomes a judge, he or she does not thereby relinquish his or her rights of citizenship, including the first amendment rights of freedom of expression. That, of course, is accurate. Furthermore, the line between what is judicially proper and what is not is hazy at best. Finally, all know or should know that judges are not intellectual eunuchs: they do have opinions and predilections. The important thing to know about a judge is his or her philosophy. Lawyers know that judges, as Justice William Douglas once observed, are not "fungible," for they often go "judge-shopping."[31]

Third, and of greatest significance, is the fact that white enrollment in Washington's public schools all but vanished as an aftermath of *Hobson.* Judge Wright could not control the wholly predictable second-order consequences of his decrees. He had no political elite that could be mobilized to support the rulings. So white students fled, and Washington's schools, for various reasons, have declined in quality since *Hobson.* They were never very good to begin with. Even Thurgood Marshall, the first black Justice of the Supreme Court, sent his children to private schools. This criticism of Wright's *Hobson* decisions presents the question of the built-in limits of courts as social planners. Said more broadly, the basic problem is the extent to which a judge can reasonably believe that those in the political branches of government will read and heed a given decree. On that score, there was little room for optimism. The District of Columbia was, and largely still is, a colonial enclave ruled by "absentee landlords"—the chairmen of the standing committees of Congress having jurisdiction over the District. Furthermore, there was no possible way that Judge Wright could stop the flight to the suburbs; his powers were confined to the District only. And within the District, those who had political power, officially or otherwise, had no interest in bettering the condition of black schools.

Knowing all of that, Skelly Wright still went on. He could not bring himself to dash the flickering hopes of blacks who were trying to bootstrap their way to a better status. Did he, then, "ruin" the Washington public schools? It is difficult to conclude that he did. As has been noted, after the 1954 Supreme Court decision desegregating Washington's schools, a massive drop in white enrollment had occurred. If the schools were in fact ruined, it is because of the failures of those who in fact ruled the District. The "system" failed, not the judge. Adequate financing of Washington's schools was simply not possible under the built-in prejudices of the white southerners who headed the congressional committees. Absolutely no attempt was made in Congress to alter the ancient system of governing the District. And no one tried to rearrange political boundaries so that Washington could be governed as a metropolitan area, which in fact it is, an area that extends into Virginia and Maryland as well as the few square miles of the District. Judge Wright is fully aware of the problem. He stated in 1975: "White flight can be slowed, and eventually reversed, only by incorporating the suburbs and the central city into a single political community, capable of removing the incentives to mass segregation. . . . Only with metropolitan government can we begin to replace fear and hate with the development of a sense that each citizen's fate is necessarily linked to that of every other citizen."[32]

The United States is unique in placing such onerous burdens upon the shoulders of lawyer-judges. Americans are notoriously litigious, as Alexis de Tocqueville observed 150 years ago. In recent years, courts have been called upon to do more and more—perhaps, as with black Americans, because the political branches of government are closed to them. The consequence, exemplified in *Brown v. Board of Education* and progeny, including *Hobson v. Hansen*, is that litigation has become a political tactic and courts are the targets of pressure groups. The meaning is clear: "Litigation is now more explicitly problem-solving than grievance-answering."[33] That is particularly true at the highest level of the judiciary, where litigants are important not so much because of the merit or lack of merit of their particular case, but because only they can trigger the system. Once the system begins its work, the litigants fade into the background as the courts—particularly the Supreme Court, but also courts of appeals and other appellate benches—seek to promulgate general rules. Judge Wright was called upon to solve a festering social problem, rather than a particularized grievance of one person, in the *Hobson* litigation.

Seen in that way, then, the problem of the decisions in *Hobson* should be considered to be systemic, aimed at shortcomings in how Americans are governed, not at J. Skelly Wright as a judge. He did his level best with the limited tools at his command. Had he ruled the other way, so as to sustain the "track" system, no doubt he would have been applauded by those he characterized as the "power structure"; but whether such a ruling would have improved the Washington schools is highly improbable.

A final criticism of Wright's *Hobson* decisions is worth mention. He was dealing with the most abrasive and most polycentric problem of all, a problem that may in time tear the nation apart. He knew that such problems are best settled politically, and so stated in his opinion. Nonetheless, many believe that he exceeded the bounds of proper judicial authority. For example, Professor Alexander Bickel wrote: "The inner city of Washington, with its slums, its poverty, its juvenile crime and its schools, is a disgrace. Against this, Judge Wright cries from the heart. But Judge Wright is a judicial officer administering the Constitution, and the Constitution does not put at the disposal of judges the resources to prevent, abolish, or even alleviate poverty, juvenile delinquency, slum housing or rotten schools."[34] Well, maybe; and then again, maybe not. Bickel, who was a leader in the cult among the professoriate who worship at the shrine of the late Justice Felix Frankfurter, knew quite well that judges do not have the resources sufficient to make their rulings stick in all types of cases; judges have neither sword nor purse, so must depend upon the cooperation of officers in the other branches of government to implement their decisions. That has always been so for the Supreme Court, particularly with respect to decisions affecting state and local governments. Bickel's mentor, Justice Frankfurter, thought that the bounds of judicial propriety were as follows:

Courts are not equipped to pursue the paths of discovering wise policy. A court is confined within the bounds of a particular record, and it cannot even shape the record. Only fragments of a social problem are seen through the narrow windows of litigation. Had we innate or acquired understanding of a social problem in its entirety, we would not have at our disposal adequate means for constructive solution.[35]

That is only seemingly a strong argument, one that was made in longer but not better language by Donald L. Horowitz:

In contemplating action in the course of litigation, lawyers and judges should ask: whether the situation they propose to control is too fluid to grasp by means short of day-to-day management, whether the case is representative of some universe of cases onto which a rule can be fastened, whether the social milieu is too diverse for a single rule, whether there are sufficient incentives to induce those formally subject to the court's orders to adopt the court's goals and implement them in other than perverse ways, whether the interaction of several targets will combine "chemically" to transform the decree on the ground, and whether the court can find out what is happening to its decree after the decree has been rendered.[36]

In that passage, Horowitz was criticizing *Hobson v. Hansen* and other recent judicial decisions. He has a point, but not much of one—for several reasons. First, Julius Hobson, the plaintiff in the case, simply had no alternative other than the courts to try to get surcease from ills that were far from imaginary. To tell him that he should have repaired to Congress and sought relief is a counsel of either cynicism or despair. The fact—the *indisputable* fact—was that Congress would not have acted. Hobson had to go to court or forever remain silent, while his children (and other black children in the District) continued to suffer the slings and arrows of racial prejudice. He worked "within the system"—the constitutional system—and targeted the judiciary as the *only* avenue that could possibly help. If he did not, he would have had to accept the *status quo* of inferior education for blacks—something he rightfully was unwilling to do. It was Skelly Wright's fate to be chosen as the specific target of Julius Hobson's shafts. Second, the Board of Education in Washington, the defendant in *Hobson*, managed to establish procedures that discriminated against black students. For Horowitz to imply that *its* policy should prevail is to take an unthinking ivory-towerish attitude toward the very real problems of very real people. Third, judges since the beginnings of the Anglo-American legal system have been making what they considered to be "wise policy" (*pace* Frankfurter) decisions. On balance, the record of judges compares very well indeed with the actions of legislators and executives. The need is not, as Bickel and Frankfurter and Horowitz would have it, to limit the power of judges in their managerial functions, but rather, so long as Americans remain litigious (and they display no signs of diminishing the flood of lawsuits), to devise means by which courts can become better suited to the accomplishment of the tasks that now are routinely brought before them. (There is little evidence of such a movement; critics of such judges as Skelly Wright would rather carp at them than help them.)

Skelly Wright's *Hobson* decisions, far from being unique, are prime examples of a new model of litigation and adjudication, one in which judges seek to become "social planners"—or, in a lesser sense, "case managers." Federal Judge Frank Johnson, drawing upon Professor Abram Chayes's studies (who stated in 1976 that "the Justices in *Brown* had committed the federal courts to an enterprise of profound social reconstruction"[37]), maintains that there is a "new model of litigation," one that "must account for the following:

— the subject matter is often not a private dispute but a public policy;
— the party structure is not rigidly bilateral but multilateral;
— the factual inquiry is not retrospective, but predictive; and
— the relief is not compensatory but ameliorative."

If federal judges are more "activist," Johnson continued, it is less because they have appointed themselves "roving commissioners to do good" than it is because new procedures have opened courthouse doors to new interests. The lawsuit, thus, has become "an instrument of reform." Those who criticize judicial activism lack historical perspective. "The courthouse door has always been open to the powerful," Johnson went on to say, "and the lawsuit has always been a ready instrument of the affluent. *I suggest . . . that activist judges may be the true conservatives.* As Edmund Burke recognized: 'People, crushed by law, have no hopes but from power. If laws are their enemies, they will be enemies to laws.' "[38] (Emphasis added.) There is no need to labor the point, save to iterate that Judge Wright's *Hobson* decrees, far from being aberrational, fit squarely into what Professor Chayes calls "public law litigation." The larger meaning, and one of greater long-term significance, is that judges are undertaking their new role with little help from the bar, and no help at all from Congress or the President. Public law litigation—the *Hobson* case is an excellent exemplar—marks a sea change in the separation of governmental powers. It makes the judiciary a primary instrument for both establishing public policies and implementing them. Skelly Wright has been a leader in that development.

For 200 years, equality has been considered in greater or lesser degree to be a moral truth given by fundamental law. In his *Hobson* decision, Judge

Wright had to confront as best he could the harsh facts that equality was still an amorphous, undefined concept, and also that, as he said at New York University, society should eliminate segregated slums and provide "cultural and educational enrichment for slum children." He should not be faulted for taking a small step in the fabled journey of a thousand miles that would reach that goal. His action was a clear signal to Congress, to people generally, that their own interests included efforts adequate to bring black Americans into the mainstream of the nation's life. That his signal went unheeded is a tragedy—initially for blacks, but also for Americans generally, who, sooner or later, will have to taste the bitter fruit of reaction to centuries of repression of 11 percent of the populace, and finally to the constitutional order itself because it has been found wanting in the achievement of a decent measure of human dignity for America's underclass. Those are high prices to pay. That they will be paid, soon or late, should not be doubted.

I have previously called Wright a pragmatic instrumentalist, and his *Hobson* decisions evidence that conclusion. Professor Robert Summers maintains that that philosophy of law "took root during the Progressive era"—and that it did.[39] A product of that age, Skelly Wright was born when it was flowering; and his professional career has spanned years of relative plenty in the United States—which enabled the ideas of Progressivism to come into at least temporary fruition. To the extent that he has a discernible philosophy, he perceives law as an instrument for human use and human betterment rather than an abstract set of norms divorced from human affairs, and conceives of social reality, as did the Progressives, as being plastic and malleable. He is a "social engineer" in black robes, willing to try to resolve difficult social problems by attempting to change, within limits, social conditions. He thus sees law in terms of its consequences—its *human* consequences. Yet, beyond that—possibly because of his Roman Catholic background (although he is no longer a believer)—he discerns fundamental values (of human needs and deserts) over and above the positive law. Oliver Wendell Holmes wrote in 1881 that the "first requirement of a sound body of law is that it should correspond with the actual feelings and demands of the community, whether right or wrong,"[40] an idea taken over, as was shown in Chapter 2, by Justice Frankfurter. Skelly Wright is not deluded by such notions; he does not pretend that he is able to discern "the feelings and demands of the community"—or, as Frankfurter said in *Willie Francis's Case*, the "consensus of society's opinion"—but does believe that he is able to determine values behind and above consensus values that he thinks are protected by the Constitution. Possibly he would agree with Holmes that the Constitution "is an experiment, as all life is an experiment,"[41] but only partially. There are certain enduring values of constitutionalism that to him are not subject to experiment—values summed up in the idea of human dignity. Wright has a fierce faith in the indomitable human spirit, and seeks to remove obstacles to the full flowering of the individual human being. In so doing, he knows that judicial decisions can be logically arbitrary but sociologically nonarbitrary. He thus would agree with Walter Wheeler Cook:

The logical situation confronting the judge in a new case being what it is, it is obvious that he must legislate, whether he will or not. By this is meant that since he is free so far as compelling logical reasons are concerned which way to decide the case, his choice will turn upon analysis to be based upon considerations of social and economic policy. An intelligent choice can be made only by estimating as far as possible the consequences of a decision one way or the other. To do this, however, the judge will need to know two things: (1) what social consequences or results are aimed at, and (2) how a decision one way or the other will affect attainment of those results. This knowledge he will as a rule not have; to acquire it he will need to call upon the other social sciences, such as economics. Note how that our traditional technique makes no adequate provision whereby counsel can furnish the court with the needed data; neither does it provide the court itself with the machinery to acquire it. Why? I take it, because the assumption that is that with nothing but his experience as a man and a judge, he can by reasoning, by logic, decide the case—it is purely a question of law, and no evidence is required after the facts of the situation have been determined.[42]

In sum, Skelly Wright considers himself—and, inferentially, other judges—able through the application of his—and their—reason to determine what should be done by society, what is best for society. The important point is that he does not do this by applying logic or deducing his decisions from the constitutional text. In his own words, his "emotional reactions are visceral, and then checked against approved principle."[43] (But principles, as we have seen, usually run in pairs of opposites.) He tries to do "what's right," which he determines by an "intuitive evaluation or guess." And further: "If I want to do something, I can find a way to do it."[44]

I would like to be very clear in what I am saying. Wright does not differ from other judges, save in one respect: He is much more candid in acknowledging the human, the personal element in the judging process. As such, he recalls Justice William Douglas's posthumous statement in his autobiography: "[Chief Justice Charles Evans] Hughes made a statement to me which at the time was shattering but which over the years turned out to be true: 'Justice Douglas, you must remember one thing. At the constitutional level where we work, ninety percent of any decision is emotional. The rational part of us supplies the reasons for supporting our predilections.' "[45] What Douglas called the "gut" reactions of a judge were the main ingredients of his constitutional decisions. To my knowledge, Douglas never made remarks such as that publicly. And one may well doubt that he was as naive as he says—that he was "shattered" at what Hughes had said. Douglas, if anything, was a hard-nosed realist, versed in Washington politics, and quite aware of how judges acted; after all, his tenure on the Securities and Exchange Commission required that he make many decisions of an adjudicatory or judicial type. Furthermore, I am not saying that Skelly Wright and William Douglas are of the same stripe. Their differences are many—on the personal level, in their relationships with others (including their families), in their devotion to the tasks assigned to them. To take the latter first, Wright acknowledges he is an "intuitive" or "gut" reactor; but his opinions are carefully written and soundly argued. Douglas, on the other hand, grew increasingly sloppy in his work on the bench as the years went by. As for their personalities, Wright is far more human, compassionate, and warm than was Douglas. Frankfurter once called Douglas one of the "two truly evil men I have known"[46]—something that no one would ever say about Skelly Wright. The point, however, is that Wright's candid statements about how he makes decisions come while he is still sitting on the bench, whereas Douglas was far less open. It is probably true, however, that Wright and Douglas would have generally reached the same decisions on issues before them. That will never be known. Douglas asserts in his autobiography that he tried to convince President Kennedy to name Wright to the Supreme Court; had Kennedy done so, Wright and Douglas then might well have been able to make a team on the High Court.

Perhaps, finally, Skelly Wright would not necessarily agree with Roscoe Pound, who, in 1913, maintained that individual interests are to be protected by law only insofar as they qualify as "social" interests.[47] Wright is interested in protecting the *self*—the individual human being—but in so doing, as has been suggested, he considers that judicial attention to individual human needs can be transmuted into the common good (the common weal). There is a close connection in his mind between personal and collective well-being. In that sense, his protection of individual interests does serve to protect social interests, but not in a mere majoritarian sense of those interests. In many respects, this means that Judge Wright adheres to a judicial version of Adam Smith's "invisible hand." Smith, writing in 1776 and influenced by the ecological and thus the social impact of the Great Discoveries, maintained that pursuit by individuals of their private economic welfare would by a mysterious means—"an invisible hand"—be transmogrified into the general good.[48] In that position, Wright is closely allied to many students of American politics—those who espouse the doctrine of political pluralism, by which is meant that through the clash of conflicting interest groups within the polity the overall national or public interest emerges. Wright, thus, is squarely in the mainstream of orthodox political thinking in the nation. Furthermore, it is fair to say that the basic assumption—the oft-times inarticulated major premise—of the American judicial system and of the adversarial method of deciding specific disputes is also a variation on Adam Smith's classic formulation. In that sense, Wright is a mainstream judge. But there is a caveat to that proposition: Within that mainstream there is a lot of room for maneuver, for individualized decision making, for choosing between inconsistent doctrinal principles both of which are relevant to a given decision.

The Principle of Reason-Directed Societal Self-Interest, thus, is the transference of both classical and Keynesian economics to judicial decision making—classical, because by the assumption that the good of all is fulfilled by the system, and Keynesian, because the quite visible hand of the sovereign—of government—acting through judges is considered to be a necessary condition of that fulfillment. In the case of *de facto* segregation, that governmental aid is "affirmative" or "positive" in nature—government doing something to help those in need—even though the courts still speak in terms of negative limitations.

But not always. This may be seen when Skelly Wright's *de facto* segregation decisions are compared with those of other courts, including the Supreme Court. *Brown v. Board of Education* merely desegregated public facilities. It was essentially negative in thrust, telling government what it could *not* do. By the 1980s that negative admonition has become an affirmative command, at least insofar as public schools are concerned. Wright's *Hobson* decisions have been discussed. They were paralleled, even exceeded, by other federal judges. The key decision came in 1968 in *Green v. School Board,* when the Supreme Court, speaking through Justice William Brennan, stated: The *Brown* decisions were "a call for the dismantling of well-entrenched dual systems tempered by an awareness that complex and multifaceted problems would arise which would require time and flexibility for a successful resolution. School boards such as respondent [in Virginia] then operating state-compelled dual systems were nevertheless clearly charged with the *affirmative duty* to convert to a unitary system in which racial discrimination would be eliminated root and branch."[49] (Emphasis added.) What type of duty? Brennan was explicit: "The burden on a school board today is to come forward with a plan that promises realistically to work *now*." Thus, in fourteen years the federal judiciary had fully nationalized civil rights, seeking to better the status of black Americans. *Brown* had been first met with belligerent defiance, which after a time became tokenism with a few blacks accorded better treatment. When Congress passed the Civil Rights Act of 1964, tokenism was supplanted by modest and tentative steps toward racial integration. The *Green* decision ushered in massive formal integration. *De facto* segregation remained.

How, then, could actual racial integration in public schools be achieved? The Supreme Court's answer: Mandatory busing. *Swann v. Charlotte-Mecklenburg Board of Education* (1971) was the turning point.[50] In this case a unanimous Court held that busing was a permissible means of

integrating schools. In an account that clearly reveals how, at the Supreme
Court level at least, the storied rule of law is in fact the rule of men, J.
Harvie Wilkinson has well summarized what took place within the Court:

Though the final *Swann* opinion was unanimous and bore the signature of Chief
Justice Burger, everything had not been harmonious on the Supreme
Court. . . . Some most unorthodox inner maneuverings [took place]. The first vote
cast by the Justices in Swann was said to be 6 to 3 *against* busing. But then, . . . in
an unusual move, each Justice went back to his chambers and drafted an opinion.
Justice Harlan's was said to have been the toughest pro-busing opinion. Then several
Justices had second thoughts and switched their votes. Soon the vote was 6 to 3 for
busing, with Burger, Blackmun, and Black dissenting. Eventually, the three
capitulated—Black being the last holdout. And Burger, who had envisioned himself
writing the opinion against busing, ended up writing the opinion for it and
incorporating much of the language from the drafts of the more liberal
Justices. . . .
 . . . On the surface *Swann* was a great liberal victory, perhaps the greatest since
Brown. The Supreme Court had upheld . . . widespread busing to desegregate black
schools. "Desegregation plans," the Court emphasized, "cannot be limited to walk-
in schools." . . . The Court . . . insisted that school officials "achieve the greatest
possible degree of actual desegregation" and show the "continued existence of any
one-race schools to be genuinely nondiscriminatory." To some, *Swann* seemed the
long awaited leap toward true integration.[51]

That hope was dashed. The United States did not, contrary to an editorial in
the *Los Angeles Times*, "definitely . . . proceed toward becoming an
integrated society."[52] To the contrary: Busing met bitter opposition, then
and now, and the Supreme Court soon began to retreat from its position.
   Chief Justice Burger led the counterattack, when, in an unprecedented
(and injudicious) action four months after *Swann*, he wrote to each federal
district judge, telling them in effect that the *Swann* decision did not mean
what he had written in it. One perfervid opponent of busing, Professor Lino
Graglia, called it "one of the strangest performances in the history of the
Court."[53] And so it was. The promise of the *Green* case—a unitary society,
a harmonious society—has not been fulfilled. Whites began to vote with
their feet and move to the suburbs; or those who could afford it sent their
children to private schools. While the rhetoric and the formal Constitution
still espoused equality, the inner parts of several large American cities
became predominantly black. The white flight got the Supreme Court's
imprimatur in 1974, when the Justices ruled in *Milliken v. Bradley* that
Detroit's schools need not be integrated on a metropolitan, as distinguished
from a citywide, basis.[54]
   Several conclusions are possible about the judicial treatment of *de facto*
racial segregation. First, judges in these cases, as in others, read their own
notions of wise public policy into the Constitution; second, those judge-

made laws are tacit invitations to others—officers in the political branches of government—to follow the lead set by the judiciary; third, those political officers, however, have discretion in administering such judge-made laws and consequently display a wide disparity in how they interpret and apply the judicial decrees; fourth, in the American system, further implementation of laws, judge-made or otherwise, is often left to individual litigants to bring lawsuits aimed at requiring appropriate action; and finally, efforts to conquer *de facto* segregation have foundered not only on the shoals of white prejudice, but also because no real effort has been made to attack the problem of equality of economic condition. Despite appearances to the contrary, federal judges have not tried to shake the social tree and rearrange the hierarchy of position and esteem within it. No doubt, most have perceived that blacks should be brought into the mainstream. But in so doing, they have erroneously assumed, without really examining the question, that places were available in that mainstream for them. The hard fact—the bedrock fact—is that likely there are not, speaking of blacks as a group and not as individuals within a group. The Second Reconstruction is ending, not with a bang, but with a barely concealed whimper, a victim of intractable white prejudice and of the fact that the ecological trap is snapping shut at precisely the time when the need is greatest—and when, as illustrated in a number of judicial and other official decisions, some efforts were being made to help them—the millions of black Americans—escape that trap. The political (that is, the constitutional) order is ever increasingly a zero-sum game; for every winner in the social struggle there must be a loser. In a meritocratic, class society there is not enough room, either at the top or in the middle classes, for many—blacks, for certain, but numerous others as well—who wish to join the affluent. That is a hard truth, an unpleasant truth, but there is no gainsaying it.

That is a bleak, even despairing assessment of the status of the Second Reconstruction (and the status of the underclass in general). It is also an evaluation of the limits of effective legal, including judicial, action. In his challenging book, *Social Order and the Limits of Law*, Professor Iredell Jenkins has concluded that law by itself cannot guarantee achievement of the goals of social justice; but law can secure certain rights and enforce duties that are indispensable preconditions of justice. More precisely:

The exact causes and cures of such social ills as poverty, inflation, discrimination, functional illiteracy, gross inequalities, corruption, and so forth are so complex and obscure that no one can say with any certainty what policy will be most effective or what its outcome will be. Unexpected factors intervene, side effects appear, benefits have their price, and people respond in ways that no one could anticipate. Thus the powers of prediction and control that the law commands are very imperfect. It is one thing to throw a bridge across a river, and quite another to get a society to exchange its present habits and values for new ones.[55]

In essence, that is what Judge Wright did in *Hobson*—"throw a bridge across a river"—but "society" did not respond. Whose, then, is the fault? Wright's? Or those who control the levers of power in the political order? Perhaps no ready, self-evident answer exists; nevertheless, it is difficult to assign blame to a judge who is sworn to uphold the Constitution and who tried, as best he could, to carry out the spirit of the fundamental law. Professor Jenkins goes on to conclude:

Law is an indispensable but supplemental instrument of order and justice. . . .

Law is indispensable because it supplies the compelling social need for a force that is at once *sovereign* and *principled*. . . . A complex society, composed of heterogeneous elements and competing interests, must have an instrument through which it can speak with a voice that will be heeded by all: it needs a locus of sovereignty that receives habitual obedience and thus is able to support its decisions with force when need be. At the same time, this sovereign power, which by definition escapes external control, must be governed by its own external principles—by self-imposed provisions and mechanisms than govern the use of this power and prevent it from becoming autocratic and arbitrary. Law is by far the best instrument devised to meet this need. (Emphasis in original.)[56]

But, Jenkins asserts, the sovereignty and indispensability of law does not mean that it is all-powerful or can act by itself; it requires, he maintains, assistance from other societal institutions for support. Law and other social institutions coexist in a symbiotic, mutually supportive relationship. In Washington, D.C., it was those other social institutions that failed, not the law itself and not the judicial process as exemplified in Judge Wright's brave, albeit eventually futile, decisions in the *Hobson* litigation. Those who, like Alexander Bickel and Donald Horowitz, criticize Wright for ruling as he did should turn their talents—in Bickel's case, should have turned his talents, for he is now dead—to developing means of energizing the institutions that complement law in bringing about social order and in effecting social change.

I do not mean to suggest that Judge Wright is typical of the judiciary. Quite the contrary: Most seem to have little interest in helping to rectify, as best they can, the dreary economic conditions of America's black populace and, indeed, of the poor and disadvantaged generally. They join others who exercise either formal authority or effective control in the nation in being complacent about the nation's large and growing underclass. Skelly Wright may remain, as he says, "an uncompromising activist" in areas affecting that class, but his is one of the few voices that can be heard in a wilderness of prejudice and unconcern. As has been noted, he is a product of the Progressive Age. "The Progressives," Professor Robert S. Summers tells us, "were not radical socialists, but they believed that democracy, corrupted by the concentration of political power in big corporations, trusts, and political bosses, must be revitalized; that the voting franchise should be extended . . . ; that industry should be regulated; that poverty and old-age hardship should be relieved and workers protected; and that steps must be taken to conserve natural resources."[57] That description fits Skelly Wright, if not precisely, at least closely enough to make it generally accurate.

IV

Judge Wright was inured to harsh criticism when he decided the *Hobson* case. What he experienced in New Orleans in the years following the Supreme Court's ruling in *Brown v. Board of Education* was far worse, both in intensity and length. His name became anathema to the white populace of Louisiana—and all because he was carrying out the decree of the Supreme Court. In theory, at least, he had far less discretion than he did in the 1960s when he was confronted with *de facto* racial segregation.

New Orleans differed: There Wright had to deal with *de jure* segregation, mandated by laws that had become unconstitutional in 1954 when *Brown* was decided. In 1954, the Supreme Court merely announced the rule—that racial segregation in public schools was invalid under the fourteenth amendment's equal protection clause. But the Justices stopped there; they did not say how the rule was to be put into effect. Not until a year later, in *Brown-II*, did it say that desegregation should take place "with all deliberate speed." That cryptic decree was in fact and in effect a delegation to the federal district judges in the Deep South to craft a remedy that would basically alter traditional life-styles of southerners. Perhaps overwhelmed by their audacity in *Brown-I*, the Justices simply did not have either the perspicacity or the courage to implement their ruling. By almost any criterion, therefore, *Brown-II* was a victory for white southerners. The district judges were to fit the principle to local needs. In legalese, those judges sat as judges in "equity," a heritage from the British legal system. (There is nothing extraordinary about that; the Constitution expressly states: "The judicial power of the United States . . . shall extend to all cases, in law and equity. . . . ") Equitable remedies can be tailored to fit the circumstances of specific cases; they permit maximum judicial discretion. The consequence should have been expected by the Supreme Court but was not. It was the realization of Justice Frankfurter's concern, stated in oral argument before the Court in December, 1952, that "nothing could be worse from my point of view than for this Court to make an abstract declaration that segregation is bad and then have it evaded by tricks."[58] That is exactly what happened. A failure of nerve on the part of the Justices produced unfortunate results, results that are still being felt. Furthermore, a political vacuum occurred. Both President Dwight Eisenhower and Congress ignored the signal from the Court. Each failed to act affirmatively to implement the *Brown* decision. Eisenhower considered the civil rights struggle to be a mere lawyers' problem and probably basically disagreed with the Court's decision. Members of Congress sat on their collective hands. State officers, at least those who sought guidance, received none. So they soon reacted to the pressures of the white majority. The burden thus fell on the district judges, and later the several judges on the Fifth Circuit Court of Appeals—all of whom were the very men who had come from the same communities that were to feel the brunt of the Court's mandate and, indeed, were often chosen from the very power structures that began to vehemently oppose the new ruling.

The Supreme Court proposed, therefore, but the 58 southern judges disposed. Small wonder, accordingly, that they met the unparalleled challenge in different ways. In many respects, what occurred in the South after 1954 was paradoxically both a breakdown of the fundamental principles of the constitutional order—an overt tearing of the social fabric that binds the nation together—and an example of how at times that same order can, given men and women of good will and courage and tenacity, adapt itself to new conditions. (Not always, to be sure, or even fully, because at this writing—1983—much of what seemed to be accomplished in the relatively roseate years of the late 1950s and 1960s is now becoming unraveled, as the nation moves into a situation of two separate, and unequal, societies, one black (and Hispanic) and poor, and the other more affluent and mostly white.) No present need exists to trace all that happened in the 1950s, for that story has been well told by a number of writers, such as Jack Bass, Robert L. Crain, and J. W. Peltason (see Bibliographic Essay for complete references).

Of course, judges saw their task differently. A few, a very few, among whom Skelly Wright was foremost, met the daunting job head-on, whereas others reflected the philosophies and mores of those who had put them on the bench. Among other examples are Judge William H. Atwell of Dallas, who refused to comply with the Court's decisions, maintaining that "the real law of the land is the same today as it was on May 16, 1954" (the *Brown* decision was announced on May 17, 1954). In South Carolina, Judge George B. Timmerman accused the NAACP of spreading "poisonous propaganda," that organization being the driving force that had targeted the federal judiciary as the means of bettering the status of blacks. And Judge Wilson Warlick in North Carolina stated: "I'm a states' rights individual and I always have been. If I had anything to do with the schools in North Carolina, I wouldn't let the federal government have any part of it."[59] All, of course, were wrong. Atwell accepted judicial lawmaking in the infamous *Plessy* decision that allowed "separate-but-equal" public facilities; to him, that was the "real law of the land." Yet it was an earlier example of Supreme Court fiat, of the Justices making up the law when they decided the case. At best, he was inconsistent; at worst, he was a bigot who knew nothing about law. As for Timmerman, for him to accuse the NAACP of spreading poisonous propaganda makes absolutely no sense; he was another bigot on the bench. Warlick was merely a latter-day spokesman for controversy between the national government and the states, one that had been settled in law during the early nineteenth century and was settled in blood during the Civil War.

Skelly Wright was of a quite different stripe. Why that was, and is, so is by no means self-evident. His prior career gave little evidence that he would become "the most hated man in New Orleans" by trying to put the Supreme Court's decree into effect. Perhaps his family and higher education (in Roman Catholic schools) had something to do with it. I do not wish, as was said in Chapter 1, to try to probe Wright's psyche. Even so, it is impossible not to wonder how much his work as Willie Francis's lawyer had to do with his later concern for the disadvantaged. He failed in his attempt to save Francis's life—a fact that still weighs heavily on his mind. Is it too far-fetched to believe that Willie Francis was on his mind when the following episode occurred?

During a Christmas Eve party in the United States Attorney's office, J. Skelly Wright sat at a window in the post office building and looked across the narrow street at the Light House for the Blind, where sightless people from New Orleans were arriving for another Christmas celebration. There, someone met them. He watched a blind Negro led to a party for blacks at the rear of the building. A blind white person was led to a separate party.

More than thirty years later, he recalled the scene. "The blind couldn't segregate themselves. They couldn't see. There was somebody else doing it for them." He continued, "It had an effect on me. It affects me even now."

"It didn't shock me. I looked at it twice, believe me, but it didn't shock me. It just began to make me think more of the injustice of it, of the whole system that I had taken for granted. I was getting mature, too, thirty-five or thirty-six, and you begin to think of things. When you go to bed at night, you think of it. That was the beginning really."[60]

That may explain Skelly Wright and how he began to change. Surely, however, it is not the full explanation about him. Surely there is more to his being able, in his mid-thirties, to see injustice than what he saw on that Christmas Eve. Even if the Willie Francis case had as much influence on his way of thinking as perhaps it did, there is still little persuasive evidence to show why he began to see the injustice "of the whole system." Why, furthermore, did he begin to change and not others? There is no ready answer. But change he did. His sense of injustice had been offended. "Law exists," Aristotle maintained, "for men between whom there is injustice,"[61] an idea superbly analyzed by the late Professor Edmond Cahn in his book *The Sense of Injustice*.[62] My point is that Skelly Wright was motivated more by his personal sense of *injustice* than by affirmative concepts of *justice*. With nothing to guide him but the Supreme Court's delphic pronouncement and his own sense of right and wrong, Wright followed his own views of what was required in New Orleans rather than those of the community. He sought to catch the consciences of the white majority: "The problem of changing a people's mores, particularly those with an emotional overlay, is not to be taken lightly. It is a problem which will require the utmost patience,understanding, generosity and forbearance and from all of us of whatever race. But the magnitude of the problem may not nullify the principle. And that principle is that *we are, all of us, free-born Americans with a right to make our way unfettered by sanctions imposed by man because of the work of God.*" (Emphasis added.)[63]

To repeat: Wright became a federal district judge in 1949 at the age of 38—the youngest judge then on the federal bench. After a short stint in Washington as a practicing attorney, he returned to New Orleans as the United States Attorney. He sought the job and got it, even though he was not a member of the New Orleans legal establishment. As was noted previously, through his friendship with Attorney General Tom Clark, he was selected for filling a vacancy on the Fifth Circuit Court of Appeals—only to have that appointment blocked by the chief judge of that circuit. That seat went to District Judge Wayne Borah, and Wright was then named to fill Borah's spot. He was easily confirmed and took office on October 26, 1949. So the accident of personality changed the course of history, at least in New Orleans and probably in Washington, D.C. Had Borah remained on the district bench, as he wanted to, he probably would not have ruled as did Wright in the New Orleans segregation cases; had Wright not been sufficiently ambitious to seek to be the U.S. Attorney, he would never have become a judge; and had he been a judge on the Fifth Circuit, he would never have been so hated in New Orleans and would never have become an appeals judge in Washington. Skelly Wright had the knack—the good fortune—of having friends who could help him and of being in the right place at the right time. His uncle, a political functionary, had assisted in getting him named as Assistant U.S. Attorney in the 1930s; his friendship with Herbert Christenberry, the U.S. Attorney, enabled him to be named to replace Christenberry when the latter went on the bench; his friendship with Tom Clark nearly got him named to the Fifth Circuit and did get him the district judgeship; and his work as a district judge so impressed Attorney General Robert Kennedy that Wright was elevated to the Court of Appeals in Washington.

I do not mean to imply that Wright was merely lucky. He was a highly successful U.S. Attorney, and his work on the district bench, in all types of cases, was of the highest caliber. He soon became respected within the profession because of his ability to clear his court's docket (that is, to decide cases rapidly). He has always had a capacity for hard and sustained work. And he became notorious and hated within Louisiana, and admired throughout the nation, because he had the courage and tenacity to take on the state of Louisiana in one of the most dramatic confrontations in American history between federal and state power. With little help, except from judges on the Fifth Circuit, Wright prevailed. He did not seek the fight; it came to him. The struggle merits extensive discussion, both for the light it sheds on racial relations in the United States and as an example of the long-continuing dispute between the national government and the states. No judge in American history ever showed more courage.

Professor J. W. Peltason has called the task of the 58 judges in the South an "awesome assignment of forcing compliance with the Supreme Court's 1954 school desegregation decisions."[64] If how its citizens are treated by government is one measure of a nation, to call the task of desegregation "awesome" tells a lot about the United States (and, indeed, about white humans everywhere). It tells us, as Peltason goes on to remark, that the basic problem involved a "major social revolution" with the contestants, black and white, having "fundamentally opposed demands." And *that* tells us that the fundamental precepts—in harsher terms, the pretenses—of the constitutional order were under attack. Given the totality of circumstances in the South since the early 1950s, and elsewhere in recent years, the constitutional order faced and still is facing its greatest challenge since the Civil War. Can more than 20 million blacks be culturally assimilated into the nation? The challenge is a continuation on a different battleground of a long-existing contentious tussle between those espousing local autonomy and those favoring a unitary nation. The struggle is far from over, at least so far as blacks are concerned. Their victories thus far have almost entirely been in the commands of *formal* law, both constitutional and statutory; not until they win in the workings of the *living* or *operative* Constitution can victory truly be declared.

The district judges had the fundamental problem of effecting basic social change through use of legal processes; they had to test, as perhaps it had never been tested before, the limits of effective legal action. To do so, the judges had not only to follow "due procedure"; they also had to read substantive values into the Constitution. Those values were found in neither the Constitutions nor statutes, but were derived from the judges' own consciences. Reordering society is a task of staggering difficulty and complexity. The "58 lonely men" had to act because, as the Supreme Court implied, the basic premises of democracy were being ignored. Too many people were being denied full membership in the American polity, not because of any intrinsic personal faults of their own but because they were "different." Despite the myth to the contrary, Americans have never suffered gladly human differentials (or dissenters) from the collective norm.

It will be recalled that Yves Simon once observed that in a democratic society "deliberation is about means and presupposes that the problem of ends had been settled." That is the nub of the problem of the "American dilemma"—ends *have not* been settled. The need, accordingly, is for ostensibly nondemocratic officers of government (the judges) to try to deal with the ends, the goal values, of the nation. In sum, the task of the district judges was to mesh the aspirations of both whites and blacks—in the South and elsewhere—into a new synthesis that would at once fulfill the reasonable aspirations of both groups. Said that way, it can readily be seen that judges had to follow the Principle of Reason-Directed Societal Self-Interest. "Democracy implies . . . that the way in which men adjust or resolve their differences is of crucial importance, that conflicts of opinion as to what constitutes the right moral and political ends are not to be resolved arbitrarily—i.e., by fiat of a stronger or allegedly superior group. . . . "[65] That is what black Americans have always faced—the arbitrary resolution of their condition. Their status in society was being determined by the accident of birth.

Skelly Wright's work in New Orleans is easily summarized. He tried to help the city and state to live up to the propaganda about America and the American Dream. Even before the *Brown* decision, he ordered desegregation of the Louisiana State University Law School, basing his decision on an earlier Supreme Court decision from Texas—that the separate law school for blacks was unequal in fact (and thus violative of the *Plessy* formulation). And he ordered LSU to admit a black student to its undergraduate school, a ruling that was at first reversed by the Fifth Circuit but, after *Brown*, sustained by the Supreme Court. His difficulties were enormous: In large part acting alone, he faced up to the city and the state and stared them down.[66] But only after a time—Judge Wright rendered some 41 separate decisions on racial integration between 1952 and 1962—and with success only in the formal law, not in the living law. The sequence of events exemplifies Professor Stuart Scheingold's observations:

Legal frames of reference tunnel the vision . . . leading to an oversimplified approach to a complex social process—an approach that grossly exaggerates the role that lawyers and litigation can play in a strategy for change. The assumption is that litigation can evoke a declaration of rights from courts, that it can, further, be used to assure the realization of those rights, and, finally, that realization is tantamount to meaningful change. The *myth of rights* is, in other words, premised on a direct linking of litigation, rights, and remedies with social change. (Emphasis in original.)[67]

Judge Wright's decrees in the District of Columbia were followed, as has been seen, by social change, but in quite different direction from the tenor of his decisions. Scheingold states, somewhat differently to be sure, the point made previously about the effective limits of law and legal action. The formal law changes, but the hearts and minds of the people directly affected are not necessarily altered. Scheingold goes on to state:

The vision of change without turmoil is part and parcel of the myth of peaceful progress. It is an illusion discredited by American history and by experience elsewhere. As Barrington Moore, Jr., puts it: "The first point to get clear is that there is no such thing as a completely peaceful reformist change, at least not in major modern industrial democracies." Similarly, there is no way in the long run to avoid testing our values in the political arena and, of course, risking repudiation or at least significant alterations.[68]

Wright was in fact and in effect repudiated by the white citizens of Washington, D.C. In New Orleans, his decisions, mainly *Bush v. Orleans Parish School*,[69] evoked violence almost without parallel in the remainder of the nation. It is important to understand why.

Judge Wright's implementation of the *Brown* decision was far from speedy. He, of course, had to await plaintiffs willing to bring actions to get judicial enforcement of the new principle. Not until 1956 did Wright direct the New Orleans school board to "make arrangements for admission of children . . . on a racially non-discriminatory basis with all deliberate speed."[70] Six years later, as he left for Washington, that order was still not carried out.

The speed in New Orleans, far from deliberate, was at best snail-like. Legal maneuverings of school officials and Louisiana politicians managed to stave off actual integration for years. One official was quoted as flatly stating : "We will not integrate. We couldn't even if we wanted to." The crucial question is why. Robert L. Crain, in his superb study *The Politics of School Desegregation*, has suggested an answer: He calls it "the failure of an elite"—the ruling class in New Orleans and Louisiana.[71] Not until violence erupted and a business slump was experienced did the elite finally decide that it was in *their* interest to rally behind Judge Wright's order. Not altruism, not a desire to follow the law of the land, but economic pressures stirred the business leaders of New Orleans. It was not until 1961 that even token integration took place, and then in a reverse way. A white minister, the Rev. Lloyd Foreman, courageously decided to obey the law and enter his child in an all-black school. John Steinbeck vividly described the "successful" effort to integrate.

The crowd was waiting for the white man to bring his white child to school [that was ordered to be desegregated]. And here he came along the guarded walk . . . leading his frightened child by the hand. The muscles of his cheeks stood out from clenched jaws, a man afraid who by his will kept his fear in check. . . .

A shrill, grating voice rang out. The yelling was not in chorus. . . . The crowd broke into howls and roars and whistles of applause. This is what they came to see and hear.

No newspaper had printed the words these women shouted. It was indicated that they were indelicate, some even said obscene. On television the sound track was made to blur or had crowd noises cut in to cover. But now I heard the words, bestial and filthy and degenerate.

The words written down are dirty, carefully and selectively filthy. But there was something far worse here than dirt, a kind of frightening witches' Sabbath. Here was no spontaneous cry of anger, of insane rage . . . no principle good or bad. . . . The crowd behind the barrier roared and cheered and pounded one another with joy.[72]

Perhaps New Orleans was so violent because it was the first large Southern city to be ordered to desegregate; but that can hardly be a complete explanation. As has been said, Judge Wright had ordered Louisiana State University to desegregate even before the *Brown* decision. So there was some experience with the idea of racial mixing. Crain has advanced these hypotheses as ways of answering the "Why New Orleans?" question:

First, we must consider that some of the difficulty arose because of the behavior of the school board. They maintained a head-in-the-sand attitude over four years, when they could have been letting the public know that desegregation was coming. It was not until the beginning of July, 1960, that the school board members decided to work to keep the schools open. . . .

Second, the school board could have avoided the fiasco caused by their choice of schools to integrate. . . . The school board knew that there were more favorable alternatives [to the schools they chose]. They had been invited to send Negro students to two silk-stocking schools, and had rejected the invitation. . . .

. . . *The New Orleans crisis arose from a general failure of community leadership, resulting in a breakdown of social control over the masses.* The school board, the mayor and civil leaders all shied away from taking action. To make a more general statement . . . the New Orleans civic elite has always been reluctant to become involved in local politics, and . . . this withdrawal contributed not only to the crises, also tended to produce the kind of mayor, and the kind of school board that New Orleans had in 1960. (Emphasis added.)[73]

Another hypothesis might be advanced: The power elite in New Orleans failed to take the true measure of the man who sat in judgment upon implementation of the *Brown* rule. They did not know Skelly Wright—his courage, his steely determination, his stubbornness, his compassion, his passion for doing "what's right," his reverence for the law, his disdain for those who through pettifogging subterfuges sought to undermine the spirit of the Constitution. No, they did not know what manner of man Wright was (and still is). But they found out.

The New Orleans elite failed or refused to act in the school crisis of 1960, and before, Crain maintains, because it did not want to wield influence in the city. That seems to mean that the city was politically disorganized, a power vacuum. That, however, is not really possible. On the one hand, Crain says that an elite had effective power in New Orleans, but, on the other hand, they did not want to use it because it, the elite, was not interested in politics. Little credence can be given to that conclusion. As with nature, politics abhors a vacuum. Someone is going to exercise power in any political community; there is no escape for that proposition. And that power in all likelihood will be oligarchic—in accordance with Robert Michels's famous "iron law of oligarchy": "Who says organization says oligarchy."[74]

What seems far more credible was that the elite was racially prejudiced, did not want to see blacks better their status, liked things the way they had been, and thought they could get away with defiance of federal judges (and thus of the federal government). They had no interest in "progress" of any type. Unlike Atlanta, the elite wanted to preserve the *status quo*, romanticized as the "southern way of life." The point is dual. First, those who wielded significant influence in New Orleans were, when defying the Supreme Court and Judge Wright, furthering their own values. But in so doing, they were, in Orwell's terms, both "wicked" and "stupid." Second, Wright for several years could not convince the elite that adherence to the *Brown* principle would work to the benefit of that very elite—if not directly, then indirectly by helping to dampen social discontent. Even today, that elite only grudgingly accepts the principle.

Judge Wright was well aware of the magnitude of the problem confronting him. In 1956, he ordered the New Orleans school board to stop requiring racial segregation. He was the first judge in the Fifth Circuit to do so. Even then, he stated that segregation would be eliminated only after such time "as may be necessary" to arrange for school admissions on a nondiscriminatory basis. He visualized that desegregation need not come "overnight or even in a year or more." That was not an enormous jump, but merely a cautious first step. He inserted the language, quoted above, in his opinion about "we are, all of us, free-born Americans with a right to make our way unfettered by sanctions imposed by man because of the work of God," because he knew that there were many religious people in New Orleans. He wanted to reach those people, to catch their consciences. He believed it did get to some of them, making them reflect. As he said in 1979: "I was looking for support. I wanted to get the job done."[75] Wright knew he had to mobilize support in the political arena. Politically astute, as always, he fully realized that law and the judicial process, far from being autonomous, were integral parts of the political process. The elite that Crain describes was not really quiescent, but their actions of resistance were less an irresistible force than was Skelly Wright's immovable determination to obey the Constitution.

Wright's work in New Orleans was, of course, not accomplished in a vacuum. Other states, notably Arkansas, were openly defying the Supreme Court. Led by Governor Orval Faubus, the citizenry of Little Rock challenged the power of the federal government to change the schools. This led to President Eisenhower finally living up to his constitutional duty "to take care that the laws are faithfully executed"—the law in this instance being one promulgated by the Supreme Court. Eisenhower used federal troops to enforce desegregation orders. There could be no doubt that the law as stated by the High Court would prevail. The Little Rock schools were desegregated, but Faubus won in the political arena. The episode led to the Supreme Court's 1958 decision in *Cooper v. Aaron*,[76] which ranks next to *Brown*, and possibly surpasses *Brown*, in significance. *Cooper* nullified efforts to avoid desegregation; the Court said that the constitutional rights of children to attend school without racial discrimination "can neither be nullified openly and directly by state legislators or state executive or judicial officers, nor nullified indirectly by them through evasive schemes for segregation whether attempted 'ingeniously or ingenuously.' " That was important in itself: Faubus was not going to get away with defiance. But the Justices went further: *Cooper* is significant because the Court unanimously stated, for the first time in express language, that its decisions are "the supreme law of the land." The Justices transmogrified a decision in a *specific* case—here, the Little Rock school situation—into a *general* rule. That logical impossibility did not deter them, because they knew that ordinary rules of logic do not determine constitutional decisions. This was, and is, a new posture for the Court, one that has had and continues to have significant consequences. In briefest terms, it means that the Supreme Court has become a third and superior national legislative chamber. *Cooper*, thus, is one of the great turning points in American constitutional history.

Of present importance, the *Cooper* ruling helped Skelly Wright in continuing battle with Louisiana politicians. For various reasons, mainly lack of funds, black plaintiffs were slow to follow up on Wright's 1956 order. The schools remained segregated. But in 1958, the *Bush* case got new life when the New Orleans school board asserted that it could not obey Wright's order because the state legislature had intervened and taken authority from the board. The judge saw through the subterfuge, dismissing the school board's argument; he said that "an artifice, however cleverly contrived, which would circumvent this [his previous] ruling, and others predicated upon it, is unconstitutional on its face."[77] When Wright was upheld by the Fifth Circuit, he found himself in direct conflict with the state legislature and governor—the same Jimmie Davis who had refused to grant Willie Francis a reprieve having been re-elected after an emotional racist campaign. What Faubus started in Arkansas left its mark on Louisiana.

The law case may have been styled *Bush v. Orleans Parish School Board*, but it could well have been called *Wright v. Louisiana*. Skelly Wright stood alone, rather like Horatius at the bridge, defending the rule of law and the command of constitutional decency against the raggle-taggle mob. "Freedom of choice," based upon Judge John J. Parker's ruling in a South Carolina case, became the slogan followed by those who refused to change.[78] It might well have prevailed had not the idea of "massive resistance" spread throughout the South. Parker had given whites a sophisticated means of evading the full impact of *Brown*; the South could have, had it followed his lead, retained segregated schools with only a few blacks attending "white" schools. But the politicians, such as Faubus and Davis and Louisiana's political boss, Leander Perez, showed that they were both "wicked" and "stupid." They outdid each other in defying Skelly Wright and the Supreme Court. Smeared with such labels as "Smelly" Wright and "Judas Scalawag" Wright, he was hanged in effigy, crosses were burned on his lawn, and the lives of both himself and family were in danger.

Wright stood fast. He would not budge. He set May 16, 1960, as the deadline for the New Orleans school board to submit a desegregation plan. The board did not do so; a referendum showed that 80 percent of the white parents favored closing the schools rather than integrating them. In addition, the state courts had ruled that the Louisiana legislature had authority to assign pupils to schools as it saw fit. Faced with those facts, a lesser man would have quailed and found some way to follow Judge Parker's lead. But not Skelly Wright. On May 16 he ordered that school desegregation begin in September 1960. He was the first judge to specify a starting date. Black children under his order were to be given the option of attending a "white" school nearest their homes. The governor and legislature were splenetic. Governor Davis assumed control over the New Orleans schools in August, an action that a three-judge federal court promptly invalidated. Wright wrote the opinion for the court, calling the statute that gave the governor control over the schools "unconstitutional on its face." Thurgood Marshall, the lawyer for Bush and the first black to be named to the Supreme Court (by President Lyndon Johnson) saw not only the specific point of the *Bush* case—that black children should be allowed into desegregated schools—but also its larger significance: "This," he told the court, "is no longer a case of Negro children seeking their constitutional right. This is now a challenge by the officials of the State of Louisiana to the sovereignty of the United States."[79] And indeed it was: Under no circumstances could the federal judiciary tolerate flagrant and continuing disobedience of lawful orders.

That should have ended the matter. But it did not. Governor Davis asserted that the court's injunction was not binding on him. School was ready to open in September, 1960, but the school board persuaded Wright to delay desegregation until November 14, the beginning of the second quarter. Wright did so, only to be met by a flurry of segregation laws passed by the legislature. That led Wright to issue an injunction against the Governor, the Attorney General, the state police, the National Guard, the state superintendent of education, "and all those persons acting in concert with them," ordering them not to enforce the new laws. That was on November 10. On November 11, the state superintendent of education declared that November 14 was a state school holiday, which caused Wright to issue a decree against the holiday and to cite the superintendent for contempt. But the dragon of official segregation was not yet dead. The legislature declared November 14 to be a school holiday, whereupon Wright added all its members to the list of those ordered not to interfere with desegregation.

On November 14, four black children entered the first grade of two white schools. This caused the legislature to pass a resolution removing members of the New Orleans school board. Again, Skelly Wright was up to the challenge to his, and the federal government's, authority; he ordered that the resolution not be enforced. White anger exploded. Leander Perez addressed a mass rally in which he shouted, "Don't wait for your daughter to be raped by these Congolese. Don't wait until the burr-heads are forced into your schools. Do something about it now!"[80] Whites threatened to boycott the schools; the legislature threatened to cut off funding. But Skelly Wright prevailed. Jack Bass in his book, *Unlikely Heroes*, concludes: "With support by the full federal judiciary and ultimately the Justice Department and by his own personal resolve, Skelly Wright broke the back of the state's effort at massive resistance and prevented the closing of the New Orleans public schools. He upheld federal supremacy under the Constitution by facing down the full force and power of the entire state of Louisiana."[81] Wright was alone, totally alone. In the summer of 1960, he could not depend upon the Justice Department; the Republican Administration did not want to take any provocative action that might affect the presidential election in November. He could not be sure of federal support for desegregation, a fact that influenced his decision to postpone desegregation from September to November 14.

By hindsight, that may have been a mistake. But Wright had little choice. He wanted to get the job done but knew that he, alone, had only the power of moral suasion. The Eisenhower Administration's desire to play election politics with the explosive situation in New Orleans forced his hand. Without Justice Department support, and, ultimately, military support, he would have been helpless. Perhaps, as in Little Rock, the Administration's mind could have been changed; but Wright did not know that at the time. Walking a thin line between law and violence, he held off the violence by bending a bit in his desegregation decrees. That he won, at least nominally, is not to be doubted. But, as I have intimated above, whether blacks have won is another matter, as yet unresolved.

The white people in Louisiana wanted to keep their hierarchical, feudal-like society, and did not want the state—that is, the federal government—to tell them how to conduct their affairs. On the face of it, that position not only has a long history, but has a certain surface plausibility. It is plausible, however, only so long as Louisiana was a true community. That it was not and still is not is obvious, for community requires, as Michael Taylor has said, "a measure of economic equality—a basic equality of basic material conditions—for as the gap increases between rich and poor, so their values diverge, relations between them are likely to become less direct and many-sided, and the sense of interdependence which supports a system of . . . reciprocity is weakened."[82] There is a lesson here that transcends Louisiana itself, and perhaps even the abrasive and unresolved question of race: If people truly want to reduce the power of the state, acting through government, they will have to further the idea of "community." Although the word *community* is nebulous and one of multiple referents, as used here it has three principal characteristics. First, the people who make up a community have a common set of values and beliefs; second, relations between community members should be direct and many-sided, with their personal affairs being settled without outside mediation or compulsion; and third, reciprocity—"a range of arrangements and relations and exchanges, including mutual aid, some forms of cooperation and some forms of sharing,"[83] in which mutual aid is routine. So seen, and remembering the importance of at least rough equality among community members, it is readily obvious that community in Louisiana has never existed—and probably is even more shattered today. The same may be said for the United States as a whole, when the relative positions of blacks and whites, of the poor and the unpoor, of the disadvantaged and the advantaged are perceived. That was the message of the Kerner Commission in 1968, and that is the message of the brave stand that Skelly Wright took in New Orleans in the 1950s. He tried, and tried desperately, to help create a true community. His was not the failure; as in Washington, D.C., after the *Hobson* decrees, the system failed. That should be a sobering thought for all who care about the health of the American body politic.

V

Soon after the violence of 1960-61 in New Orleans and the belated decision of its elite to do at least some of what was right and just, Skelly Wright was named by President John F. Kennedy to the Court of Appeals in Washington, D.C. He had no trouble being confirmed by the Senate, even though the chairman of the Senate Judiciary Committee, James Eastland of Mississippi, had called him "a no-good son of a bitch."[84] As is the Senate's custom, Eastland deferred to Louisiana's senators, who were glad to get Wright out of New Orleans. (His replacement, Frank Ellis, was a political hack who promptly cut back on or reversed some of Wright's decisions.)

Enough has been seen, in this and in previous chapters, to be able to conclude with a sociological truism (but one that is far from accepted in the legal profession): The legal system and the state are closely intertwined. This means that law and politics are closely connected, with politics being the superior. Laws, however promulgated, derive from the governing coalition in any society, and are administered and implemented by members or representatives of that coalition—including judges. "Law thus," Professor Scheingold concludes, "serves the *status quo* in a kind of dual capacity. Legal processes are linked to the dominant configurations of power. At the same time, in its ideological incarnation, the law induces acquiescence in the established order by suggesting that the political system is beneficent and adaptable."[85] Judge Wright knows this very well. He knew, for example, that he had to mobilize the governing coalition of New Orleans if his decrees were to be put into effect. He was quite aware of the fact that judges can propose, but that politicians dispose. Judicial decisions are arrows shot into the sky, aimed at particular targets, but where they fall depends in large part upon how they are subsequently steered (interpreted) by those who exercise effective control in the political order.

The meaning for blacks is obvious: They gain enhanced status and economic opportunities in direct proportion to the political power that they exert. This, in turn, means that the Voting Rights Act of 1965 has had as much or more to do with their improved status as did judicial opinions. When cities such as Atlanta and Philadelphia, Detroit and Los Angeles, Chicago and Newark elect black mayors, something important has happened. But the American dilemma still abides. The hearts and minds of most whites have not been changed. Blacks targeted the courts as the only means of gaining enhanced status, but they knew that whatever rights they might get judges to acknowledge had, as Scheingold argues, to be followed by political mobilization. That mobilization in fact took place, as witness the Civil Rights Act of 1964. But even it has not been enough. The lesson, however, is unmistakable: Blacks will prevail only to the extent that they are able to wield significant political power. On that question, the jury, as lawyers say, is still out.

Professor Orlando Patterson has noted three great historical movements in the contact and enmeshment of blacks with European civilization:

The first movement is concerned with the detribalizaton and rural proletarianization of the diaspora blacks in the New World. The second movement, which was no less traumatic in its impact, involves the massive urbanization of the black community, a process that has very nearly worked itself out in the United States and is now in full swing in other parts of the Americas. The third movement only now shows signs of beginning: it concerns the critical catalytic role of black Americans in the coming post-industrial period of American civilization. . . . This last movement . . . is conjectural. It is more a scenario of one likely course of development, given certain clearly identified trends in the development of American society and the present condition of the black minority.[86]

During the first period, black slaves were indispensable to the agricultural economy of the South. After the Civil War, growing industrialization attracted many former slaves and their children to what soon became the nauseous *barrios* of the inner northern industrial cities. The consequence, says Patterson, was the "lumpenproletarianization of the black community"—a condition that still exists.

The Civil War merely freed the slaves; it really did not change their status fundamentally. Blacks (and poor whites) were submerged in a feudalistic, sharecropping economic system, out of which there was little chance to escape and which differed little from the pre–Civil War economy. Douglas F. Dowd tells us:

The profits of Southern industry were dependent upon cheap and abundant labor. The self-respect of the mass of Southern whites was dependent to a critical degree on the existence of the underprivileged and oppressed position of the Negro. The power of Southern business and political leaders rested on the creation and maintenance of the one-party system, a post-bellum development of the South. The maintenance of the South as an economic preserve of the North was dependent to an important degree on the continued political sterility of the South in national affairs. All these, of course, were interconnected.[87]

The southern ruling elite, Dowd maintains, particularly in its new middle class, cooperated with the northern industrialists and sunk blacks and poor whites even lower and insured that the South would remain backward. That, of course, helps to explain why the New Orleans elite failed to meet the challenge of racial desegregation. Dowd goes on to say that the new white middle class "gave as a *quid pro quo* easy access to the natural resources of the South to those on the outside, a process that greatly furthered the economic domination of the South by the North." There was a political trade-off: The middle class of the South profited from a one-party system, and the North sacrificed its penchant for abolition of slavery for the right to plunder the South and to ignore after 1877 the fact that blacks became members of a *de facto* caste system.

Only one way was available for blacks to escape the social and economic morass: flight to the cities. Migration began slowly and peaked during the early twentieth century. The push came from the caste system in the South; the pull was provided by northern industries looking for cheap labor at a time when the supply of Europeans was being cut off. Not all blacks left the South—about half of the black population still lives there—but those who did concentrated in a few cities. There they were met with racism and discrimination and promptly "ghettoized." They became a *lumpenproletariat,* working at relatively menial jobs (except for a small black middle class). "A large minority are trapped in a secondary labor market where there is no reward for tenure and where wages and working conditions are barely preferable to street life and welfare."[88] At this writing (early 1983), theirs is the highest rate of unemployment in the nation.

The principal beneficiary of recent changes in law is the black middle class. Richard B. Freeman maintains that blacks moved closer to whites in education, in jobs, and in income. But that is true only for a relative few.[89] The mass of blacks remain in the underclass. That is a harsh, even unpleasant assertion, nonetheless accurate. Professor Herbert Reid maintains that the black middle class is in fact a "second-class middle class," and continues:

The underclass is a real, existing class in current capitalist development. It is not a "limited lumpen" class, nor is it "surplus" in the Marxist sense. It is a class created by structural and social barriers to improvement of mobility. For example, blacks have often been the first fired in the current recession because they were the last hired and many will not be rehired because their jobs are being eliminated as the U.S. shifts from traditional industry to the high-technology age. Lacking the skills to meet the demands of the changing job market, their future as viable workers is in doubt. This threatens to produce an even larger and more permanent underclass within the black population. It is this which needs immediate and *urgent* attention if blacks are to join the mainstream of American society. (Emphasis in original.)[90]

Joining the mainstream of American society: That was precisely what Judge Skelly Wright sought to help blacks accomplish. As I have repeatedly argued, he tried, however unsuccessfully, to convince the white majority that *their* interests would also be furthered if blacks joined the mainstream. His point was that "those integrated into the system will be tempered by the stake in the existing order"—another way of stating the Principle of Reason-Directed Societal Self-Interest.

Professor Patterson perceives blacks as constituting a "radical catalyst" in the emergent postindustrial nation. He notes that the limits of reformism in dealing with poor blacks have been reached and there is an "open revolt" by many formerly sympathetic whites against affirmative action programs designed to help blacks as a group. He then asserts that special efforts are required, more than merely eliminating former and present racial discrimination. Poor blacks must be enabled to develop skills at an accelerated rate, as Christopher Jencks has remarked:

Unfortunately . . . skills are not absolute but relative—and hence, competitive. If the least adept students are given slightly better instruction, while instruction of the most adept gets substantially better, the competitive position of the least adept will deteriorate rather than improve. If that happens, poverty will grow more widespread. If the schools want to end poverty, they must not only improve the position of the poor pupils; *they must improve it faster than they improve the position of the rest of the pupils.* (Emphasis added.)[91]

What, then, might be done? Three alternatives may be suggested: (1) continuing to neglect the basic problem, while proffering such tentative and ineffectual "answers" as affirmative-action programs; (2) brutal repression; and (3) completely restructuring society.

The third alternative, though perhaps the most desirable, can be summarily ruled out. There will be no radical realignment of the positions of power and wealth and privilege that have existed since the beginnings of the Republic. A hard fact must be faced: *Whites will not accept blacks as a group in any position of social or economic equality*. No evidence exists that any fundamental change in attitudes and behavior patterns toward blacks by whites has occurred. Professor Patterson observes that it is impossible to neglect the 20 million blacks living in America's ghettos and it is not possible to use repression as a response to their demands. He thinks there is only one long-term alternative—"a fundamental change in social policy involving a restructuring of the American occupational structure." But he concedes that the likelihood of such a change is remote at best, that "before conditions can get any better they will certainly get much worse, for the black poor in particular and class relations in general." His vision is gloomy: violence on a large scale. The American poor are no longer passive.

Where do Skelly Wright's views fit into this scenario? Several conclusions are possible. First, he firmly believes in reform, because he has an abiding faith in the "democratic" system and its ability to work if the channels of participation are kept open. To that end, second, Wright has, in nonjudicial writings, severely castigated the Supreme Court for rulings that he considers to unduly favor those with wealth and money in the political process.[92] Third, he has come down squarely in favor of affirmative-action programs. Fourth, he would doubtless be strongly against use of repression to curb black unrest. The net conclusion is that he is willing, on and off the bench, to try to advance the cause of black Americans (and others who are disadvantaged) *incrementally*, with the hope and faith that eventually everyone's interests will be furthered. He has expressed no willingness to restructure society; his dislike of corporate money in electoral campaigns does not, for example, lead him to advocate the breakup of the giant corporations.

As a pragmatic instrumentalist, Judge Wright illustrates both the shortcomings and the merits of such an approach to the judging process. He is imbued with the idea that law has a high potential for social engineering; that is a consequence of his being born in the Progressive Age. His is a fundamental, albeit rudimentary, optimism about the human being and the human condition. He grew to maturity when law was being used wholesale to build the American version of the welfare state. Wright has an abiding faith in the general idea that law can restructure society, and is willing, insofar as the cases he decides allow, to remove obstacles to the full participation of everyone in the social and political order. On the other hand, if he has thoughts about the law's limited effectiveness or its inherent capabilities and limitations, he has not published them.

Skelly Wright knows that he can work only incrementally. He tries, by throwing out signals of what legally-concretized decency—the Constitution's basic premise—means in specific cases, to bid his fellow citizens to aspire to greater heights. Rightly or wrongly, he sees the Constitution as a moral imperative. He is not naive; he knows that those signals can be and often are misinterpreted or ignored. But he tries—which is much more than many other judges do. Wright knows that the American dilemma is not that of the blacks, but a problem in the hearts and minds of white Americans. White treatment of blacks is one of the world's great injustices. Skelly Wright has not passed it by.

4

Judge Wright and the Bureaucracy

The reform of administrative procedure is a large task, and Congress, the agencies, and the courts all have roles to play. . . . The courts should control discretion by vigorously reasserting their inherent role as the interpreters of legislative enactments and guardians against invidious and irrational exercises of governmental power. . . . While all branches of government must join in the fight to limit discretion, I believe it is the courts which will have to bear the primary burden.
—J. Skelly Wright (1972)[1]

I believe the judges should retrench from their disposition to act as final arbiters of the public good. We should . . . be more reluctant than we have about filling the void when, in our judgment, the elected branches of government should have acted and failed.
—J. Skelly Wright (1980)[2]

I

Whether Judge Wright is as "activist" as many believe, and perhaps even he thinks, may well be doubted. It is one thing to single out a few isolated decisions and point to them as prime examples of hyperactivism; but it is another to consider the full sweep of Wright's decisions. Skelly Wright as reluctant activist or even "passivist" is perhaps best seen in his rulings involving judicial review of administrative action. This chapter develops the ways in which he has met the continuing problem of what to do about rulings of the bureaucracy that, for one reason or another, are challenged in court. This is a generalized evaluation; other chapters, such as those devoted to national security and freedom of expression, are concerned with specific substantive areas. The basic conclusion is that, as his 1980 Harvard speech (note 2 above) indicates, Wright has indeed retrenched from substituting his judgment for that of administrators. Except when minorities and the environment are concerned, he appears to be content usually to defer to the bureaucrats. (The terms "bureaucracy" and "bureaucrats" are not used invidiously; rather, they are employed synonymously with "administration" and "administrators.")

Why is Judge Wright a reluctant activist, even a passivist, in questions of review of administrative action? There is no ready answer. If indeed that characterization is accurate, two hypotheses may be advanced. First, it is possible that with the growing complexity of problems dealt with by government, he believes that the expertise—his own as well as that of other judges—is not sufficient to the need when compared with that of administrators. That may have *some* validity; but how much is difficult to determine. As will be shown, he does not hesitate to substitute his judgment for that of administrators when environmental questions are involved—and surely they are among the most complicated of all that come before Wright's court. Second, he may see the problem of checking the bureaucracy as one peculiarly within the province and competence of Congress, the "democratically" elected—and thus "representative"— branch of government. To the extent that this is so, it could derive from Wright's fervent belief in the essential goodness of "the people" and, thus, of their capacity, through their representatives, to make wise policy decisions. But could it be traced to the fact that he, like Justice Hugo Black, may be becoming more "conservative" as he grows older? Could criticism by colleagues on the bench and by the professoriate be getting to him—subtly, at least—so that he has a growing uncertainty in the essential correctness of his answers to pressing social problems? These are hypotheses that may explain his swing, if that it be, to a posture of judicial passivism when the public administration is challenged.

To understand his decisions and off-bench writings about the public administration, it is necessary at the outset to outline the basic nature of modern America. That the United States in the twentieth century has become the "administrative" or "bureaucratic" state cannot be doubted. However much some may deplore the rise of organizations, both private and public, to prominence and dominance in the nation, their existence—their *continuing* existence—is one of the fundamental facts of the present day. Bureaucracy is characteristic of all industrialized societies, the principal factor that makes the U.S. and the U.S.S.R. resemble each other. Although it is, of course, not presently possible to discuss the question of bureaucracy in full, this section of Chapter 4 develops these propositions: that bureaucracy is both public and private; that there are close connections in fact between these two ostensibly disparate types; and that the law as made by judges and Congress and the president alike is concerned with both types—although what travels under the banner of "administrative law" is almost entirely devoted to judicial review of the public administration. (Section II is concerned with Judge Wright's published views about the bureaucracy.) The unifying theme of the present exposition is that the United States has traveled down the road toward an indigenous form of "corporatism"; America today, and predictably even more so in the future, exemplifies neither capitalism nor socialism but the third "ism"—corporatism.

"The twentieth century," Phillippe G. Schmitter once maintained, "will be the century of corporatism just as the nineteenth century was the century of liberalism."[3] If that is true about the United States, as I think that ever increasingly it is, then it may be concluded that we are experiencing, without benefit of formal amendment, a massive realignment of constitutional powers. The suggestion is that the emergent Constitution of the United States is corporatist in nature; that "constitution" is seen mainly in the fundamental law's "living" or "operative" senses and is a consequence of the growing merger of public and private power within the polity. That merger, in sum, is the creation of a new type of state in the United States, namely, the corporate state, American style. No one, whether judge or commentator, has yet to come to grips with the emergent phenomenon of corporatism, although Professor Howard J. Wiarda has suggested in an important essay that much of the debate about capitalism and socialism or between liberals and their critics is irrelevant and misses the point. To him, the fundamental issue is what form American corporatism will take: "It is time for Americans . . . to begin putting away their narrow and ethnocentric biases, to terminate the literature and thinking that sees the United States as superior and more 'developed' not only in the economic sense (also now questionable in a way it wasn't a decade ago) but politically, socially, and morally as well, to begin comprehending our own condition in the light not of some ancient and now largely imaginary or mythical liberal model but from a truly comparative perspective and in the light of the European-Iberic-Latin corporatist model which socially and politically we now also approximate."[4] The "liberal model" Wiarda mentions is classical liberalism—that of John Stuart Mill and others—rather than that of modern "Keynesian" liberals.

Professor Schmitter identifies two type of corporatism—*societal* and *state*. The former is "embedded in political systems with relatively autonomous, multilayered territorial units; open, competitive electoral processes and party systems; ideologically varied, coalitionally based executive authorities," featured in the postliberal, advanced capitalist welfare states. The latter Schmitter defines as polities that have political systems in which territorial subunits are controlled by a central bureaucracy; elections, if held, tend to be farcical; a single party state; and narrowly recruited executive elites.[5] I suggest that, ever increasingly, the United States is taking on the characteristics of societal corporatism. Government exercises directive intelligence (usually called regulation) over much of private business, and has close and continuing contractual ties to some private enterprises (notably in the arms and space industries). Yet, private initiative and corporate discretion is subject only to minimal restraints.

John Maynard Keynes, writing in 1925, noted the need for control over currency and credit, widespread dissemination of data relating to business, judgments as to the scale at which the nation should save, the scale at which savings should be exported, and rationalization of investment markets—exactly what is taking place today. In his language:

> I believe that in many cases the ideal size for the unit of control and organization lies somewhere between the individual and the modern state. I suggest, therefore, that progress lies in the growth and recognition of semi-autonomous bodies within the state—bodies whose criterion of action is solely the public good as they understand it, and from whose deliberations motives of private advantage are excluded, though some place it may be necessary to leave, until the ambit of man's altruism grows wider, to the separate advantage of particular groups, classes or faculties—bodies which in their ordinary course of affairs are mainly autonomous within their prescribed limitations, but are subject in the last resort to the sovereignty of democracy expressed through parliament. I propose a return, it may be said, towards medieval conceptions of separate autonomies.[6]

That is a call for a modern form of feudalism—which, with the rise of giant corporations and other pluralistic groups within the polity, has already occurred. Keynes, however, went astray when he thought that those groups would pursue "the public good" and would be ultimately subject to legislative control. As matters have evolved, the groups pursue their narrow, private interests and have little or no concern for the overall public or common weal. Further, the legislature (Congress), rather than being able to control the groups, all too often is the prisoner of those "semi-autonomous bodies within the state."

The modern state and modern interest groups seek each other out and cooperate more than they conflict. This means that the modern state is in fact a symbiont, with public and private governments acting syzygetically. Each retains its identity, but they are so closely intertwined that one could not exist without the other. Andrew Shonfield has shown in his magisterial *Modern Capitalism* that the state seeks to further maximum employment, promote economic growth, curb inflation, smooth out business cycles, regulate conditions of work, help alleviate individual economic risks, and resolve labor disputes. This he calls corporatist: "The major interest groups are brought together and encouraged to conclude a series of bargains about their future behavior, which will have the effect of moving economic events along the desired path."[7] That adds up to at least a primitive form of economic planning, even though the term is eschewed by those who wish to pretend that America is different.

The movement toward the third "ism" is occurring when the tenets of liberal democracy, private enterprise, and normative constitutionalism are still the operative belief system of most constitutional commentators, including judges. Their assumptions are taken for granted without inquiry into their worth. Those assumptions, or postulates, include the following:

The United States is a representative democracy; whatever was done in the past, particularly by the Supreme Court, has a special significance, so that it carries with it the presumption that, if at all possible, it should be repeated today; those who wrote the Constitution had a unique wisdom and a rare prescience—they acted not only for themselves but for generations yet unborn; lawyers are best qualified to discern and articulate the meanings of the words written in 1787; national uniformity in public polity is a "good"; in America, process is what counts—following proper procedures will result in desirable decisions; man is capable, through the exercise of reason, of moving steadily toward perfecting the good life on earth; there is no problem, however novel or complex, that cannot be handled within the confines of the Document of 1787; and there is such a thing as a pure legal problem, separate and apart from the political economy of the nation. Other postulates may exist, but those will suffice to make the point. Constitutional commentary is valid to the extent the postulates are valid. I believe that most, perhaps all, are faulty in some degree.

Whether Judge Wright adheres to those assumptions is the question. We have seen in Chapter 3 that, insofar as racial segregation is concerned, he rejects one of them—the idea of the pre-eminence of process. He was and is willing to go beyond the decisions reached by "due procedure," to determine whether those decisions accord with his sense of justice (or of injustice). He seems to accept some of the others, at least tacitly. But those postulates, I maintain, were in large part derivative from an outmoded paradigm. More succinctly, they were consequences of the Great Discoveries that began with Columbus.[8] Taken together, they are the tenets of liberal democracy and its economic counterpart, private-enterprise capitalism. They have become obsolescent.

Normative constitutionalism is the bedrock idea—the view that government should be limited. But that belief arose out of the unique, fortuitous, and nonreplicable circumstances that characterized the United States up to at least the beginning of the twentieth century. The consequences are becoming all too apparent. As the social—the ecological—bases of normative constitutionalism vanish one-by-one, a definite movement away from liberal democracy has become obvious; and private business finds itself ever increasingly tied in with public government. The meaning should be clear: Much of today's constitutional commentary misses the point of the nature of the true Constitution today. That includes, be it said, that of Judge Wright—as well of the judiciary generally. A new politico-economic order is being created. In my judgment, this is "corporatist"; its general characteristics are set forth here as a basis of assessing Judge Wright's administrative law decisions—how, that is, he has reacted to the rise of the bureaucratic state. Sophisticated discussion of the role of the judiciary vis-à-vis the judiciary must, in sum, consider the nature of the modern state. The corporate state, American style, has ten principles.

The first principle is: *There is a fusion of political and economic power in society.* This occurs in two ways. First, the giant corporations and other social groups are themselves political orders. They are private governments for members of the "corporate community." Second, public policies are usually a resultant of a parallelogram of political and economic forces. The myth to the contrary notwithstanding, policies emanate from the "subgovernments" or the "iron triangles" of Washington, rather than in the schoolboy version of Congress making the laws, the president administering them, and the courts interpreting them. The terms refer to the symbiotic relationships between congressional committees, administrative agencies, and affected interest groups.[9] Each subgovernment is interested—usually, at least—in only one segment of public policy. Says Professor Grant McConnell: "The distinction between the public and the private has been compromised far more deeply than we would like to acknowledge. . . . The very idea of constitutionalism sometimes seems to be placed in question."[10]

The second principle is: *The group is the basic unit of society.* Although the Constitution of 1787 recognizes only two entities—the natural person and government—since then an organizational revolution has occurred, one that has produced a society in which the group is dominant. Both in politics and in economics, the lone individual counts for little. Even in the Supreme Court's constitutional decisions, a person is important mainly because the High Bench is not a self-starter. It cannot reach out and seize policy issues, but must await the accident of litigation. Once the process starts, and particularly once a case is accepted for decision on the merits, the litigant becomes insignificant. Those 150-plus Supreme Court decisions made each term are for the development of the law—in other words, for larger legislative purposes. Constitutional cases, accordingly, are *de facto* class actions, although not brought as such, with the class being all others similarly situated throughout the nation. The diminution in importance of the person *qua* person, furthermore, has produced a growing body of "status rights" developed around an emergent concept of status in constitutional law. In net, neo-feudalism is coming to the law.[11]

The third principle is: *The state is a metaphysical entity—a "super-group person"—larger than the arithmetical sum of its parts (the units of public and of private governance).* Despite the myth to the contrary, the state is sovereign in the United States and is recognized as such by the Supreme Court. That may not be liked, because it cuts across the grain of the idea of popular sovereignty, but it cannot be gainsaid. The *state*, moreover, should be distinguished from its apparatus, *government* (which, as has been said, is both public and private), and those who are ruled, the citizenry that travels under the name of *society*. (Few commentators and no judges, to my knowledge, make that careful but necessary distinction.) The state as "group person" is a conception based upon Otto von Gierke's analysis of society. To him, "groups were real persons—real 'unitary' persons, existing over and above the multiple individual persons of which they are composed."

Just as corporations are constitutional persons by Supreme Court fiat, so, too, with the state; it is "a sort of high reality, of a transcendental order, which stands out as something distinct from, and superior to, the separate reality of the individual"[12]—and, one might add, the separate realities of government and social groups. Ernest Barker has pointed out the dangers of such a view:

If we make groups of real persons, we shall make the national state a real person. If we make the state a real person, with a real will, we make it indeed a Leviathan—a Leviathan which is not an automaton, like the Leviathan of Hobbes, but a living reality. When its will collides with other wills, it may claim that, being the greatest, it must and shall carry the day; and its supreme will may thus become a supreme force. If and when that happens, not only may the state become one real person and the one true group, which eliminates and assimilates others; it may also become a mere personal power which eliminates its own true nature as a specific purpose directed to law or right.[13]

The most cursory survey of American policy and judicial decisions in recent decades quickly reveals that the state does indeed "carry the day" and that, accordingly, it is pre-eminent.

The fourth principle is: *The Supreme Court is an arm of the state.* Courts are unquestionably a part of the political order. Professor J. A. G. Griffith has said it well: "The judiciary in any modern industrial society, however composed, . . . is an essential part of the system of government and . . . its function may be described as underpinning the stability of that system and as protecting that system from attack by resisting attempts to change it."[14] The Supreme Court, and other courts, are parts of the governing coalition of the nation, and cannot long—or, indeed, ever—be out of synchronization with the other segments of government. Put bluntly, the state *always* wins in litigation when the issue is considered important by those who wield effective control in the nation. I can think of no exception to that broad proposition.

The fifth principle is: *"Communitarianism" is replacing individualism as the primary American ideology.* This follows from the second principle and anticipates the sixth. The term *communitarianism* is taken from Professor George Lodge's *The New American Ideology.* "America," he maintains, "now appears to be heading into a return to the communal norms of both ancient and medieval worlds," going on to remark that the individualistic ideology was an aberration.[15] It will not do to shrug off such a view, for Lodge, himself a pillar of the northeastern establishment, is on the faculty of the central organ of the business establishment, the Harvard Business School. Lockean individualism, the ideology that permeates much modern constitutional commentary, is being replaced—whether one likes it or not—by the new ideology. In many respects, communitarianism is synonymous with corporatism. The individualistic basis of law, both public and private, is vanishing. Individualism as an operative ideology is simply not possible in a nation dominated by huge public and private bureaucracies.

The sixth principle is: *Society is bureaucratized.* Bureaucracy is one of the commonplaces of the day. It exists and is dominant, ever more so, yet learned scholars and judges still write and speak in terms of individualism. A person is significant in the United States, both in politics and in economics, only as a member of a group—a bureaucracy. More than sixty years ago, Max Weber maintained: "The bureaucratization of society will, according to all available knowledge, some day triumph over capitalism, in our civilization just as in ancient civilizations. In our civilization also the 'anarchy of production' will be supplanted in due course by an economic and social system similar to that typical of the late Roman Empire, and even more so of the 'New Kingdom' in Egypt or the sway of the Ptolemies."[16] Once rapid capitalist expansion has halted, the dynamism of capitalist competition would give way to bureaucratized techniques of regulating the economy. Weber, writing *circa* 1920, presciently forecast the shape of things to come. Even though he thought that charismatic leadership could be a creative revolutionary force that would help alleviate the emergent problems he perceived, he nevertheless maintained that in the long run "the seemingly irresistible advance of routinization, rationalization and bureaucratization" would be dominant. As of 1983, and the future so far as it can be foreseen, that domination is increasingly more obvious. It is worth mention that the need for Weber's "irresistible advance" complements very well the end of the 400-year boom brought about by the Great Discoveries. Internalization—the management of existing resources rather than constantly searching for new resources—is characteristic of the age.

In modern times, Jacques Ellul takes Weber a giant step further. Focusing on what he calls "technique," he notes in *The Technological Society* "the transition from the individualist to the collectivist society." Ellul defines *technique* as more than machines, technology, or procedures for attaining an end. "In our technological society, technique is the totality of methods rationally arrived at and having absolute efficiency (for a given stage of development) in every field of human activity. Its characteristics are new; the techniques of the present have no common measure with those of the past."[17] Technique imposes centralism upon the economy. So, too, with politics: The technician—the technocrat—perceives the state as an enterprise that must function efficiently. And efficiency requires administration (bureaucracy). Ours, then, is an age of collective action—as John R. Commons noted several decades ago.

The seventh principle is: *Corporatism is mercantilist.* Mercantilism was the economic theory appropriate for the medieval period, the time of feudalism and the beginnings of nationalism, roughly the period of the fifteenth to the eighteenth centuries. It had five primary characteristics: it was nationalistic; it saw in gold and other precious metals an important economic force; it promoted exports over imports; imports were limited by tariffs and nontariff barriers to trade; it was both a political and an economic policy. The economic objective was a favorable balance of trade or at least a balance of trade, whereas the political goal was a balance of power.

Mercantilism gave way to classical economics and the notion of a natural equilibrium. No special insight is required to perceive parallels between mercantilism and the economies of major nations today. Other than the fact that currencies have been cast adrift from the gold standard, the modern age may accurately be termed neo-mercantilist. The other four characteristics of the older version are clearly evident in American policies. This, of course, was not an abrupt shift from the past. In many respects, mercantilism never really died out. The difference today from the political economy of the nineteenth century is far more one of degree than of type.

The eighth principle is: *A growing social stratification characterizes corporatism in America.* Society in the United States is increasingly one of a managerial elite at the top (those with expert knowledge), beholden in large part to a moneyed and propertied aristocracy, and with a larger and larger underclass. The elite is fed by the system of education, which is the ninth principle.

The ninth principle is: *Universities, rather than being centers of independent knowledge, tend to be "service stations" for the institutions of corporatism.*

The tenth principle is: *The distinction between law and politics is disappearing.*

These last three principles of American corporation will be discussed together. There is little need to do more than expand a bit on the suggestion in Chapter 3 that a permanent underclass is being created in the United States. In significant part, that "new class"—it is really not so new; rather, the perception of it is—is a consequence of the scientific-technological revolution, which, among other things, has managed to create a terminal sense of the loss of work itself among increasing numbers of people and which, through improved health measures, keeps more people alive longer than ever before in history. What Thorstein Veblen foresaw at the turn of the century and what Aldous Huxley put in his novel, *Brave New World*, and what Orwell affirmed in *1984*, is fast becoming reality. Brain power, not manual labor, is the main requirement. Technicians are needed, but only a relative few, even of them, are necessary. A technological elite manages a technological society, one dominated by Ellul's *technique*, and, at the bottom, are increasing masses of people to do the menial tasks that have not yet been mechanized. Far too many exist for those jobs. As a consequence, a *de facto* class of Huxleyan "proles" is being created. Castes are not mandated by formal law, but the result of accidents of birth and intelligence in an increasingly stratified society. Those castes are to be seen in the living or operative law.

Education in the emergent corporate state, American style is closely tied in with societal groups. Schooling is mandatory, not for the students as individuals, but for the general good of society as a collectivity. A close tie-in exists between universities and the groups of society. Rather than being disinterested centers of learning, universities all too often exemplify what Julien Benda called *La Trahison des Clercs* (translated as "The Treason of the Intellectuals"). To Benda, treason did not mean subversion against the state, but the adherence of intellectuals *(les clercs)* to the ideas of nationalism and to the centers of power within the nation (including public government).[18] Although Benda wrote in the mid-1920s, his observations are particularly cogent today.

Today's intellectuals—far too many of them, at least—are apolitical only in the sense that lawyers are: They will, they do, sell their talents to the highest bidder. During recent decades, knowledge "has become the central capital, the cost center, and the crucial resource of the economy." A knowledge explosion is indeed taking place, but the holders of knowledge, far from being dispassionate observers dedicated to the pursuit of truth, are, speaking generally, beholden to those who exercise real power in the nation. Says Professor Victor V. Ferkiss: "The action of technicians has an inevitable social dimension. It seems permissible to suggest that, on average, this activity, even if carried on in an autonomous manner, tends to work in favor of that part of the system benefiting the ruling classes."[19] It should not be forgotten that, in his famous farewell address warning about the dangers of the "military-industrial complex," President Eisenhower coupled intellectuals into that complex. Perhaps the classic example of *la trahison des clercs* in modern times is the way in which brilliant scientists and engineers bent their talents to producing the atomic bomb (and later on, a thermonuclear bomb). The process continues: "Many industrial social scientists have put themselves on auction. The power elites of America, especially the industrial elite, have bought their services."[20] We like to think that universities are centers for the disinterested pursuit of truth. But that is really not so: They are service stations for the institutions of American corporatism.

As for the Rule of Politics rather than the Rule of Law, little need be said. The point, said bluntly, is that law is not and indeed cannot be a substitute for politics. For millennia, political philosophers have sought for ways to create a society in which government was by laws and not by men. The ideal persists, but it is unattainable. Written constitutions do not make it possible, even with a bill of rights and other putative limitations on government. Those constitutions merely take political decisions out of the hands of politicans and pass them into the hands of judges or other persons. The fact that courts, even the Supreme Court, make certain kinds of political decisions does not mean that they are any less political. Furthermore, as Professor Martin Shapiro has told us, "No regime is likely to allow significant political power to be wielded by an isolated judicial corps free of political restraints."[21]

To sum up this section: The United States has traveled well down the road toward a form of societal corporatism. The idea is resisted. Corporatism is a difficult label to swallow, both politically and conceptually. It is difficult politically because the very word recalls the specter of fascism, of Benito Mussolini and other tyrants. Societal corporatism is not yet overtly authoritarian, but it could become so. The idea is conceptually difficult because of the several meanings that are given the term. Schmitter distinguishes, for example, between societal and state corporatism, as we have seen. It is accurate to say, however, that the United States has always been corporatist to some degree, in the sense of close and continuing relationships between government and business. American history can be read as an exemplification of the principles of Alexander Hamilton put into effect; in his economic theories and in the expressed need for government to aid business, Hamilton was the most important of all the Founding Fathers. In turn, private business has always fulfilled functions of government (the state). I am not suggesting that corporatism was overt in the sense of being codified in statutes expressly designed for that end. The only attempt to do so came in the National Recovery Act of the early New Deal of President Franklin D. Roosevelt, which was declared unconstitutional (although not because it was corporatist) by the Supreme Court. More basically, judicial review of administrative action—the focus of this chapter, as seen through Judge Wright's decisions—should be evaluated in the larger *constitutional* context—namely, the type of government that is evolving in the United States. The most appropriate label for the emergent government is corporatism.

II

Judge Wright shares with others who study and comment on the role of courts vis-à-vis the public administration, and other judges who are called upon to make decisions concerning that relationship, adherence to an outmoded paradigm of the nature of the constitutional order. Not that the so-called Constitution of Rights (of Limitations) was ever an accurate label. To the contrary; government in the United States has always been precisely as strong as conditions required, able to fulfill the desires of those who exercise effective control in the polity. Franz Neumann said it well:

No society in recorded history has ever been able to dispense with political power. This is as true of liberalism as of absolutism, as true of laissez faire as of an interventionist state. No greater disservice has been rendered to political science than the statement that the liberal state was a "weak" state. It was precisely as strong as it needed to be in the circumstances. It acquired substantial colonial empires, waged wars, held down internal disorders, and stabilized itself over long periods of time.[22]

Said more bluntly: A principle of constitutional relativity runs throughout American history. The limitations the orthodoxy perceives are more ostensible than real. A generation ago, Professor Edward S. Corwin noted the decline of the ideal of limited government and the emergence of a Constitution of powers in a secular state. Surely he was accurate. Surely, too, government in the United States is tilting toward authoritarianism, as the next chapter will show.

Federal judges perceive government and the administrative process only in a piecemeal fashion. As cases come to them, they are deeply concerned with the manifold details of the emergent corporate state, operating through its apparatus, government; however, they not only proceed on an outmoded paradigm of American constitutionalism, but are unable to view the public administration systemically. Furthermore, they are constrained by the "given"—the fact that the public administration is largely a creation of Congress and thus subject to the ultimate authority of Congress. The meaning is clear: The "supreme court" of administrative law is not the High Bench; it is Congress, which can and does act as a "super court of appeals" in administrative matters. As for private bureaucracies, judges on lower federal courts are further limited by the Supreme Court's conception of "state action." The Constitution, the saying goes, runs against governments only. It is only on extremely rare occasions that the actual—the *de facto*—governing power of "private" groups is acknowledged by the Supreme Court.

Of all federal judges, no one has been more concerned with the problem of how courts should treat administration than Judge Skelly Wright. His numerous opinions have been supplemented by several law journal articles. In briefest terms, he believes that the judiciary has only a limited role to play. Consider these statements, the first in 1972 and the second in 1980:

> It is ultimately impossible to talk sensibly about administrative law outside the framework of a theory of democratic government. Such a theory would determine how loud a voice the citizenry should have in various kinds of decisions as properly legislative, others as administrative, judicial, and so forth. I do not propose, even if I could do so, to put forth such a theory. . . . But the core of the argument may be stated. I have argued elsewhere that the Constitution deliberately places certain decisions—notably those affecting minority rights—outside the domain of the majority and its elected representatives. . . . Precisely because of this restriction, it is all the more necessary that those matters reserved for majority decision be done through majoritarian process. It is in this sense that legislative decisions are democratic: unlike a judge, whose decisions purport to be "principled," a legislator may trade off a vote on one question for the support of a colleague on another issue of greater importance to his constituents; decisions are made by vote, with the winning side presumably representing a greater number of citizens. Most important, legislators are subject to electoral control.[23]

In net, that is a statement of a romantic view of the governing process; in it, Judge Wright accepts the postulate or assumption, noted above, that the United States is a representative democracy. Therefore, the judiciary should have only a limited role in supervising the other branches of government, whether legislative or administrative. Compare his 1980 view (a part of which was set forth in the headnote to this chapter):

> I believe the judges should *retrench* from their disposition to act as final arbiters of the public good. We should . . . be more reluctant than we have been to fault the other agencies of government and, also, more hesitant about filling the void when, in our judgment, the elected branches of government should have acted and failed. . . . We tend to forget that, once upon a time, it was not self-evident that judges had *any* business overseeing the work of departments or other agencies of government, except only as it was charged that constitutional rights had been violated. I am now wondering out loud why that is not the right rule, why the courts should do no more than keep administrators within constitutional bounds. (Emphasis in original.)[24]

That is far from the voice of committed judicial activist, eager to impose his own values upon the governing process.

A tension or inconsistency exists, however, between what Judge Wright called "the right rule" in 1980—keeping administrators within constitutional bounds—and some of his decisions. In the *Three Mile Island* case, discussed below, he was quite willing in 1982 to oversee the work of the Nuclear Regulatory Commission in a problem that was purely one of statutory, not constitutional, interpretation. That case, however, dealt with environmental concerns—a category of law that Wright tends to be willing to "fault the other agencies of government."

Other members of his court tend to see things differently. For example, the late Judge Harold Leventhal once wrote that "the court is in a real sense part of the total administrative process, and not a hostile stranger to the office of first instance."[25] The courts, said Leventhal, must join with the administrative agencies in a partnership in furtherance of the public interest as "collaborative instrumentalities of justice." There can be little doubt that he thought judges should be the senior partner. Judge David Bazelon also is willing to go further than Wright in supervising the bureaucracy.

Wright's position on administrative law is best seen in the area of "informal rule-making" by the agencies. Placing great emphasis on cutting down delay in the process, he often is at odds with his colleagues in specific cases. He strictly construes the congressional mandate in the Administrative Procedure Act (APA)—the general statute that governs the public bureaucracy.[26] Under the APA, there are two general types of rule-making—formal and informal. A rule is "an agency statement of general or particular applicability and future effect designed to implement, interpret, or prescribe law or policy or describing the organization, procedure, or practice requirements of an agency."

Formal rule-making is much like litigation in courts, except that the goal is to promulgate a general rule rather than merely to settle a dispute. It is required when Congress says that rule-making should "be made on the record after opportunity for an agency hearing." As in the judiciary, parties involved have an opportunity to cross-examine witnesses, to submit and rebut evidence, and to have a decision that is based on the written record at a hearing. Obviously, that can be a long process; so there should be little wonder that many prefer informal rule-making.

Certainly Skelly Wright does. He believes that use of it, in accordance with the Administrative Procedure Act, protects the public interest and enables agencies to act with relative dispatch. Under the APA, informal rule-making procedures need only be "openly informed, reasoned and candid." Often called "notice and comment" rule-making, because the agency drafts a proposed rule and sends it out for comment by interested parties, informal rule-making under the APA requires that public notice be given of the proposed rule and interested persons given at least thirty days to comment. This comment can come by written presentations or oral testimony. The record in an informal rule-making case thus consists of the basis and purpose statement of the proposed rule, the comments received, and a transcript of any hearings that may have been held. Wright maintains that such rules "will be made through a genuine dialogue between agency experts and concerned members of the public."[27]

Precisely what a "genuine dialogue" might be, and how it is to be determined, are questions that Judge Wright has not discussed extensively. Nor has he suggested how such a dialogue can take place absent something akin to true adversary procedures (as in formal rule-making). Moreover, he goes on, a court in reviewing agency informal rule-making should simply "satisfy itself that the requisite dialogue occurred and that is was not a sham." Just how one is to prove, on judicial review of an informal rule, there was no "sham" is a question that Wright has not confronted. Given the fact that the record—the basic data before the reviewing court—is merely the collection of documents noted above, it seems to be all too easy for agency personnel to load that record with statements that appear to sustain the agency action. One does not denigrate public administrators in asserting that they can, if they wish, easily make the record look good for the end they desire. The situation is not helped by Wright's further assertion that "if the subject-matter of a rule falls within an agency's delegated authority [from Congress], there are only two grounds for a court upsetting it": if "the basis and purpose" statement includes "no reasons or merely conclusory reasons"; or if "the agency has relied on important findings, assumptions, or techniques not made public prior to the rule's promulgation."[28] As Wright pointed out in *Rodway v. United States Department of Agriculture*,[29] the failure of an agency to agree to *all* of the procedural requirements of informal rule-making will result in the absence of an adequate record for purposes of judicial review.

This, again, sounds much better than it actually is. It places difficult, perhaps insuperable, burdens upon the persons contesting the rule. How do they and, indeed, how can a judge, determine whether the record contained all that actually occurred within an agency? Wright seems to assume that *all* relevant data are in the record or are so obviously not in the record that their absence can be easily detected. The assumption is unwarranted. One need not be considered a cynic or unduly harsh on administrators to suggest that the record may not—likely, will not—reflect all that transpired in the agency. After all, when Supreme Court Justices admit that they do independent research and concede in one way or another that their personal philosophies are instrumental in their decisions, why should one expect administrators to act differently? There is, in sum, simply no way that a reviewing court can ensure that the "dialogue" the APA requires is not a "sham."

I have suggested above that Skelly Wright has a romantic view of the governing process insofar as he adheres to a notion of the viability of representative democracy in the United States. His "romance" with informal administrative rule-making stems from 1973 and 1974 when panels of his court (on neither of which he sat) adopted what he calls an "ad hoc approach to procedural review" of rule-making. In *International Harvester Co. v. Ruckelshaus* and *Mobil Oil Corp. v. Federal Power Commission*,[30] he witnessed what he considered to be excessive formalities placed upon informal rule-making by his colleagues, requirements that went beyond what Congress had thought necessary. The cases led Wright to publish an article in the *Cornell Law Review* in which he set forth his views on the matter.[31] The cases and article deserve considerable attention.

First, the cases. In *International Harvester*, the Environmental Protection Agency (EPA) had decided not to suspend for one year the statutory standards for auto emission control. Suspension was permitted only if the administrator determined that the necessary technology to meet the standards was not "available." EPA determined that the technology was available, but through a complex method not revealed to the auto companies. When challenged in court, the panel said that the parties should have an opportunity "to address themselves to matters not previously put before them." The case was sent back to the EPA, with directions to allow the parties to comment and criticize the method EPA used to reach its decision. Of more importance, the court went on to say: "We require reasonable cross-examination as to new lines of testimony, and as to submissions previously made to EPA in the hearing on a proffer that critical questions could not be satisfactorily pursued by procedures previously in effect."[32] The problem, as Judge Wright saw it, was that the statute did not require any cross-examination procedure for rule-making. The court's panel in effect amended the statute "in the interest of providing a reasoned decision."[33]

Skelly Wright saw this as an example of "judicial fiat"—as he also saw the decision in the *Mobil* case. There, the court's panel again in effect amended the statute by requiring that the Federal Power Commission (FPC) hold "some sort of adversary, adjudicative-type"[34] hearing, with opportunity for cross-examination and written interrogatories. Other cases from other courts led Wright to the conclusion that agencies may have been held to abuse their discretion if they failed to hold an evidentiary hearing even when Congress had not made such a hearing a requirement. Wright concludes (in his article): "Thus, after an agency has fully completed its consideration and promulgation of a rule, the reviewing court may demand reconsideration under any procedures which, in retrospect, strike the court as being appropriate to the issues raised. This curious 'ad hoc' approach to procedural review is not authorized by the APA or by any other statute; nor should it become the law by judicial fiat."[35] But here, again, Wright seems to place an inordinate confidence in the bona fides of public administrators. He does not view them with a skeptical eye, but tends to accept their version of what took place in the agencies. He justifies this in his conclusion to his *Cornell Law Review* article:

> What reviewing courts can realistically do to improve rule-making is just what the APA asks them to do—open the agencies to outside information, challenge, and scrutiny. Before dismissing this as a demeaning or trivial task, we should recall how many agencies have become captives of private interests, closed to new methods or regulation and planning, and dedicated to obscuring their policies from the public and Congress. . . . The APA provides the courts with powerful tools to attack these abuses. We should learn to use these tools and give up playing arcane procedural games authorized by neither statute nor common sense.[36]

This is Skelly Wright the reluctant activist, the person who sees a limited role for the judiciary vis-à-vis the bureaucracy. This, in other words, is Wright as the Establishment judge pure and simple. Labels, however, are meaningless. The question is whether his views on informal administrative rule-making are valid.

There is no easy answer to that question. Clearly, Wright is correct in his view that requiring administrative agencies to follow procedures not mandated by Congress makes informal rule-making akin to formal rule-making. What he calls the "ad hoc approach" allows the judiciary to follow "a relentlessly 'activist' role." While noting, in an obvious understatement, that he does not always find judicial activism "uncongenial," he maintains that the ad hoc approach "can claim no constitutional mandate, and it certainly protects no minority interests which the political system would ignore."[37] Therefore, he asserts, it "lacks those foundations in law and reason which an activist posture requires." That, however, is not necessarily correct. A "constitutional mandate" certainly can be found in the due process clause, which is a command that those affected by governmental action be given an opportunity for "some kind of hearing." Judge Wright correctly says that the will of Congress prevails over that of the administrator, and then goes on to observe: "If the APA precludes the ad hoc approach, then that approach can survive only if the Constitution requires it."[38] But he quickly states that "there is not even a colorable claim to this effect," citing a 1915 Supreme Court decision concerning Colorado tax officials as persuasive authority.[39] In essence, the Supreme Court is saying (it repeated the 1915 holding in 1973), and Judge Wright concurs, that when administrators act as *legislators* they are not held to due process norms—just as Congress is not. Wright concedes that "all government actions must be surrounded by procedures representing a reasonable balance between fairness and efficiency."[40] But he then goes on to assert that for rule-making, the fairness is owed to the public generally and not to the particular individuals.

Serious problems attend such a position. For one thing, agencies may be mini-legislatures, but they act to fill in the interstices of a statute—a general rule—promulgated by Congress. For example, in *International Harvester*, only a handful of companies were directly affected by the EPA action. It would not be difficult to give them a full day in court. Second, how can fairness be owed to the public generally, without permitting some person (natural or corporate) to contest the agency decision? Who speaks for "the public"? If the answer to that question is that the agency does, then anything the agency might do is in the public interest. Fairness, furthermore, is by no means an easily definable concept. Be that as it may, it is certain that Judge Wright is basically concerned with undue delay in the administrative process. To allow the "ad hoc approach" means to him that the informal rule-making process is overjudicialized. Witness this comment:

The administrative process would . . . be completely predictable. Fearing reversal of his substantive initiatives, each administrator would clothe his agency's actions in the full wardrobe of adjudicatory procedure. By demanding procedural refinements on an ad hoc basis, reviewing courts would inadvertently induce agencies to adopt maximum procedures in all cases. Seeking administrative variety, we would obtain administrative paralysis. The inherent virtues of rule-making . . . would be forfeited. Like adjudicatory regulation today, rule-making would become a lawyer's game.[41]

The result, as Wright sees it, is undue delay in the administrative process. The will of Congress is being frustrated.

That may well be so. Judge Wright was not on the panel for either *International Harvester* or *Mobil Oil*. It was not until *Ethyl Corp. v. EPA*[42] that Wright was able to translate his law journal ruminations into judicial prose. In *Ethyl*, review was sought of EPA regulations requiring reduction in the average lead concentration in gasoline. The decision turned on the question of whether the EPA had introduced enough evidence to support its determination that leaded gasoline was a threat to public health. Ethyl argued that it had not been able to introduce sufficient evidence on its behalf. Wright wrote for an *en banc* court, and upheld the regulations. He found that the APA's informal rule-making requirements had been satisfied. He refused to hold that interested parties had a right to cross-examine witnesses in informal rule-making proceedings. "Petitioners," Wright wrote, "were afforded a meaningful opportunity to be heard and to controvert the evidence. Fairness demands no more." That fairness ranks high in his scale of values may also be seen in his opinion in the *Home Box Office* case, where he inveighed against *ex parte* communications to administrators as being basically unfair.[43]

The difficulty with Judge Wright's fairness position is obvious. Nowhere is *it* mandated by statute. Furthermore, giving one an opportunity to be heard and to controvert evidence does not, by any means, mean that administrators will listen *and* heed. Of course it is true that if one has the chance to be heard—to present testimony in his own behalf and to controvert opposing testimony—he or she will not necessarily win. The contrary is emphatically accurate. All that legal process provides, whether it is judicial or administrative, is the opportunity to present one's views. That, however, is based on two assumptions—first, that the decision maker is unbiased and will not decide on the basis of data other than that presented in the hearing; and second, that the proceedings themselves meet some minimum standard of rationality. Those assumptions may well fall of their own weight. Those who make governmental decisions carry their predilections along with them, as premises that are either articulated or, more likely, not articulated. Rationality comes into the proceedings only in the sense that decisions, when fully analyzed, may be considered to be logical derivations from those premises.

The point, for present purposes, is simple yet profound: Judge Wright's fairness criterion cannot reasonably ensure that decisions are made with bias eliminated and with premises articulated. Perhaps there is no way that such decisions can be made with assurance. It does seem likely, however, that those other judges who believe that informal proceedings should be made more formal sense, however imperfectly, that something is awry in the administrative process, and that more formality is the way to remedy it. They appear to believe that only through completely open adversary proceedings will better decisions come from the public administration.

Be that as it may, the present Supreme Court does agree with Judge Wright. In *Vermont Yankee Nuclear Power Corp. v. National Resources Defense Council*,[44] the High Bench unanimously rejected the notion that a reviewing court could impose additional rule-making procedures upon an administrative agency. Finding that requiring supplemental procedures would nullify "the inherent advantages of rule-making," Justice William Rehnquist, speaking for the Court, cited Judge Wright's *Cornell Law Review* article to support the decision. Rehnquist went out of his way to chastise the lower court (a panel of judges on Wright's Court of Appeals), saying that the panel "seriously misread or misapplied the statutory and decisional law cautioning reviewing courts against engrafting their own notions of proper procedures upon agencies entrusted with substantive functions by Congress." Maintaining that the lower court "has unjustifiably intruded into the administrative process," Rehnquist asserted that the Court of Appeals "fundamentally misconceives the nature of the standard of review of an agency rule." He criticized Judge David Bazelon's opinion for being an egregious example of "Monday-morning quarterbacking," "Kafkaesque," and "judicial intervention run riot."

As with politics, administrative law seems to make strange bedfellows. Rehnquist and Wright agree on little else. By no means, however, is it certain that they are correct, and Bazelon wrong, in cases such as *Vermont Yankee.* Bazelon seems to have been pursuing ideas of social justice, whereas Rehnquist and Wright opted for efficiency as the overriding value. To Rehnquist, the agency was, in effect, a part of Congress—and to be treated as such. Since the judiciary does not seek to force additional procedures upon Congress, it therefore follows that judges should not do so for Congress's delegates. It is accepted law, of course, that "courts should defer to the experience and judgment of the agency to whom Congress has delegated appropriate authority."[45] Indeed, the Supreme Court holds administrative expertise in high regard, for it has long held that " 'cumulative experience' begets understanding and insight by which judgments not objectively demonstrable are validated or qualified or invalidated."[46] Only when agencies act arbitrarily or capriciously, abuse their discretion, or act contrary to law should their actions be set aside by reviewing courts. These standards of review all "presume agency action to be valid . . . and require affirmance if a rational basis exists for the agency's decision."[47]

That posture of judicial deference ultimately poses a fundamental constitutional question. After all, agencies are part of the "headless fourth branch of government" rather than arms of Congress; and it is not necessarily valid to treat them as mini-legislatures with all the deference due to a *constitutional* branch of government (Congress). The agencies, furthermore, are all too often, as Judge Wright wrote, "captives of private interests" (an observation that has been repeated many times by numerous other commentators), and it is more than a little difficult to perceive how the *public interest* is served by adherence to the procedural regularity that Wright advocates and Rehnquist requires. In fact, as was said in discussing the principles of American corporatism, public policies tend to be set by the iron triangles or subgovernments of Washington. That is an extraconstitutional means of formulating policy, something that neither Wright nor Rehnquist have been willing to confront. Again, it is a romantic view of governance that they articulate. They fail to come to grips with the realities of power in the emergent corporate state. With iron triangles in effect, the public interest (however defined, itself a difficult task) is furthered only by happenstance. The elites of those triangles pursue narrow goals, with little or no regard for the larger issues of statesmanship. The consequence is that political pluralism, as theory and practice, is in disarray. That has long been known to perceptive political scientists, such as Henry Kariel, Grant McConnell, Theodore Lowi, and Robert Dahl,[48] but has not yet been accepted by, or even known to, many lawyers and judges. The rise of bureaucracy, public and private, has produced a new political and constitutional order; but is is one which is dealt with by judges employing ancient notions that have little or no relevance to modern America. Finally, there is much more to the concept of expertise than that of the putative expertise in the agencies. Judges, too, are expert—but in a different way—theirs is an expertise in general societal values, values that transcend the technical aspects of administration.[49]

The exaggerated deference to the agencies that Judge Wright advocates thus poses the crucial question of who is to rein in the excesses of administrators? The answer Wright gives is Congress—and, indirectly, the courts. He believes that "there must be some limit to the extent to which Congress can transfer its own powers to other bodies without guidance as to how those powers should be exercised."[50] This means that he is willing to second-guess Congress and tell it that proper limits must be placed upon the powers of the agencies. In effect, he is thereby calling for resurrection of the moribund "delegation of powers" doctrine. "At the risk of seeming antiquarian," he wrote in 1972, "I think the reported demise of the delegation doctrine is a bit premature." The doctrine "retains an important potential as a check of unbounded, standardless discretion by administrative agencies."[51] Congress has often legislated broadly and left the drafting of detailed standards and guidelines to the bureaucracy. Wright observes that it is no doubt much "easier to pass an organic statute with some vague language about the 'public interest' which tells the agency, in effect, to get the job done." Wright goes so far as to maintain that the courts should resurrect the delegation doctrine "as a matter of constitutional morality if not constitutional compulsion." In net, the doctrine provides that Congress can delegate its powers to the bureaucracy, provided that an "intelligible principle" canalizes the discretion that Congress gives over. It has not been employed by the Supreme Court since the mid-1930s—and then only twice—with the result that it is a dead letter in the law.[52] Congress routinely delegates enormous chunks of governing power to the public administration; far from rarely, the delegations are completely absent any "intelligible principle." The courts go along.

That Judge Wright can see a constitutional question when Congress delegates unbridled power to the agencies is difficult to reconcile with his stated inability to see a due process constitutional question lurking in the informal rule-making process. If it is accurate to say that many public policies are the results of bargaining within the iron triangles of Washington, then certainly adherence to the minimum requirements of informal rule-making cannot by any means improve the process (as Wright maintains). The suggestion, in sum, is that the position of the courts vis-à-vis the bureaucracy is just as much a constitutional question as the relationship of the courts to Congress. Wright maintains that the role of the judge is merely to "keep administrators within constitutional bounds." But what are those bounds? There is no ready answer. The Constitution is an evolving instrument of governance, which must be adapted to new social and political conditions. It will not do to employ a 1915 decision dealing with a Colorado administrative action as controlling authority to say, as did Wright, that rule-making raises no constitutional question. In administrative law matters, the federal judiciary deals largely with questions emanating from the federal bureaucracy, a far cry from what Colorado was in 1915 or is today. Since due process of law is a constitutional precept, and since most administrative law decisions are variations on the due process theme, it is apparent that keeping administrators "within constitutional bounds" is the norm and not the exception (as Wright maintains).

It may well be that Skelly Wright knows this. Consider, for example, the case of *Chisholm v. Federal Communications Commission.*[53] During the 1976 presidential primary season, a Court of Appeals panel, on which Judge Wright sat, upheld reversal of a 10-year old statutory interpretation by the FCC. Under the statute, any licensee of broadcasting facilities who allows one political candidate to "use" his or her facilities must allow "equal time" to all other candidates for that particular office. At first, the FCC interpreted the law as requiring that electronic coverage of a debate among candidates include all legally qualified candidates or an offer of equal time at a later date. In 1975, the FCC changed its interpretation to say that debates between qualified candidates would be excluded from the equal time requirement. This decision allowed Gerald Ford and Jimmy Carter to debate on television, without any requirement for participation by other candidates—in this instance, Shirley Chisholm.

This was too much for Judge Wright. He dissented, contending that "the Commission, in rejecting its own prior opinions as to the intent of Congress . . . has substituted its own judgment for decisions made by Congress, and has acted without regard to the procedures it was required to follow." He concluded that notions of judicial deference "cannot insulate this exercise in administrative abrogation of power from judicial review." That is not the language of a committed judicial passivist in administrative law matters. It was, furthermore, by no means clear that the FCC had disregarded the procedures Congress said it should follow. Was there, however, a constitutional principle lurking somewhere in the dispute? Wright did not allude to one in his 30-page dissent. Nevertheless, it is possible to argue that one did exist. Under the old FCC rule, a television station was obligated to invite *all* candidates to a debate; but under the new one, two candidates could stage their own debate at, say, the behest of the League of Women Voters, and the television station could then cover the debate as a "news event." That, of course, was a subterfuge to evade the old rule. Its effect was to eliminate a candidate with a small following. Judge Wright, therefore, was protesting a limitation on political speech, which surely is a first amendment question. Constitutional principles *can* be found buried in administrative law cases.

The point became overt in Wright's dissent in *Capital Broadcasting Co. v. Mitchell*,[54] where a panel held that "Congress has the power to prohibit the advertising of cigarettes in any medium," locating that power in Congress's constitutional control over interstate commerce. Wright refused to agree: Although he denounced the advertisers of cigarettes as "merchants of death," he asserted that the first amendment "does not protect only speech that is healthy or harmless." I shall return to Judge Wright and the first amendment in Chapter 6. It is enough now to point out that his absolutist position about first amendment freedoms did not carry over to protect a fundamentalist preacher who had been denied renewal of a radio license by the FCC. The case is *Brandywine-Main Line Radio, Inc. v. FCC.*[55] Against a first amendment argument by the licensee, Wright rested his approval of license denial upon grounds that the licensee had mispresented material facts. The two positions are difficult to reconcile. On the one hand, "merchants of death" receive constitutional protection; on the other hand, a dissembler does not.

Skelly Wright tends to take a hard look at disputes involving environment concerns. Justice Lewis Powell of the Supreme Court has written that in matters involving the environment, "the only role for the court is to insure that the agency has taken a 'hard look' at environmental consequences"; it should not "interject itself within the area of discretion of the executive as to the choice of action to be taken."[56] As a reviewing judge of administrative matters concerning the environment, Wright goes further; he takes a hard look and thus tends to "interject" his personal views into the dispute. Take, for example, *Calvert Cliffs Coordinating Committee v. Atomic Energy Commission*,[57] where Wright found that the AEC had failed to comply with the National Environmental Policy Act and, therefore, "must revise its rules governing consideration of environmental issues." He outlined a crucial role for the judiciary in such cases: "Our duty is to see that important legislative purposes, heralded in the halls of Congress, are not lost or misdirected in the vast hallways of the federal bureaucracy." This is Wright the activist rather than Wright the passivist. To him, the environmental law was not a "paper tiger," but rather a federal law that "sets a high standard for the agencies, a standard which must be rigorously enforced by reviewing courts." And in *Wilderness Society v. Morton*,[58] Wright strictly interpreted a statute concerning rights-of-way for companies building the Alaskan pipeline. The congressional statute called for rights-of-way of not more than 50 feet; the companies wanted 146 feet in some places. Even though the Department of the Interior had often granted licenses wider than 50 feet, Wright asserted that "it is our firm belief that a line must be drawn between according administrative interpretations deference and the proposition that administrative agencies are entitled to violate the law if they do it often enough." On the other hand, Wright was on a panel of his court that held that "we are faced with an unusually impressive administrative interpretation supporting the conclusion we reach, first adopted as long ago as 1949 . . . and until now, we believe, not questioned by the Courts or Congress. This interpretation . . . is entitled to great weight." Consistency, it seems, may be a jewel, but not necessarily so in the judicial process.

Three other environmental decisions, authored by Judge Wright, merit attention. In *Students Challenging Regulatory Agency Procedure v. United States*,[59] Wright found that an environmental impact statement of the Interstate Commerce Commission was defective; he chided the ICC for preparing a statement written in a "combative, defensive and advocatory language and style." And in *Sierra Club v. Morton*,[60] he found such a statement was required for the Department of the Interior's national coal leasing program. Both decisions reversed administrative determinations. Judge Wright indeed has a concern for the environment.

That concern was particularly evident in *People Against Nuclear Power (PANE) v. Metropolitan Edison Co.*,[61] which involved two nuclear reactors at Three Mile Island in Pennsylvania. In March, 1979, Three Mile Island Unit 2 nuclear reactor (TMI-2) suffered a major accident. At the time of the accident, Three Mile Island Unit 1 nuclear reactor (TMI-1) was shut down for refueling and routine maintenance. The Nuclear Regulatory Commission (NRC) ordered both units to be kept closed, pending an investigation of the accident. In September, 1981, the NRC voted to allow TMI-1 to be restarted, rejecting a contention by PANE that serious psychological problems would result, and that the stability of the community would be damaged. The decision was reached even though the NRC's Safety and Licensing Board had recommended that psychological distress of a restart be considered. PANE took an appeal, and won in the Court of Appeals for the District of Columbia Circuit. Judge Wright held that although the National Environment Policy Act (NEPA) "does not encompass mere dissatisfactions arising from social opinions, economic concerns, or political disagreements with agency policies," it does apply to "post-traumatic anxieties, accompaneid by physical effects and caused by fears of recurring catastrophe." Wright attempted to narrow his decision by noting that, unlike other NEPA cases, this one presented "the holocaust potential of an errant nuclear reactor." Judge Malcolm Wilkey strongly dissented, criticizing Wright's opinion as "unwarranted, unprecedented, and inconsistent with relevant decisions in this and other circuits." Wilkey considered Wright's opinion to be "well designed to delay the development of nuclear power (contrary to the national policy determined by Congress and the Executive). . . ." The Supreme Court agreed with Wilkey; in April, 1983, it unanimously overturned Wright's decision, saying that it was for Congress and not the courts to determine whether psychological factors should be considered by the NRC.[62] The people living around Three Mile Island thus lost a battle to be free from the mental harm of possible accidents in nearby nuclear plants. The larger lesson is clear: Implicit in the Supreme Court's opinion is that nuclear plants are a "good thing" for people generally, and that the few must suffer for the benefit of many others. If so, then it is a decision in accord with Machiavellian principles. Said the Florentine: "It is not the well-being of individuals that make cities great, but the well-being of the community"; and "the common good can be realized in spite of those few who suffer."[63]

That, however, is not the present point. Rather, it is that Judge Wright was quite willing in the *PANE* case to rewrite, in effect at least, the National Environmental Policy Act. The deference he displays toward administrative judgments (discussed above) was quietly shelved. There is at least an apparent inconsistency in his rulings. His romantic view about governance does not extend to nuclear matters. Consistency with his other decisions is not the true issue: As Emerson said, "a foolish consistency is the hobgoblin of little minds." Wright's deference to administrators would have been "foolish"; after all, the question of nuclear power is exponentially different from other areas of governmental concern. That Wright was basically wrong in his *PANE* decision is by no means self-evident. Certainly, he was wrong in the sense that the Supreme Court unanimously overturned his decision. But surely it is not obvious that possible psychological harm should not be taken into consideration in licensing nuclear plants. As Justice William Brennan said in a concurring opinion: "There can be no doubt that psychological injuries are cognizable under NEPA. . . . As the Court points out, however, the particular psychological injury alleged in this case did not arise, for example, out of the direct sensory impact of a change in the physical environment . . . but out of a perception of risk. . . . In light of the history and policies underlying NEPA, I agree with the Court that this crucial distinction 'lengthens the causal chain beyond the reach' of the statute." Justice William Rehnquist, speaking for eight members of the Supreme Court, cavalierly dismissed PANE's concerns (and Judge Wright's opinion):

Risk is a pervasive element of modern life. . . . Many of the risks we face are generated by modern technology, which brings both the possibility of major accidents and opportunities for tremendous achievements. Medical experts apparently agree that risk can generate stress in human beings, which in turn may rise to the level of serious health damage. For this reason, among many others, the question whether the gains from any technological advance are worth its attendant risks may be an important public policy issue. Nonetheless, it is quite different from the question whether the same gains are worth a given level of alteration of our physical environment or depletion of our natural resources. The latter question rather than the former is the central concern of NEPA.

Time and resources are simply too limited for us to believe that Congress intended to extend NEPA as far as the Court of Appeals has taken it. . . . The scope of the agency's inquiries must remain manageable if NEPA's goal of "ensuring a fully informed and well-considered decision" . . . is to be accomplished. (Emphasis added.)

The Supreme Court, it seems, is quite willing to opt for efficiency over possible, even probable, "serious health damage" in nuclear matters. Judge Wright is not: The delays attendant to adding procedural requirements in informal rule-making matters are also present had his *PANE* decision been sustained. That, however, does not worry him as much as an errant nuclear reactor might. Were this a perfect world, those reactors—if built—would be constructed in areas remote from populated areas. But this is an imperfect world, one in which considerations of administrative efficiency prevail over the "well-being of individuals."

In some environmental cases, Judge Wright has apparently gone out of his way to validate agency actions *aiding* the environment that were opposed by major industries. One is the already discussed *Ethyl Corp. v. EPA*; the other is *Amoco Oil Co. v. EPA.*[64] In *Ethyl*, Wright allowed the EPA to take regulatory action based on negative health effects that were not conclusively proved. Those health risks, said Wright, involve questions that are "particularly prone to uncertainty." As a result, the statute allows the EPA "flexibility to assess risks and make essentially legislative policy judgments." The regulators need not demand the same degree of certainty that the scientific community would require. "The administrator may apply his expertise to draw conclusions from suspected, but not completely substantiated, relationships between facts, from trends among facts, from theoretical projections, from imperfect data not yet certifiable as 'fact' and the like." It is quite obvious that Judge Wright is willing to allow administrators a great deal of discretion when decisions favorable to environmental improvements are made.

His concern, it seems, transcends the mere procedural, and gets into the substantive aspects of a case. In that sense, his *Ethyl* and *PANE* decisions are consistent, even though he upheld administrative action in the former and struck it down in the latter. As for the Supreme Court, if one may infer a conclusion from the two cases, it is that the Justices have opted for deference to the bureaucracy. In *Ethyl*, they refused to review Judge Wright's decision; whereas, as previously noted, they overruled him in *PANE*. Administrative efficiency, without judicial second-guessing, appears to be the *summum bonum* to the High Court.

Skelly Wright's interest in environmental improvement may also be seen in the *Amoco Oil* case. There, he upheld EPA regulations under the Clean Air Act that prohibited use of leaded gasoline in automobiles without catalytic converters and required national marketing of at least one grade of unleaded gasoline. Distinguishing the Act's requirement for regulations based upon "findings," Wright concluded that when regulations were of a policy-making nature or were predictions of matters on the "frontiers of scientific knowledge," the statute was satisfied with "adequate reasons and explanations, but not 'findings' of the sort familiar to adjudication." He saw the process as "quasi-legislative in nature," and therefore stated that a "rule-making agency necessarily deals less with 'evidentiary' disputes than with normative conflicts, projections from imperfect data, experiments and simulations, educated predictions, differing assessments of possible risks, and the like." Again, deference to the administrator in a situation in which the agency sought to improve the environment. Seeing his job as determining whether the EPA had acted arbitrarily or capriciously, Wright considered it critical that the court "give due deference to the agency's ability to rely on its own developed expertise. . . . The immersion in the evidence is designed solely to enable the court to determine whether the agency decision was rational and based on consideration of the relevant factors. . . . It is settled that we must affirm decisions with which we disagree so long as this test is met." (An appropriate question is this: What happened to that sentiment when Judge Wright had to decide the *PANE* case?)

Wright went on in *Amoco Oil* to explain that a reviewing court should look at agency decisions not as scientists or statisticians alien to a judge's training and experience, but as an exercise of "our narrowly defined duty of holding agencies to certain minimal standards of rationality." This means, as has been previously discussed, that judges should sit as members of lunacy committees so as to determine the reasonableness, the rationality of an administrator's acts. Judge Wright, however, proffers no precise criteria by which that determination can be made. What he did say is this:

There is no inconsistency between the deferential standard of review and the requirement that the reviewing court involve itself in even the most complex evidentiary matters; rather the two indicia of arbitrary and capricious review stand in careful balance. The close scrutiny of the evidence is intended to educate the court. It must understand enough about the problem confronting the agency to comprehend the meaning of the evidence relied upon and the evidence discarded; the questions addressed by the agency and those by-passed; the choices open to the agency and those made. The more technical the case the more intensive must be the court's efforts to understand the evidence, for without an appropriate understanding of the case before it the court cannot properly perform its function. But that function must be performed with conscientious awareness of its limited nature. *The enforced education into the intricacies of the problem before the agency is not designed to enable the court to become a superagency that can supplant the agency's expert decision-makers.* (Emphasis added.)[65]

That presents the question, avoided by Judge Wright, of where a judge and staff, even as aided by lawyers in briefs and argument, can obtain the requisite expertise to become sufficiently expert in complex technical and economic problems. I have previously alluded to the different types of expertise in such matters—the technical expertness of agency personnel and the expertise of judges in general societal values. There is nothing in legal education or legal practice that, speaking generally, will make a lawyer who becomes a judge privy to the esoterica of technical matters. To think that a judge, even as helped by law clerks and counsel, can do so is to indulge in what has been called "the lawyer as astrophysicist fallacy"—the notion that lawyers as generalists can, with a little time and effort, master the intricacies of any subject matter, including that of astrophysics. In sum, the lawyer as generalist can read a text on astrophysics over the weekend and know enough to launch a rocket on Monday. The point is general, and certainly not limited to Judge Wright. The judiciary taken as a whole has no special expertness or abilities than enable judges to master the details of complex economic and technological questions.

What is one to conclude about Judge Wright and administrative law? In most general terms, whether he is activist or passivist seems to depend upon the issue being litigated. On some constitutional and environmental questions, he can and does find ways to supervise the bureaucrats. At times, as in the *Ethyl* case, he seems to look at what the administrator decided—the substantive as distinguished from procedural issues—and rule accordingly. He, thus, is a sometime activist in this area of public law. I shall return to specific aspects of Wright vis-à-vis the bureaucracy in subsequent chapters, particularly those relating to national security and freedom of expression.

If the principal conclusion is accurate, then it follows naturally that J. Skelly Wright is a result-oriented judge. This is said not to denigrate one of the great judges of modern times, but to iterate that, as with all others who are chosen to sit in judgment on their fellow humans, Wright is concerned with who wins and who loses in litigation. His personal values are up-front; and he does not hesitate to further them. So do others, even though result-orientation, as was discussed in Chapter 1, is a term of opprobrium among those who think or say they think that "reason" and "principle" determine—at least, should determine—the outcomes of law cases. Those commentators—their name is legion—fail to consider the "pragmatic instrumentalist" theory of law, the theory that Professor Robert Samuel Summers avers is the "fourth great tradition" in Western legal theory (the others being analytical positivism, natural law philosophy, and historical jurisprudence).[66] Judge Wright is the pragmatic instrumentalist *par excellence* among contemporary American judges. (Summers's neologism seems to be merely a fancy and less pejorative way of saying result-orientation.)

III

"The fundamental question," James L. Sundquist of the Brookings Institution recently asserted, "is whether . . . the U.S. government can be made to work—under any leadership."[67] He did not define what he meant by "work," but apparently the word refers to effectiveness or efficiency. That indeed is a basic question, but it is only half of one. The problem essentially revolves around two complementary goals—efficiency and account-ability—and how to resolve the tensions between them. That, in the final analysis, is the important question about administrative law, however much its details get buried in turgid legalisms. It has yet to be answered by anyone. In this brief final section, I should like to suggest that the complementary goals of government are really questions of constitutionalism. They cut to the very core of the constitutional order. "Severe institutional and structural problems" exist deep "in the traditions of American political behavior and the constitutional structure itself," Sundquist concluded.

What, first, is accountability? And what is efficiency? No extensive disquisition can be undertaken here; but a few generalized remarks are in order. Consider Madison's famous statement in *Federalist No. 51*:

But the great security against a gradual concentration of the several powers in the same department, consists in giving to those who administer each department the necessary constitutional means and personal motives to resist encroachments of the other. The provision of defense must in this, as in all other cases, be made commensurate to the danger of attack. It may be a reflection on human nature, that such devices should be necessary to control the abuses of government. But what is government itself, but the greatest of all reflections on human nature? If men were angels, no government would be necessary. If angels were to govern men, neither external nor internal controls on government would be necessary. *In forming a government which is to be administered by men over men, the great difficulty lies in this; you must first enable the government to control the governed; and in the next place oblige it to control itself.* (Emphasis added.)

Madison's is a powerful statement in favor of accountability—the prevention of political power being concentrated in one branch of government. One branch checks another—so the theory goes. More precisely: Accountability, if it means anything, means that those who wield power have to answer in another place and give reasons for decisions that are taken. This is basically a procedural concept; it assumes that if the rules are followed about giving a hearing or if, say, Congress can theoretically overrule the bureaucracy, no more is required. Procedural regularity is considered to be sufficient to the need. (We have seen that Skelly Wright, except in administrative law cases dealing with equality and the environment, adheres to this view.)

There is more to accountability than procedure alone. Attention must also be paid to *substance*—to the content of the decisions themselves. In other words, accountability perceived as procedure only assumes the unassumable—that there is a common acceptance of "right" moral and political ends. Such a common acceptance is, however, not true of modern America: The goals of social action are frequently the very subject of dispute. If that be so, as surely it is, then the problem of accountability becomes extraordinarily difficult. Those who exercise power must be checked—answer in another place—not only for the *way* their decisions are made, but also *for the decisions themselves.* The need thus becomes one of identifying an external set of standards by which the *content* of those decisions can be weighed and, if found wanting, rejected. The problem is that no consensus exists about those standards. As has been seen, Judge Wright at times locates in his hierarchy of personal values standards to evaluate administrative performance, although he generally adheres to accountability as a procedural concept.

Administrative agencies combine the functions of all three branches of government—legislative, executive, judicial. Their core guiding concept is not "due process," but the "public interest"—itself an undefined term. No one quite knows what it means, although it seems to be basic to the idea, adumbrated above, of the state as a "super-group person." Two presidents, John F. Kennedy and Jimmy Carter, have said as much. Said Kennedy in 1962 concerning a question about the "public interest" in collective bargaining negotiations: "These companies are free and the unions are free. All we [the Executive] can try to do is indicate to them the public interest which is there. After all, the public interest is the sum of the private interests, or perhaps it's even sometimes a little more. *In, fact, it is a little more.*" (Emphasis added.) In his farewell address, Carter echoed that sentiment: "The national interest [a synonym for the public interest] is not always the sum of our single or special interests."[68] This means that the interests of the state, which agencies in theory seek to further, are superior to the arithmetical sum of the private interests of the nation. I do not say that Judge Wright has, consciously or subconsciously, thought about such abstract matters; I do suggest, however, that judges sooner or later will have to confront the manifold problems of accountability as matters of substance as well as procedure. Wright, as has been said, does this at times but not systematically.

When the Supreme Court struck down the so-called legislative veto in June, 1983, it in effect turned the bureaucracy loose.[69] Although Congress still can enact statutes to "veto" or overrule administrative decisions, those statutes are subject to the constitutional presidential veto, and thus would be extremely difficult, perhaps impossible, to do on anything other than a sporadic basis. Given the extreme deference that the judiciary routinely pays to administrative decisions, this means that no one is left to watch the watchmen. The "fourth branch of government" is not only headless; it is in fact now subject to few checks. There is no way, in Madison's words, "to oblige" the bureaucracy "to control itself."

That, in sum, is a critical constitutional problem of the present day. So, too, is efficiency. Again, this is a most difficult subject to corner and corral. I do not wish to do more here than to suggest a way of thinking about it. Efficiency refers to costs, but much more than mere *economic costs*—in funds, in human effort, in the energy used to achieve a desired result. Those costs are relatively easy to calculate. Much harder, and of much greater significance, are *social costs*, namely, "all direct and indirect losses suffered by third parties or the general public" as a consequence of specific activities—here those of the public administration. Says Professor K. William Kapp: "Social losses may be reflected in damages to human health; they may find expression in the destruction or deterioration of property values and the premature depletion of natural wealth; they may also be evidenced in an impairment of less tangible values."[70] Any diminution in the quality of life is a social cost. Here, again, the legal system, and certainly that part called administrative law, is inadequate to the need. This is the second part of the constitutional problem presented by the rise of bureaucracy.

"An essay on the criticism of law," Felix Cohen said a half-century ago, "must be fundamentally an essay on ethics." So, too, in an essay on a judge (such as this book), a person who interprets and makes the law: His is essentially an ethical task. Cohen says:

The instrumental value of law is simply its value in promoting the good life of those whom it affects, and . . . any law or other element of the legal order which has effects upon human life can be judged to be good or bad in the light of those effects. . . . The total valuation of law resolves itself into a judgment upon the life of human beings insofar as it is involved in the law itself or is affected by law. *The evaluation of law must be in terms of the good life, and to demonstrate the nature of this standard is the task of ethics, and, more particularly, of morality.* Difficult as this task is and uncertain as its conclusions have been, it is a vicious illusion to suppose that the task of the statesman is less difficult or that his conclusions can be more certain. (Emphasis added.)[71]

The meaning is that in administrative law matters, as elsewhere in the constitutional order, a pragmatic instrumentalist such as Judge Wright, a man who is interested in "doing what's right," must also be a moralist. "Moral philosophy," Professor Joel Feinberg states, is "the foundation of constitutional jurisprudence, . . . and one cannot fully understand the latter without studying the former."[72] In America, we have married litigation to legislation and look for statesmanship in our courts. That statesmanship must, as Feinberg says, encompass views of moral philosophy; and the law that judges make must be evaluated, as Cohen says, "in terms of the good life." Efficiency in government is not enough. Nor is a government that overemphasizes accountability, for that could end in political paralysis.

Moral philosophy may seem to be remote from the routine operations of the congeries of agencies, public and private, that make up the modern bureaucratic state (such as the United States). But I suggest that it is far from irrelevant. Lurking in the shadowy crevices of the Constitution, and particularly in the great silences of that document, is the foundational idea of personal autonomy. A moral imperative of the Constitution is that the *self* is to be protected against undue intrusions from others (the fields of tort and criminal law) and from government (the fields of constitutional and administrative law).

In his decisions in administrative law, Judge Wright seeks to protect the individual in his personal autonomy against the overweening power of the state. He has come out squarely and explicitly for such a position in some of his nonjudicial writings; and many of his decisions, as this and other chapters reveal, see him applying that moral principle in specific cases. His *PANE* opinion (on the Three Mile Island situation) is proof positive of that conclusion. There are numerous other examples of the same position. Two of them, *Zweibon v. Mitchell* and *Halkin v. Helms*, will be discussed in the next chapter. They, too, are decisions in the area of administrative law, but decisions with a distinct overtone of constitutionalism. They will show even more clearly Skelly Wright's deep concern for the personal autonomy of lonely individuals in a thoroughly bureaucratized nation.

His task is made all the more difficult because of the persistent refusal of the Supreme Court to recognize the fact that giant corporations and other social groups are "private" governments that have as much, and at times more, influence on the way that Americans act as do the public bureaucracies. That corporations are instruments of governance has long been recognized by perceptive observers. For example, as long ago as 1908, Arthur Bentley remarked: "A corporation is government through and through. . . . Certain technical methods which political government uses, as, for instance, hanging, are not used by corporations, generally speaking, but that is a detail."[73] Corporate growth in America "signifies nothing less than a social revolution," observed John Davis in 1897.[74] As the organizational society *par excellence*, America's political economy is dominated by business enterprises not even remotely in the contemplation of the Founding Fathers. Some corporations overshadow, in economic importance, most of the fifty states and many of the nations of the world.

The consequence, as has been suggested above, is the emergence of a new constitution—that of the third "ism," corporatism, which is neither capitalism nor socialism—as a layer on the palimpsest that is the Document of 1787. By creating a national common market, corporations have contributed to the decay of traditional federalism; by becoming transnational, they are progressively blurring the line between foreign and domestic in American policy; and as major interest groups, they are breaking down original precepts of separated governmental powers. They are private governments for several reasons. Primary institutions for the authoritative allocation of value, corporations largely determine how prices are set and economic rewards bestowed, and are changing the nature of property itself. They "legislate" the terms and conditions of most contracts, through use of standardized forms. As hierarchical bureaucracies, they are political orders, the local self-governments of much of American society—"the logical successor to manor, village, and town."[75] Increasingly, the identifications and loyalties—the attributes of citizenship—attach to groups. Corporate citizenship is no figment of a sociologist's imagination. As the basic units of "economic" or "functional" federalism, corporations routinely interact with congressional committees and federal agencies in the iron triangles of Washington that formulate policies for the nation and are creating a new separation of powers between government and industry. Furthermore, corporations often use private judiciaries (arbitrators), have extensive intelligence services (even for industrial espionage), and utilize private "armies" (their security forces). Their internal orders are political systems. If authority is the central concept of politics, and property of economics, a corporation embodies both in one collective entity. In everything except name and constitutional theory, corporations are governments. (I speak here mainly of the giants.)[76]

The myopic refusal of the Supreme Court to perceive the obvious makes it impossible for the governing power of the corporations to be legitimated. It also makes it impossible for lower court judges, such as Skelly Wright, to tackle the problems of making private governing power accountable. A few courts have edged in that direction, but the general picture is otherwise: A corporation is considered to be a species of private property and, as such, not amenable to constitutional proscriptions. As a consequence, the organizational sector of America, including corporations, is "the black hole of American rights"—as Professor David Ewing of the Harvard Business School has written.[77] At odds with democratic theory and vision, it is increasingly difficult to reconcile the undoubted power of corporations with the ideal of democracy.

As will be shown in Chapers 6 and 8, Judge Wright knows at least intuitively that the power of corporate wealth and privilege has significant consequences for the personal autonomy of Americans. He has inveighed against the disproportionate power of corporate money in electoral campaigns (one of the themes of Chapter 6) in law journal articles, but he has been able to do little more; and he perceives the amount of corporate crime to be of great significance to the social order (Chapter 8). But he is blocked in going further by a Supreme Court all too willing to give corporations constitutional protections (by designating those disembodied economic entities as "persons" within the meaning of the Constitution), but wholly unwilling to impose constitutional duties upon them.[78] This is a threshold problem of American law. Skelly Wright intimates that he is fully ready to cross that threshold. The Supreme Court is not. Led by Justice William Rehnquist, that court insists against the overwhelming evidence to the contrary that there is an "essential dichotomy" between public and private acts and corporations are indubitably private. That, in brief, is nonsense, but it is nonsense with which we and Judge Skelly Wright have to live. Professor Paul Brest has encapsulated the basic, the essential point: "The Court's state action doctrine seems a crude substitute for addressing and accommodating the concerns to prevent abuse of power on the one hand, and to protect individual autonomy and federalist values on the other. . . . The [state action] doctrine has seldom been used to shelter citizens from coercive federal or judicial power. More often, it has been employed to protect the autonomy of business enterprises against the claims of consumers, minorities, and other relatively powerless citizens."[79] That, in a nutshell, is one of the major problems of the relationship of courts and the bureaucracies.

5

Judge Wright and the National Security State

Undoubtedly the President . . . is imbued with vast and indispensable powers for dealing with the vital problems generated by our relations with foreign powers, including the duty to protect this country from foreign aggression or subversion. The very existence of such tremendous power, however, renders it susceptible to abuse and endangers those fundamental personal liberties which the Government was instituted to secure for its citizens and whose exercise elevates the nation to a stature worthy of defense. Thus, although the attempt to claim Executive prerogatives or infringe liberty in the name of security and order may be motivated by the highest of ideals, the judiciary must remain vigilantly prepared to fulfill its own responsiblity to channel Executive action within constitutional bounds.

—J. Skelly Wright (1975)[1]

I

Beginning with World War II, and perhaps even before, the United States became the National Security State (NSS)—or what Professor Harold Lasswell hypothesized as the emergence of the Garrison State, one in which "specialists on violence are the most powerful group in society."[2] Although the relative power of groups in America is impossible to measure precisely, Lasswell's insight has been validated since he wrote in 1937. The military and paramilitary forces—the Department of Defense and the intelligence community—are without doubt extremely powerful. Not that they act alone; they do not. They have close and continuing ties with congressional committees and industrial organizations as well as centers of higher learning. Of all of the iron triangles that operate in Washington, this one is indubitably the most significant and influential.

The basic concept of the NSS is just that—national security. This chapter is concerned with Judge Skelly Wright's handling of national security questions in the post-World War II period. The emergence of the NSS poses grave dilemmas to the very nature of constitutionalism and to the role of the judiciary in a society that insists it is a democracy. The NSS, rather than springing full grown like Aphrodite during the turmoil of the past four or five decades, has had a long history. Only by viewing that history can a full understanding of what the NSS means today become apparent. Of necessity, therefore, reference will be made to America's past in order not only to illumine the present, but to put Judge Wright's decisions in context.

I begin, not with the distant past, but with the following assumption: Since 1939, the United States has been in a continual state of war—undeclared, and partly secret, before Pearl Harbor; declared in the Second World War; "cold," beginning either in late 1944 or early 1945 when the enemy switched from Germany and Italy and Japan to the Soviet Union; undeclared (by Congress) in Korea and Indochina, plus divers other encounters in the Third World (notably the Dominican Republic in 1965); and covert, as in the subversion of Iran and Guatemala and Chile by American intelligence operatives. This condition—it is not a theory—is perhaps, with the advent of nuclear weapons, today's overriding peril to fundamental constitutional rights and liberties. The clear and continuing challenges to a judiciary to limit governmental action within what Judge Wright calls "constitutional bounds" are all too obvious. I shall conclude that the judges generally have failed the test, although Wright may be said to have gotten passing grades. That conclusion, I shall emphasize, means that courts are, when the talismanic incantation of national security is uttered, part of the governing coalition—independent only in theory but not in fact.

My assumption is easily validated, but that is not our present concern. Suffice it to say that World War II really began for the United States in 1939 when President Franklin Roosevelt secretly aided England against Hitler; and that World War III can be said to have begun not later than 1945 when Hitler was defeated. The enemy became the U.S.S.R.[3] The United States and the Soviets have been locked in mortal combat since that time—not in a shooting sense, to be sure, although in Korea and Indochina American forces engaged in bloody combat with what were said to be Soviet surrogates. The process continues and has intensified in recent years. True enough, "World War III" is a misnomer, because there has been and still is considerable interchange between the two superpowers and their competition has in many respects been nonviolent. That condition of combined violent and nonviolent antagonism creates the tensions between constitutionalism and national security, tensions that at times, but far from routinely, are presented to federal judges for consideration and decision. Should there be doubt about the *de facto* state of war with the Soviet Union, consider what Richard Nixon wrote in 1980 in his book, *The Real War:*

During all of my presidency we were engaged in "war" with the Soviet Union. . . . We are at war. . . . World War III began before World War II ended. . . . World War III has gone on now for a third of a century, since those closing days of World War II. . . .

Korea and Vietnam were battles in the war, as were the coups that brought Soviet satellite regimes to power in places as remote as Afghanistan and South Yemen. So, too, have been the struggles to keep Communist parties from taking control in Italy and Portugal, and to contain Castro's export of revolution in Latin America.

World War III is the first truly global war.[4]

There is no need to labor the point, although it should be said that all presidents since 1945 were or are in essential agreement with Nixon, and to note that the strange nature of World War III derives from nuclear weapons. Battles that appear to be local are, in fact, segments of the larger struggle. That is the only way World War III can be fought without jeopardizing civilization itself.

What, then, is the National Security State? A beginning might be made by defining national security itself: The term, as Arnold Wolfers has said, is an ''ambiguous symbol.''[5] (That ambiguity, I argue below, is intentional.) Even so, it does have some meaning. Consider this definition: ''National security is that part of government policy having as its objective the creation of national and international political conditions favorable to the protection or extension of vital national values against existing and potential adversaries.''[6] That is not entirely satisfactory, but it does point up some of the essential characteristics of the phrase. First, national security is a governmental monopoly, the most complete of all such monopolies (even though purportedly private organizations, such as corporations and universities, are part of the national security apparatus). Second, in the American constitutional order it is the general government that is overwhelmingly important in national security matters. State and local governments are not only secondary, they are insignificant, in the process. Third, within the central government, power over national security matters, although splintered under the formal Constitution, is ever increasingly a prerogative of the Executive. Congress has some, and the courts even less, actual power; both of those branches have in practical effect abdicated to the Executive. Fourth, the values that national security is to protect or extend are those considered ''vital.'' Of them, survival of the nation-state is doubtless highest in the hierarchy. Physical survival is most important but so, too, are the cultural—the constitutional—values of, say, the United States. (The tension between physical and cultural values produces conflicts and, thus, litigation, in a part of which Judge Wright has had a major role.) But survival also means ''extension'' values as well as ''protection'' values; in simplest terms, this means territorial imperialism—the drive of one nation-state to dominate others both to enjoy the benefits of conquered territory and to extend its ideology.[7]

The United States today is a state that makes considerations of national survival and enhancement of national well-being the overriding desiderata of policy. I do not, of course, suggest that this makes the United States unique; nor do I say that the NSS today is basically different from the USA of the past. But what I do say is that the NSS since 1945 is characterized by the pervasive belief, carefully nurtured and cultivated by the state's propaganda and ideology, that a devil-like external force constantly threatens our most cherished values and our very physical survival. That force, of course, is the abstraction labeled "communism" and its physical exemplification in the U.S.S.R.

The fundamental problem presented by the NSS is the extent to which the individual must defer to the interests of the state when matters of important state policy are concerned—important as defined by those who control the state and its apparatus, government. I shall conclude that the state *always* prevails when such questions are litigated. There is nothing really new about that conclusion; it merely restates a basic Machiavellian principle: "It is not the well-being of individuals that makes cities great, but the well-being of the community"; and "the common good can be realized in spite of those few who suffer."[8] Or, to repeat what Franz Neumann said:

No society in recorded history has ever been able to dispense with political power. This is as true of liberalism as of absolutism, as true of laissez faire as of an interventionist state. No greater disservice has been rendered to political science than the statement that the liberal state was a "weak" state. It was precisely as strong as it needed to be in the circumstances. It acquired substantial colonial empires, waged wars, held down internal disorders, and stabilized itself over long periods of time.[9]

That challenge by Machiavelli, echoed by Neumann, is a knife thrust deep into the body of the notion of limited government—of liberal democracy as it was known (at least in the myth). It will continue to be felt for the indefinite future.

The challenge, in essence, is constitutional in dimension, involving the need to reconcile "reasons of state" with "reasons of freedom and liberty." The core principle of the NSS is reason of state (*raison d'etat*), which has been defined as "the doctrine that whatever is required to insure the survival of the state must be done by the individuals responsible for it, no matter how repugnant such an act may be to them in their private capacity as decent and moral men."[10] Not mentioned in the Constitution, it is a basic principle of America's fundamental law. The "father" of the Constitution, John Locke, called it the *prerogative*: "This power to act according to discretion, for the public good, is that which is called the prerogative. . . . There is a latitude left to the executive power, to do many things of choice, which the laws do not prescribe."[11]

So there is, as Judge Wright at least inferentially conceded in the headnote to this chapter. He, however, refuses to kowtow to the magic phrase, "national security"; he insists on trying to preserve personal rights and freedoms, as his opinions in *Zweibon v. Mitchell* and *Halkin v. Helms*[12] reveal. Because of the paucity of cases dealing with national security that get judicial cognizance and because he has not yet articulated his views on either national security or reason of state in an off-bench writing, Wright's views must be gleaned from a few opinions. Some of these are discussed in Chapter 6 (dealing with freedom of expression); in this chapter, principal attention will be accorded the *Zweibon* and *Halkin* rulings, plus those in *Halperin v. Kissinger* and *American Security Council Education Foundation v. Federal Communications Commission.*[13]

The NSS burst forth full-panoplied during the Second World War, and was continued in the Cold War. The key decisions were mainly Executive in origin. One of the more obvious was President Harry Truman's authorization to drop atomic bombs on Hiroshima and Nagasaki in August, 1945, supposedly to force the Japanese to surrender. The Cold War may be said to have begun when the crew of a B-29 bomber unleased its lethal payload on August 6, 1945. Strictly military considerations did not require it; the American Strategic Bombing Survey concluded in 1945: "Based on a detailed investigation of all the facts and supported by the testimony of the surviving Japanese leaders involved, it is the Survey's opinion that certainly prior to 31 December 1945, and in all probability prior to 1 November 1945, Japan would have surrendered even if the atomic bombs had not been dropped, even if Russia had not entered the war, and even if no invasion had been planned or contemplated."[14] The mists of history have obscured that conclusion. Historians speak glibly about one million American lives being saved because the bombs were dropped. To his dying day, President Truman defended his decision. In hard fact, there was no need to obliterate the two cities. The real target was psychological—to throw fear into the Soviet Union.

So began the Cold War (Nixon's World War III). It not only continues to this day but seems to be intensifying. Today the world lives in dread of a nuclear holocaust. Says Professor Marshall Goldman of Harvard's Russian Research Center:

No one ever claimed that the world is a rational place, but the behavior of both the United States and the Soviet Union today is remarkably self-destructive. There is only the remotest chance in the wake of Brezhnev's death that either Andropov or Reagan will seek a softer or more conciliatory tone. Both talk about detente, but neither has done anything about it. Mutual distrust is so rampant that any statement concerning weapons, no matter the drift, has the unfortunate result of accelerating the arms race. Not only has the rivalry strained the economics of these countries, but it is increasing the tension and the risk of conflagration.

Of even greater danger is the fact that each side has created an unrealistic image of the other, which only serves to fuel the intensity of the race. The lack of realism reflects not only passion but large doses of naivete, which makes for an increasingly unstable condition. . . . We have the makings of an international game of chicken with the consequence being global catastrophe.[15]

A parlous situation, indeed. Should it continue, as it will, the result will be not one Rome but two Carthages—and of immensely greater import, the end of civilization itself.

Nuclear weapons, however, did not create the NSS. America would be a garrison state today regardless of what weapons the specialists on violence have at their disposal. Considerations of security have always been foremost in the minds of political officers. The United States grew and prospered during the nineteenth and early twentieth centuries because of a favorable concatenation of circumstances—an empty continent, available for exploitation at minimum cost; protection by two oceans and the British navy; and no external enemies—in sum, an environment both fortuitous and nonreplicable. So the specialists on violence—the military forces—were needed only sparingly (except for the Civil War), and did not attain their predominance until those favorable circumstances had vanished and the United States undertook all of the difficult problems of other nation-states.

A basic question posed by the NSS is whether security, like other national goals, is *intermediate* or *ultimate*. That, in essence, is the question that national security presents to the judiciary in the handful of cases that get judicial attention. We shall see that Judge Wright appears to believe that it is an intermediate goal, one that should be justified in terms of the higher values that it is expected to serve. He sees his task as finding a way between Abraham Lincoln's two unpalatable extremes; Lincoln asked on July 4, 1861: "Is there in all republics this inherent and fatal weakness? Must a government of necessity be too *strong* for the liberties of its people, or too *weak* to maintain its own existence?"[16] The task of those who govern, particularly judges, is to find a way of reconciling those apparently inconsistent ends. That, to anticipate, has not yet been done. Judges have not produced a unifying principle that welds the inconsistent demands of security and freedom. Nor has anyone else. What has been done and is being done may be simply stated: Security interests always prevail over individual freedoms in any situation considered important by those who wield effective power within the polity.

Judge Wright is concerned about that situation. He believes with Arnold Wolfers, that "political formulas such as 'national interest' or 'national security' . . . [are] to be scrutinized with particular care. They may not mean the same thing to different people. They may not have any precise meaning at all. Thus, while appearing to offer guidance and a basis for broad consensus they may be permitting everyone to label whatever policy he favors with an attractive and possibly deceptive name."[17] That is Wolfers speaking; but Judge Wright seems to agree. As will be shown in this and the next chapters, he elevates such values as freedom from unreasonable searches and freedom of expression to a parity with national security and tends to favor those constitutional values. For example, he wrote in 1979, using language quite similar to that of Wolfers:

The amorphousness of national security . . . defies any attempt to cast the notion with sufficient specificity. . . .

That "national security" means different things to different people is incontestable. . . . To some, national security means devoting the bulk of our national resources to creating the ideal society—one, that is, whose economic dynamism and social amenities are attractive to citizens of foreign powers and thus likely to channel the currents of world ideology in our direction. To others, this is nonsense: national security translates literally into military superiority. Still others take a more discriminating view and seek to arrive at a secure compromise between domestic improvements and military might. And within each of these conceptions of national security there is a sufficient number of allocational configurations to correspond to the multiplicity of individual visions of a "secure" nation.[18]

That was written in the context of a case involving first amendment values of expression; Wright came down on the side of expression. For him, it was not an aberration.

The National Security State had its formal birth in 1947 when Congress enacted the National Security Act. Among other provisions, that statute created a National Security Council in the White House with the mission to integrate "domestic, foreign and military services and other departments and agencies of the Government to cooperate more effectively in matters involving national security."[19] Three important structural changes were made in government. First, the Central Intelligence Agency was created as a permanent body, thus legitimating secrecy and intelligence gathering for the first time in peacetime as a necessary and vital function of government. That activity was greatly increased in 1952 when, by a still secret executive order, President Truman created the National Security Agency (NSA). Second, the military services were reorganized in a Department of Defense. Each service kept its identity, but the Joint Chiefs of Staff were to give overall guidance. Third, the statute was designed to make sure that the domestic economy was able to provide resources and materiel for national security purposes. Strangely enough—or perhaps not so strangely—the concept of national security itself was left undefined. The term was left to gather content from experience—the experience, it is important to note, of those in positions of power in the national security apparatus. No national debate of any consequence took place. New governmental mechanisms were created by a statute that surely can be called "quasi-constitutional" in nature. By altering the structure of government, it ranks in importance with the Sherman antitrust law, the National Labor Relations Act of 1935, the Employment Act of 1946, and the Budget and Impoundment Control Act of 1974. In practical effect, furthermore, the National Security Act was an abdication by Congress over large segments of public policy. The CIA, for example, operates almost as a "state within a state," having well-nigh unfettered discretion.

The NSS, in sum, is the American version of the Dual State, one in which considerations of national security often collide with considerations of personal freedoms and liberty. It sets its own rules, with its governing apparatus by no means subjected to the rules of interdictory law. The Executive is in control, and no one is watching the watchmen. It is precisely there that the courts, particularly those in Washington, D.C., come into play. Rather, they *should* come into play. Judge Wright and colleagues have wrestled with some but by no means all of the problems brought by the NSS. That wrestling match, speaking generally, has been lost by the judges. It is important to understand why. To do so requires discussion of the judicial decisions, specifically those that involved Judge Wright. Others, however, will be mentioned.

II

I have discussed at some length the idea that the United States is the National Security State because an understanding of that development is necessary to an understanding of the way that judges have decided national security issues. All nations, of whatever stripe, have two basic goals—external security and internal order—and in that sense the United States is no different from any other. Where it differs from many, perhaps most, others may be found in the fundamental concept of the formal Constitution: that ours is a limited government, a government circumscribed by the rule of law. Enough now is known for everyone to realize that the formal Constitution's precepts often, perhaps usually, are undercut by contrary principles of the living or operative Constitution. This is particularly true in national security matters. I have argued elsewhere that national security is one of the primary reasons for the emergence of a new informal fundamental law that can be called the Constitution of Control.[20] This constitution exists as a layer on the palimpsest that is the Document of 1787.

The discussion of Skelly Wright and national security begins, not with his judicial decisions, but with one of his actions as United States Attorney in New Orleans. At about the same time that Congress enacted the National Security Act and the Taft-Hartley Labor Relations Act, President Harry Truman, by executive order, established the nation's first loyalty-security program. One of the goals of the Taft-Hartley Act and the loyalty program was the identification and elimination of members of the Communist Party from labor unions. Robert Himmaugh, an employee of the Federal Barge Lines (an agency in the Department of Commerce) and an active waterfront labor leader, was interrogated by a Commerce Department loyalty board, in the course of which he denied ever have been a Communist. Following investigation by a grand jury, he was indicted for making false official statements. The Department of Justice in Washington viewed the matter quite seriously, as did Wright. A special assistant attorney general was dispatched from Washington to conduct the prosecution. The real target, apparently, was the National Maritime Union. Said Wright at the time: "This investigation shows beyond doubt that the NMU from its inception in 1936 until late in 1946 was nothing more than an arm of the Communist party, and through the NMU, the Communist party could control shipping from the East coast and the Gulf coast of the United States. This control was to be exercised in behalf of Russia in the event of war between the United States and that country."[21] In a speech before the New Orleans Junior Chamber of Commerce, he repeated that charge.

The Himmaugh prosecution was started by the Department of Justice, which sent a team from Washington to exercise supervision over it. Wright's feelings at the time may be gleaned from the quotation above. When I asked him in 1983 how he knew that communist members of unions would help the Soviet Union in war, and specifically that Himmaugh would do so, he could not recall that any evidence was produced to validate that conclusion.[22] It was the beginning of the Cold War. President Truman's loyalty board procedures proceeded on the assumption that membership in the Communist Party would mean disloyalty should war come with the U.S.S.R., and, therefore, that there was no need to provide probative evidence for that assumption. Few contested the assumption; and, indeed, in 1951 the Supreme Court in *Dennis v. United States* upheld convictions of Communist Party leaders on the theory that even though no "clear and present danger" to the United States existed, there was a sufficiently strong probability of a future danger that the men could be imprisoned.[23]

The Himmaugh episode showed that Skelly Wright accepted the norms of his superiors in Washington. He was willing to go along with what Truman's Department of Justice wanted[24]—although it is important to note that today (1983) he maintains that had he had freedom of action in 1948, he would not have prosecuted Himmaugh. We will see in Chapter 6 that as an appeals judge, Skelly Wright in 1972 perceived an essentially similar factual situation differently from his quoted remarks (above). In dissent, he maintained that the government had no need to know about past affiliations of a government employee, and, therefore, that it had no "constitutionally legitimate interest in a correct answer."

What may be concluded from these events a generation apart? Most obviously, Wright in 1948 and 1949 was seeking to attain a solid position in his profession, and with his superiors in Washington, whereas in 1972 he had been freed from those invisible but nonetheless binding chains. As a senior member of the Court of Appeals, he did not hesitate to dissent from his colleagues. It was quite easy in 1948 for someone fresh from military service, and trying to establish himself, to go along with the status quo. Wright knew, as the saying goes, that to "get along" one has to "go along." Only those with the perfect vision of hindsight will fault him for that. When, however, he became a judge, it was a different matter. He was able to see public and legal affairs from a different perspective. By no means, for example, did he "go along" with the power structure of New Orleans during the 1950s. We have seen in Chapter 3 that he took on and stared down the entire state of Louisiana, as well as the city of New Orleans, in his struggle to apply the law as he understood it. In the Himmaugh prosecution, furthermore, he was under the direct control of the Department of Justice. Wright did not initiate the proceeding. It would have been folly for him to refuse to cooperate with the men from Washington. Finally, by 1972 most of the grosser aspects of the Cold War had been ameliorated, and the Supreme Court had cast serious doubt upon its holding in the *Dennis* case. Calmer minds prevailed, often at least, and Skelly Wright was a sane voice of reason.

Skelly Wright as district judge in New Orleans was not confronted with any important national security issues. Only when he was elevated to the Court of Appeals did he occasionally rule in such cases. The word "occasionally" is used advisedly; few national security issues ever get to court. When they do, the government is usually sustained. In the fundamental contest between reasons of state and reasons of personal freedom and dignity, the state is the clear winner. The basic problem is accountability. Judges, speaking generally, are loathe to hold government officers accountable for their actions when the case involves assertions of national security. Skelly Wright is perhaps the major exception to that generalizaton.

"National security," as such, is generally not a separate category of scholarship about the Constitution. Those who author text books and coursebooks subsume their analyses under specific constitutional provisions. Thus it is that much of what are national security issues are considered under the first amendment's freedom of expression requirements. For example, *United States v. O'Brien*,[25] concerning prosecution for publicly burning one's draft card, is thought to be a free speech case, and that it is. But it is even more so a dispute over national security. So, too, with *Barenblatt v. United States*[26] and *Dennis v. United States*;[27] the former is pigeonholed as a problem involving Congress's power of investigation, and the latter is seen as a freedom of expression case. Again, that is correct; but the more fundamental issue in both cases was national security. (Discussion of *O'Brien* is deferred until the next chapter.)

Barenblatt and *Dennis* both deal with the Cold War obsession with the external devil that justifies the rise of the NSS—the so-called Communist menace. In the former, Barenblatt argued that his conviction for contempt of Congress for refusing to answer questions about possible Communist Party affiliations was barred by the first amendment's freedom of expression provisions. Not so, said the Supreme Court: Congress had the power to investigate Communists and "the balance between the individual and governmental interests here at stake must be struck in favor of the latter." Said Justice John Harlan for the Court: "In the last analysis," Congress's power "rests on the right of self-preservation, 'the ultimate value of any society.' . . . Justification for its exercise rests on the long and widely accepted view that the tenets of the Communist Party include the ultimate overthrow of the United States by force and violence, a view that has been given formal expression by Congress." In net, that was a form of governmental thought control, legitimized by a slim Supreme Court majority (5-4) that, as Harlan's statement reveals, was in fact an arm of the avowedly political branches of government. How Barenblatt's silence had anything to do with an overthrow of government, imminent or deferred, is completely mysterious. As Skelly Wright's friend (and judicial role model), Supreme Court Justice Hugo Black said in dissent: "Ultimately all the questions in this case really boil down to one—whether we as a people will try fearfully and futilely to preserve democracy by adopting totalitarian methods, or whether in accordance with our traditions and our Constitution we will have the confidence and the courage to be free." That is a sentiment with which Wright would fully agree.

This is not the place to analyze such matters in full. It is enough to mention that *Dennis* is another example of thought control. Communist Party leaders were imprisoned and their convictions upheld by the Supreme Court for advocating the overthrow of government at some indeterminate future time. No evidence was adduced that they planned the imminent or even future overthrow of government. *Dennis* and *Barenblatt* are not aberrations. They typify a Supreme Court ever ready to defer to Congress, a tribunal that in such cases is part of the governing coalition of the nation, a court to which Judge Wright as a member of a lower court must in theory defer.

As a judge, Skelly Wright has not often dealt with cases concerning membership in the Communist Party. His national security opinions have come in cases dealing with such matters as wiretapping without a judicial warrant (*Zweibon v. Mitchell*), the so-called state secrets privilege (*Halkin v. Helms*), wiretapping of a former government employee (*Halperin v. Kissinger*), and whether a television network had fairly presented national security matters (*American Security Council Education Foundation v. Federal Communications Commission*). They will be discussed in that order.

Zweibon is really three cases decided over a four-year period. The facts are relatively simple. In the late 1960s, members of the Jewish Defense League (JDL) staged violent demonstrations against the Soviet installations and personnel in New York as a protest against the treatment of Jews in Russia. Certain JDL actions also violated several criminal statutes. Wiretaps were placed on JDL headquarters in New York and telephone messages intercepted by the Federal Bureau of Investigation. The taps became known during criminal trials of JDL members, who promptly sued for violation of their fourth amendment rights (against unreasonable searches and seizures). The defendants included John Mitchell, both individually and as Attorney General of the United States. Mitchell argued in defense that the wiretapping was lawful because it was "authorized by the President of the United States, acting through the Attorney General, in the exercise of his authority relating to foreign affairs and was deemed essential to protect this nation and its citizens against hostile acts of a foreign power and to obtain foreign intelligence information deemed essential to the security of the United States." In other words, national security was supposed to validate the wiretaps. The district judge agreed, finding that the governmental action was reasonable within the meaning of the fourth amendment. But the Court of Appeals, with Judge Wright writing an opinion for a plurality of judges, reversed. Wright held that a judicial warrant was required before wiretaps could be placed on a domestic group that was neither the agent of nor acting in collaboration with a foreign power. The national security argument did not prevail. (That should have ended the matter, but did not, for the district judge when the case was sent back to him held that Zweibon was not entitled to a jury trial. So in 1977 the Court of Appeals, in *Zweibon II*, reversed that holding. Back before the district court, Mitchell again prevailed; and in 1979, with Judge Wright again writing the opinion for the court—in *Zweibon III*—the district judge was reversed in part. Our interest here lies principally in *Zweibon I*'s 1975 plurality opinion of Judge Wright, and all references below are to that opinion.)

Zweibon I, as opinion and decision, shows Skelly Wright at once at his best and his worst. He is at his best in the decision reached and the monumental argumentation written to explain and justify it. The decision was correct and the argumentation impregnable (even though some of his colleagues found parts of it not to their liking). Wright, however, is at his worst in the extreme length of the opinion—some 84 pages of not particularly well written prose, larded with 279 footnotes, most of which have additional textual material. He had enough time, so he could have written it shorter. The case was argued on October 23, 1974 and not decided until June 23, 1975—precisely eight months later.

Be that as it may, *Zweibon I* was Wright's first important national security ruling. He had no apparent difficulty in dealing with what he called in 1979 the "amorphousness of national security." Readily acknowledging that the President had "vast" but undefined powers in protecting the nation, he forthrightly rejected the argument that national security was an absolute value, highest in the hierarchy of constitituonal values. The courts had to remain vigilant in channeling Executive action within constitutional bounds. To him, the case embodied that problem "in a particularly acute form," because the court was confronted with the delicate task of reconciling the need of the Executive to gather foreign intelligence information with "the citizen's cherished right to maintain his privacy and associations inviolate against unreasonable governmental intrusion." (The distance between that statement and his part in the prosecution of Robert Himmaugh in New Orleans is obvious.) In *Zweibon*, Judge Wright did not hesitate to make a national security determination. Quoting Justice Robert Jackson's comment that "security is like liberty in that many are the crimes committed in its name,"[28] he distinguished internal or domestic security from foreign security. The latter term, *foreign security*, he considered to be synonymous with *national security*. Conceding the President's pre-eminence in the conduct of foreign relations, Wright nonetheless rejected the argument that *warrantless* wiretaps in this instance were necessary to protect that power. The Supreme Court denied review.

Halkin v. Helms is different. It dealt with the activities of the National Security Agency (NSA). Located in the outskirts of Washington, D.C., the NSA is probably the most secret of all the intelligence agencies. And it probably has the largest single collection of computers and sophisticated electronic machinery in the world. Data are collected from the planet over, with the cooperation of cable and telegraph companies.[29] In *Halkin*, Adele Halkin and other former Vietnam war protestors challenged the fact that their overseas messages had been intercepted without a warrant. A panel of the Court of Appeals sustained the intercepts, with Judge Roger Robb asserting that judges must pay "utmost deference to executive assertions of privilege upon grounds of military or diplomatic secrets." Why that was so, Robb did not explain; he merely concluded that the "state secrets" privilege was absolute. The privilege, which is a rule of the law of evidence, permits the nondisclosure of matters considered to be vital to the national security. Therefore, even though it was conceded that Halkin's privacy had been invaded, she had no remedy. There was no way to prove her case.

That is bad enough; but the larger meaning is even worse. The NSA was released from any likelihood of judicial intervention into its affairs. Robb made national security, as asserted by executive officers, an ultimate value. Judge Wright did not agree; he joined in a dissent (from denial of a petition for a rehearing *en banc*), in which Judge David Bazelon accused Robb of totally disregarding the importance of the "Fourth Amendment interest," and thus immunizing conduct that appeared to be proscribed by that amendment. Said Bazelon:

The [state secrets] privilege becomes a shield behind which the government may insulate unlawful behavior from scrutiny and redress by citizens who are the target of the government's surveillance. . . .

The state secrets privilege, weakly rooted in our jurisprudence, cannot and should not be a device for the government to escape the strictures of the Fourth Amendment. "Our system of jurisprudence rests on the assumption that all individuals, whatever their position in government, are subject to federal law." The [majority of the court] employs an evidentiary privilege to carve out an exception to this basic principle of constitutional limitations on government.

Bazelon's opinion was eloquent, but did not state the usual judicial response to national security matters. With Skelly Wright, his was a voice crying in the wilderness, unheeded and unsung.

The courts in such matters are paper tigers. Consider, for example, *Jabara v. Webster*,[30] a 1982 decision of the Sixth Circuit Court of Appeals, where the NSA's interception of overseas telegraphic message was challenged on fourth amendment grounds. Again, the NSA won, with Judge Bailey Brown saying for the panel of three judges: "The question . . . is whether [Jabara] has an expectation of privacy that society is prepared to recognize as reasonable." Brown answered the question in the negative. The point, as summarized in the *New York Times*, is that "the National Security Agency may lawfully intercept messages between United States citizens and people overseas, even if there is no cause to believe the Americans are foreign agents, and then provide summaries of these messages to the Federal Bureau of Investigation." The fundamental conclusion that must be drawn is that the NSA, and the intelligence community generally, is not constrained in any significant way by law or by courts—or, for that matter, by Congress or the Executive. The NSA can, and apparently does, routinely intercept every telephone, cable, and telex message sent from and into the United States (as well as messages throughout the world). For many years, this was justified on the basis of a theory of "inherent presidential authority." In 1978, however, Congress enacted the Foreign Intelligence Surveillance Act (FISA) in an effort to control what the judges would not control. Activities long without controls from outside—that is, without accountability—were to be brought under the rule of law.

That statute in large part is a mere charade. It gives the appearance of control over the NSA without the reality. Surveillance now has to be approved by the courts, but in a Kafkaesque way, through a special Foreign Intelligence Surveillance Court. That tribunal is a modern Star Chamber. Not only does it act in secret, its very existence is kept a secret; it is listed in neither the *Government Organization Manual* nor the *United States Court Directory*. No adversary hearings are held, and its decisions are not published. James Bamford in *The Puzzle Palace* has managed to learn more about it than anyone outside of a small circle in government. The Foreign Intelligence Surveillance Court has seven judges, all appointed by Chief Justice Warren Burger, who, says Bamford, have traded "in their robes and gavels for cloaks and daggers." The FISC has never refused a NSA request, which makes it "an Executive Branch rubber stamp"—a category that differs only in degree, it would seem, from standard federal courts. Bamford concludes: "Like an ever-widening sinkhole, NSA's surveillance technology will continue to expand, quietly pulling in more and more communications and gradually eliminating more and more privacy."[31] Justice Louis Brandeis foresaw exactly that in his oft-quoted dissenting opinion in *Olmstead v. United States* (1928), which held that the fourth amendment did not apply to wiretaps of telephone conversations:

Subtler and more far-reaching means of invading privacy have become available to the government. . . . The progress of science in furnishing the government with means of espionage is not likely to stop with wiretapping. Ways may some day be developed by which the government, without removing papers from secret drawers, can reproduce them in court, and by which it will be enabled to expose to a jury the most intimate occurrences of the home. . . . Can it be that the Constitution affords no protection against such invasions of individual security?[32]

The flat and correct answer to Brandeis's question is: No, it does not. Technology has overtaken the law. Institutions created for the pre-technological age—courts and legislatures and the like—are simply not sufficient to the need of curbing the new technology of the intelligence community. Everything can be monitored. There is, as Winston Smith learned in *1984*, literally no place to hide. I am not suggesting that the United States resembles the Oceania of Orwell's anti-utopia. Far from it—thus far at least. But I do say, with Senator Frank Church, that "the technological capacity that the intelligence community has given the government could enable it to impose total tyranny, and there would be no way to fight back, because the most careful effort to combine together in resistance to the government, no matter how privately it was done, is within the reach of the government to know. Such is the capability of this technology."[33]

That is the fear that underlies Judge Wright's opinion in *Zweibon* and his agreement with Judge Bazelon's dissent in *Halkin*. He perceives national security not only as important in itself, but as an intermediate goal that is indispensable to his ultimate goal—the protection of the autonomy of the individual person. That conclusion is evidenced by his opinion in *Halperin v. Kissinger*. Halperin had his home telephone tapped for 21 months during and after the time he was an assistant to Kissinger in the White House. The justification given for the taps was that security leaks were occurring. Warrants were not obtained; here, as in *Zweibon* and *Halkin*, the actions were justified on the basis of the President's "inherent" power to protect national security (another way of saying "reason of state"). Halperin won at the trial level, but was awarded only nominal damages. He promptly appealed. The damage award was overturned, with Judge Wright saying:

This case presents the conflict between the government's need to act decisively to safeguard the nation's security and those individual rights that are implicated in any surveillance situation. In such a case we must carefully consider any impact that our decision might have on the nation's ability to defend itself and its vital interests. Equally, as the Supreme Court has said, "It would indeed be ironic if, in the name of national defense, we would sanction the subversion of one of those liberties . . . which makes the defense of the nation worthwhile." . . .

The question presented by this case is when may constitutional rights be overborne by the Executive to protect the security of the entire nation. Unfortunately, the inherent vagueness of the term "national security" hampers careful analysis. . . .

We believe . . . that whatever special powers the Executive may hold in national security situations must be limited to instances of immediate and grave peril to the nation. Absent such exigent circumstances, there can be no appeal to powers beyond those enumerated in the Constitution or provided by law. Any security from one danger purchased with our individual rights would be but an illusion, for its price would be those protections against all other threats to our liberty. (Emphasis added.)

Although the thrust of that decision and opinion is clear, problems about the quoted portion are evident. Several may be mentioned.

First, how does Judge Wright (or anyone else, for that matter) determine the impact of a judicial decision on the nation's ability to defend itself? Where are the data relevant to that determination? Is a judge or a court left to accept—or, as in *Halperin*, reject—the Executive's mere assertion that there would be an adverse impact? Second, as has been noted, Wright a few years before had no difficulty in cutting through the inherent vagueness of the concept of national security. *Halperin* was decided in 1979, only four years after *Zweibon*. Third, it is fair to say that at no time has Wright proffered a careful and detailed delineation of the factors that go into national security decisions. For example, we are not told, save in a phrase, precisely what are the "instances of immediate and grave peril to the nation" or what are "exigent circumstances." A basic problem here is that the data adequate to evaluate such matters are controlled by the Executive (as *Halkin* indicates). Moreover, as the Pentagon Papers episode reveals—it is not unique—those data can be and are manipulated by Executive officers.[34] How, then, can others, such as judges, make an accurate and fair assessment regarding the national security implications of a given action? Judge Wright does not tackle that difficult question. The point is not that the term "national security" is too vague to permit careful analysis; rather, it is that judges are prisoners of the adversary system; neither they nor their staffs have the expertise requisite for making such judgments. And Wright does not tell us how possibly could a tap of 21 months on Halperin's telephone have anything to do with the "need to act decisively." Finally, here as elsewhere, Judge Wright saw the case as involving far more than the immediate litigants before the bench. The question was not what he said it was but whether a citizen can recover damages for violation of his constitutional rights by government officers. In other words, the case could—should—have been limited to the specific facts before the Court of Appeals. It was not a time to make a legislative judgment, to set down a general rule covering all types of wiretaps that were placed for alleged national security reasons.[35]

I do not mean to imply that Wright's decision in the *Halperin* case was wrong. Of course he was correct in deciding as he did, although it may be noted that Halperin was fortunate in the judges who sat on the panel (Spottswood Robinson and Gerhard Gesell, in addition to Wright). Had Wright been joined by, say, Nixon's appointees Roger Robb and Malcolm Wilkey, it is quite possible that they would have ruled the other way—and Wright would have been relegated to composing a dissent. Nor do I mean to suggest that the *Halperin* decision has made any marked difference in the way that government agencies operate. If anything, since 1979 the situation has worsened, as President Ronald Reagan by executive order—without noticeable dissent from Congress—moved to unleash the intelligence agencies from even the minimum restraints that were placed on them in the post-Watergate and post-Vietnam period.[36] One judge, even one as important as Skelly Wright, makes little difference in that overall pattern. He tries, but his powers are strictly limited. Courts are not self-starters, with roving commissions to do good and to rectify all of the wrongs of an imperfect society. Judges must await the accident of litigation to be able to rule at all. And when lawsuits are filed, appellate judges such as Wright are generally limited in their information—in this instance, about the intelligence operations of government. Secrecy is another barrier: Morton Halperin, for example, learned about wiretaps on his telephone only after the fact was disclosed in the trial of Daniel Ellsberg. Fortuities are no way to ensure accountability to constitutional norms. Still another factor is the cost of litigation. Halperin's legal expenses ran into hundreds of thousands of dollars. The lone person, even if aided by groups such as the American Civil Liberties Union, simply cannot afford to tackle the government with its enormous resources and platoons of lawyers. The consequence, in sum, is that Judge Wright in *Halperin* struck a blow for freedom and decency and against unconstitutional government behavior; but the decision and opinion are far from the norm in either the judiciary or the bureaucracy.

Perhaps Judge Wright's most extensive discussion of national security came in *American Security Council Education Foundation v. Federal Communications Commission* (1979). An extract of Wright's concurring opinion, dealing with what he considered to be the "amorphousness" of the term "national security," was previously quoted. The ASCEF is a nonprofit institution with the self-assigned mission of improving public understanding of the facts and issues of national security. Its case is not constitutional; it fits better into the broad category of administrative law. But is is discussed here because of the subject matter. ASCEF charged that the Columbia Broadcasting System aired news programs with a decidedly "dovish" slant on national security. To remedy that, the Foundation requested the FCC to require CBS to afford a reasonable opportunity to present contrasting views—presumably of a "hawkish" nature. The FCC denied the request, and ASCEF appealed to the Court of Appeals, which upheld the Commission. Under the so-called fairness doctrine, television and radio stations are required to give equal time on controversial issues. Judge Edward Tamm, for the court majority, found no evidence of a fairness violation. (The fairness doctrine is designed to give the public "suitable access to social, political, esthetic, moral, and other ideas and experiences," as the Supreme Court stated in 1969 in upholding its validity.)

Judge Wright would have gone further than Tamm; he found first amendment aspects in the case. His basic position, however, was his belief that the term "national security" defies precise definition: "*by its very nature* [it] cannot be reduced to a definable core." That is because it is "preambulary in nature," and preambulary terms "defy reductionist attempts to specificity because each such term represents a cluster of ideas, not all of which are in harmony and some of which may be in rank discord."

What is one to make of such statements? Several comments are appropriate. First, it is worth mention that Wright stood alone in his *ASCEF* concurrence, not even garnering his close ally in most cases, Judge David Bazelon, to his position. Second, and of more importance, national security—in whatever guise, whether it is called that or the national interest or the interests of society—*is* employed by lawyers and judges—as, indeed, Wright did in the *Zweibon* case. So it was simply wrong for Wright to call it "unthinkable" to try to give the term specificity. Decisions are made in the name of national security. It may not have a precise meaning, but it is something other than "preambulary." The term, third, is no more vague than others routinely employed by judges, not excluding Skelly Wright, *as if* they had some sort of common meaning. Examples are many, as Judge Learned Hand once observed: When invalidating governmental acts, Hand said, judges

do not, indeed may not, say that, taking all things into consideration, the [act] is too strong for the judicial stomach. On the contrary, they wrap their veto in a protective veil of adjectives such as "arbitrary," "artificial," "normal," "reasonable," "inherent," "fundamental," or "essential," whose office usually, though quite innocently, is to disguise what they are doing and impute it to a derivation far more impressive than their personal preferences, which are all in fact lie behind the decision.[37]

Judges, of course, are hardly as innocent as Hand would have it. They are far more likely to be hard-bitten realists, fully aware of what they are doing and in fact wanting to do it. Surely Judge Wright knew what he was doing in the *ASCEF* case. He dressed his concurrence in language that, though not "preambulary," certainly was designed to obscure his personal preferences.

III

What, then, may one conclude about the role of judges in national security questions—generally (as with all federal judges) and specifically (as with Skelly Wright)? Several conclusions, admittedly tentative, seem possible. These conclusions speak to the nature of the dilemma that the rise of the National Security State presents in a constitutional state, the long-standing tradition of judicial deference to the avowedly political branches of government when it is asserted that matters of security are involved, the limited character of litigation to date, the role of judges as members of the governing elite, and the lack of specific criteria by which judges can make decisions in national security cases.

First, the dilemma: The National Security State is characteristic of the modern age. The problem is how to reconcile its imperatives with the values associated with traditional ideas of constitutionalism that, speaking generally, are concerned with limitations on government. The NSS is the direct antithesis of that concept. It legitimates a government of virtually unlimited powers, powers that are rationalized as essential to the preservation of the nation-state. Stated another way, the dilemma is between those who perceive national security as the ultimate goal and those who, like Judge Wright, see it as intermediate to the achievement of even more fundamental goals—all the while acknowledging that national security is indispensable to realizing those other goals (which may be subsumed under the concept of human dignity). No one has yet produced a unifying principle that will at once recognize the inconsistent demands of security and constitutionalism. That dualism, it should be noted, is nothing really new; it runs throughout American history. I have argued elsewhere that our constitutional history is characterized by two inconsistent moralities—a pagan morality and a Judeo-Christian morality.[38] The first morality values security, both internal and external, which might be called the ultimate value of social order. The second morality involves human dignity, that which Felix Cohen called the "good" and Skelly Wright called "goodness," the notion of legally reified decency that is a distillation of the Bill of Rights and the ideals of American constitutionalism. The "national interest" is the core of the first morality, due process of law and equal protection of the laws of the second. There are, thus, two goals of official behavior, two ideals of human endeavor, both used as norms by identifiable human beings, that are in the last analysis incompatible with one another. This dichotomy causes intellectual confusion and a gap between pretense and reality in official behavior. At times, the goals merge in judicial opinions; when they do, the courts usually choose the first over the second morality. The judges, however, often try to rationalize their decisions in terms of the second morality. So, too, do other government officers. The unavoidable conclusion is that if there is a single morality in American constitutionalism as it operates in fact, it is that of the pagan values embedded in the concept of national security. It is a conclusion, however, that Judge Wright has not yet confronted in comprehensive detail. We have seen examples of his unwillingness to accept unquestionably assertions of national security by the Executive; but he has not yet examined in depth the imperatives of the NSS. It is fair to say that his decisions denying national security arguments deal invariably with relatively minor questions. The only exception to that generalization is his views in *Halkin v. Helms*, where he clearly saw the portentous consequences of an unleased and unfettered National Security Agency.

Second, the tradition of judicial deference: National security is a function of the avowedly political branches of government, and of them, the Executive. Judges are reluctant to intervene in such complex and arcane matters, a reluctance born both of an acknowledged lack of expertise in judges and a realization that whatever judges might say about specific issues will be overruled by the national security establishment should a judicial decision run contrary to its desires. *Halkin* and *Jabara*, both discussed above, are typical of the judicial attitude, as is *United States v. Butenko*[39]—where the Third Circuit Court of Appeals sustained a warrantless wiretap of a Soviet agent. *Butenko* is roughly analogous to *Zweibon*, where Judge Wright, as has been seen, held that a warrant was necessary. The meaning is clear: Recall the words of Professor Martin Shapiro, "No regime is likely to allow significant political power to be wielded by an isolated judicial corps free of political restraints." In that respect, courts differ little, if at all, from other governmental institutions; all are subjected to the "rule of politics" rather than the "rule of law," as the myth would have it. The point is not that judges do not have *some* latitude to act independently to check the abuses of the NSS. In the judicial rhetoric, at least, there is a long-standing tradition of willingness to intervene in the national security process. The rhetoric, however, must be carefully distinguished from what courts do in fact. Judges *say* one thing but often *act* differently. The classic example is Justice David Davis in *Ex parte Milligan* (1866):

The Constitution of the United States is a law for rulers and people, equally in war and in peace, and covers with the shield of its protection all classes for men, at all times, and under all circumstances. No doctrine involving more pernicious consequences was ever invented by the wit of man than that any of its provisions can be suspended during any of the great exigencies of government. Such a doctrine leads directly to anarchy or despotism, but the theory of necessity upon which it is based is false; for the government, within the Constitution, has all the powers granted to it which are necessary to preserve its existence, as has been happily proved by the result of the great effort to throw off its just authority.[40]

That is a nice sentiment, were it true; but it is not. An evident piece of arrant hypocrisy, Davis's statement was a futile attempt to mesh the demands of reasons of state with reasons of freedom. The holding in *Milligan*—that civilian courts must be used, even in time of war, if they are open—was neatly undercut by the Supreme Court's ruling in the 1942 case of *Ex parte Quirin*.[41] As for Judge Wright, he has not yet confronted the problem where, as stated in his *Halperin* decision, the nation itself was in "grave peril" and where "exigent circumstances" may give the Executive "special powers." Those special powers, as I have previously noted, may be subsumed under the concept of reason of state. Wright is unwilling to make the mental leap and perceive danger to the nation merely on an executive officer's assertion, absent an obvious and immediate threat. Wright, furthermore, apparently does not believe that the Constitution is relative to circumstances, for he is able to locate great and enduring—and superior—values either in the express words of the Constitution or lurking somewhere in its interstices. To the extent that is accurate, he is a judicial voice crying in the wilderness of obeisance to the Natonal Security State. But Wright has not yet developed a satisfactory substitute, sufficient to convince his colleagues on the bench, to counterbalance what usually are their knee-jerk reactions to "national security."

Third, the limited range of litigation: Only a relative few national security cases ever get to court. Despite the pervasive nature of the NSS, its activities are one of the least litigated areas of governmental action. Why that is so is an important and difficult question. It is testimony to the efficacy and potency of the ideology of the NSS that very little litigation has emerged questioning the validity of its basic assumptions, premises, and operations. Not only are many of the operations of the NSS kept secret, its basic assumptions are seldom challenged in litigation because people have been propagandized by the state, through the media and other devices, to accept those assumptions. This might be called ideological control by elites—what Marxists label as the "manipulation of consciousness"—and it is the most effective and, indeed, indispensable kind of political control in any system. Ideological control is potent because it obviates the need for elites to resort to more direct, explicit and physical forms of coercion. Since litigation represents a formal, explicit and direct challenge to the state, its frequency must, accordingly, be kept within bounds thought tolerable by the elites. Another reason for the nonuse of litigation by those who otherwise question the imperatives of the NSS is the absence of any organized national groups operating in the national security area with both the will and the resources to mount court battles. The main, and perhaps only, exception is the American Civil Liberties Union, and its ability to pay the enormous costs of litigation is quite limited. This stands in sharp contrast to the numerous organized interest groups that operate in other areas of public policy and routinely challenge, pester, question, and influence the state. In short, there is no anti-NSS lobby or litigation group. There is nothing that Skelly Wright, as an appellate judge, can do to change that picture, however much he might want to do so. He must await the accident of litigation to rule on national security matters—and that often is, as was true in *Zweibon* and *Halperin*, purely an accident that the cases were ever brought in the first place.

Fourth, judges as members of the governing coalition: I have mentioned above the tradition of judicial deference to the Executive in national security issues. Little more need be added here. "Judges," as Professor Martin Shapiro maintains, are in fact "incorporated into the governing coalition, the ruling elite, the responsible representatives of the people, or however else the politcal regime may be expressed."[42] In his important book, *The Politics of the Judiciary*, Professor J. A. G. Griffith of the London School of Economics has shown how the legal system and the judiciary generally reflect the values of the power structure of the state.[43] Griffith was, of course, writing mainly about the British judiciary, but his observations have a wider relevance. He effectively showed that a legal system cannot be regarded as operating in a political vacuum. That surely is accurate for the United States. Where, then, does Judge Wright's national security view fit into such an analysis? The answer is easy: Although he has run against the mainstream at times, he is still a member of the politico-legal Establishment of the nation. Should an actual and obvious danger threaten the United States, Skelly Wright would not say nay to those who would mount an adequate defense. What he does not like, and rightfully so, are the uncritical widespread uses of national security as a talisman for the automatic approval of every exercise of national security in all circumstances. He has a skeptical eye, and demands proof—as indeed all judges should—that the nation's security is really at issue.

Fifth, the lack of criteria to judge national security issues: How and why Judge Wright comes down on the side of reasons of freedom, as against reason of state arguments, is by no means clear. Perhaps the most that can be said is that his personal predilections run in that direction. He requires proof positive that some lone and often impecunious individual is in fact such a threat to the state and its interests that his or her interests must give way. Most judges seem to react similarly—putting *their* preferences into legal form. This means that there is a dearth of identifiable criteria of judgment on national security issues, criteria that are external to both the Executive and the judiciary and that would permit evaluation of the claims of the NSS in as objective a manner as is possible. To the extent that such an external criterion exists, it lies within the capacious and ill-defined concept of reason of state. The bulk of the judiciary accepts that principle, although they do not use the term. Rather, they usually will speak of the interests of a nebulous and never defined entity called "society" or will maintain that equally vague terms such as "public policy," the "public interest," or the "national interest" should prevail. No one knows what those terms mean. The result is to maximize discretion in the Executive, a condition that complements the other aspects of the role of judges in national security matters that are discussed immediately above. Professor Alfred Vagts once observed that "there is in the American system of government and politics no fixed or final arbiter on the question of what constitutes national interest"[44]—which was not quite correct. That "fixed and final arbiter" tends, with the rise of the NSS, ever increasingly to be the Executive branch of government.

IV

The impotence of judges in national security matters is part of the much larger inability of our political institutions or impotence of our political institutions. That greater incapacity stems from the burgeoning problems produced by the convergence of the end of the 400-year boom and a runaway science and technology. At the very time that the politico-economic institutions derivative from the Great Discoveries may well have run their course, the scientific-technological revolution is creating new problems of immense portent. We have noted above how the technological capabilities of the intelligence community can, if the desire is there, make the personal value of privacy moribund; analogous technologies are producing weapons of unparalleled power of destruction.

The law, however and by whomever created, cannot keep up with these developments. We have come to the end of an epoch—and are effecting a transition to a new one, the contours of which cannot be determined at this time. Judges are prisoners within the confines of the institutions of the old order. They must act without breaking free, for that break—if and when it comes—will have to be by other means. The political order is in obvious disarray. It cannot deal adequately with an entire range of problems, the foremost being that of national security in the nuclear age—an age when constitutional institutions designed for resolving essentially domestic questions must confront an interdependent and shrinking world. To the extent that judges make law, they are by far the most impotent of all the branches of government. Nothing they can or will do is likely to alter the basic features of the National Security State, even though its emergence presents a constitutional problem of the first dimension.

Skelly Wright knows that, at least intuitively. But if he has thought deeply about the manifest failures of the political (the constitutional) order, it is only in the occasional case that comes before his court or, as will be shown in the next chapter, when he believes that the Supreme Court has been badly mistaken in some of its decisions. Wright does what he can. In the companion case to *Halperin v. Kissinger*, he wrote in *Smith v. Nixon* (1979) that "courts may not simply accept bland assurances by the

Executive that a situation did, in fact, represent a national security problem requiring electronic surveillance.''[45] That is something, he said, that courts must discover for themselves. Yet he is fully cognizant that he tends to march to a different drummer from other judges in matters concerning the NSS, and realizes full well that only a paucity of national security questions are ever litigated. He is quite comfortable with the fact that he is a relative rarity among federal judges concerning the NSS; he displays no desire to do more than protect individual rights and liberties. Although he would not dismantle the National Security State, Skelly Wright would ameliorate, insofar as his powers as a judge allow, its excesses and pretensions.

6

Judge Wright and Freedom of Expression

The theory of free speech is grounded on the belief that people will make the right choice if presented with all points of view on a controversial issue.

—J. Skelly Wright (1971)[1]

I

The first amendment speaks in simple, austere terms: "Congress shall make no law respecting an establishment of religion, or prohibiting the free exercise thereof; or abridging the freedom of speech, or of the press, or the right of people peaceably to assemble, and to petition the government for a redress of grievances." Clear enough, one might think; yet lurking beneath that simplicity and austerity is a bewildering reality. Although written in absolute language, it is in fact a relative admonition. The first five words, by Supreme Court interpretation, read something like this: "Congress may make some laws . . . "; furthermore, both the states and Congress are bound by the amendment—again by Supreme Court interpretation. Moreover, the amendment contains a seemingly incongruous pairing of limitations: freedom of expression (speech, press, assembly, and petitioning the government) *and* freedom of religion and a prohibition against a state religion. Those several provisions have spawned numerous controversies, mostly in this century. Judge Skelly Wright has participated in many of them. This chapter develops his views on freedom of expression (speech and press); the next chapter deals with a still-controversial decision concerning freedom of religion.

At the outset, it is desirable to set forth some general ideas about the reasons for and the functions of the first amendment. What, first of all, is its derivation? Professor Thomas Emerson, perhaps the leading academic commentator on the amendment, has observed:

The right of the individual to freedom of expression has deep roots in our history. But the concept as we know it now is essentially the product of the liberal constitutional state. It is an integral part of the great intellectual and social movement beginning with the Renaissance which transformed the Western world from a feudal and authoritarian society to one whose faith rested upon the dignity, the reason and the freedom of the individual. The theory in its modern form has thus evolved over a period of more than three centuries, being applied under different circumstances and seeking to deal with different problems.[2]

Emerson thus limits the concept of freedom of expression in space and time. His observation bears striking resemblance to the emergence of the "liberal constitutional state" during the 400-year boom following the Great Discoveries. If he is correct, and I believe that he is, then the first amendment as a way to limit government and enhance freedom of expression should be seen as a unique phenomenon in known human history. No other nation outside the Western world knew it; and historically, it is only some 300 years old. By no means can freedom of expression be called inherent in either human nature or human governance. It may well be an aberration, a moment of human history. With the emergence of the National Security State and with the ecological trap apparently once more closing, freedom of expression may well be seen as a mere "pip" on a graph rising sharply from zero to maximum and then declining. How far that decline will go is not yet known; that will, as I have previously argued, only come when conditions so warrant, the Constitution now and always being relative to circumstances.

As Professor Emerson tells us, the amendment was designed to protect the human self and its personal autonomy against governmental infringements; and truth in the political arena is considered to be a product of the clash of opposing ideas. This latter conception is quite remarkable: it is ultimately based on faith and on the assumption of the essential benevolence of mankind. It is also predicated on the assumption that the goals or ends or purposes of society have been settled, and all that remains is to work out the details through "rational" discourse. Neither assumption holds water.

In 1919, some 128 years after the first amendment was ratified, Justice Oliver Wendell Holmes articulated the underlying premise of freedom of expression. Borrowing from John Stuart Mill and Adam Smith, Holmes stated:

Persecution for the expression of opinions seems to me perfectly logical. If you have no doubt of your premises or your power and want a certain result with all your heart, you naturally express your wishes in law and sweep away all opposition. To allow opposition by speech seems to indicate that you think the speech impotent, as when a man says he has squared the circle, or that you doubt either your power or your premises. But when men have realized that time has upset many fighting faiths, they may come to believe even more than they believe the very foundations of their own conduct that *the ultimate good desired is better realized by free trade in ideas—that the best test of truth is the power of the thought to get itself accepted in the competition of the market, and that truth is the only ground upon which their wishes safely can be carried out. That at any rate is the theory of our Constitution.* It is an experiment, as all life is an experiment. Every year if not every day we have to wager our salvation upon some prophecy based upon imperfect knowledge. While that experiment is part of our system I think we should be eternally vigilant against attempts to check the expression of opinions that we loathe and believe to be fraught with death, unless they so imminently immediately interfere with the lawful and pressing purposes of the law that an immediate check is required to save the country. (Emphasis added.)[3]

"What is truth?" Pilate asked, and did not expect an answer. "What is truth?" Justice Holmes asked, and stayed to give an answer: whatever emerges from the clash of interests in the political arena, in the marketplace of ideas.

Several comments may be made about the Holmesian oft-quoted statement. First, to allow "opposition by speech" may mean, in addition to what he said, that societal ends (goals) have been settled and largely accepted, so that the speech is merely about ways to achieve commonly accepted ends. Second, it is obviously a transfer of Adam Smith economics to the realm of politics. At least inferentially Holmes adhered to the notion of an "invisible hand" through the operation of which proper public policies would be produced. Third, that 1919 dissent by Holmes is still the basic theory of the first amendment, as revealed both in judicial opinions and scholarly comment. Fourth, Skelly Wright, to the extent that he has a consistent philosophy about the first amendment, is a stout adherent to what Holmes said. Finally, Holmes's views, and thus the prevailing theory of the first amendment, are demonstrably faulty in actual practice. His statement may be, as he said, "the theory of our Constitution," but that is so only for the formal as distinguished from the living or operative fundamental law. His was—and still is, for most people—a touching faith that all was, or would be, for the best in the world.

It is important to understand why the Holmesian view of freedom of expression is faulty. First, one must realize that a gap always exists between myth (or pretense) and reality in American constitutional theory. The formal Constitution—"of the books"—bespeaks a system of untrammeled expression; the living Constitution bespeaks a system of manipulation of the public by means of a pervasive system of propaganda, with the mass media the principal instruments employed by government for that purpose. Second, with information available in plethoric quantity and with public issues becoming ever increasingly complex, it is simply impossible for individuals, singly or *en masse*, to be informed on all—even most—matters of national or even local importance (hence the rise in recent years of "single-issue" politics). Third, it is far from demonstrable—in fact, it is highly unlikely—that people generally want to be informed; the lack of knowledge about elementary factual matters readily available to all is so well known as not to require documentation. Fourth, a media monopoly (or oligopoly) exists. Control over the dissemination of information is highly concentrated, with the main sources being the television networks, some news magazines, and a few newspaper chains. Furthermore, that oligopoly has close ties with the corporate world, with numerous interlocking directorships, and thus shares and disseminates the values of corporate capitalism. The media in the United States have three major functions: to make money, to help sell consumer goods (through advertising), and to operate as a socializing influence on the people—to accept and believe in the values of corporate capitalism. An aspect of the latter, as Robert Carl Manoff has shown, is that the media, however "responsible" or "adversarial" they might think they are, in fact are instruments employed by the state to further national security interests.[4] Finally, in important matters of public concern, government (the apparatus of the state) pursues policies of secrecy which artifically limit the range and character of public debate.

The Holmesian statement, with its myth of unfettered expression, is the ideology of the first amendment. Ideology, Clifford Geertz tells us, provides "a symbolic framework in terms of which to formulate, think about, and react to political problems."[5] Further: "The function of ideology is to make an autonomous politics possible by providing the authoritative concepts that render it meaningful, the suasive images by means of which it can be sensibly grasped."[6] The myth of the first amendment offers a comprehensible set of assertions, of beliefs, about the nature of the American political order. At its core is "the legal paradigm—a social perspective which perceives and explains human interaction largely in terms of rules and of the rights and obligations inherent in rules." There are, so it is believed, "rules" about the first amendment; and correlative obligations on government—*public* government, for the reasons set forth in Chapter 4—to adhere to those rules. The right of free expression is part of what Professor Stuart Scheingold has called the "myth of rights" (see Chapter 3), the notion that legal processes play a significant independent role in the governing of America. Scheingold asserts, however, and I agree, that

At all points, law and politics are inextricably intertwined and in this combination politics is the senior partner. Laws are delivered to us by the dominant political coalition as are the judges and other officials responsible for interpretation and implementation. As a consequence our rights are always at risk in the political arena and therefore provide very little independent leverage.

Law thus serves the status quo in a kind of dual capacity. Legal processes are closely linked to the dominant configurations of power. At the same time, in its ideological incarnation, the law induces acquiescence in the established order by suggesting that the political system is beneficent and adaptable.[7]

Holmes and his intellectual followers, which include not only Judge Wright (as the headnote to this chapter indicates) but most who write about the first amendment, have a romantic view of the amendment's provisions for freedom of expression. The faults (listed above) of the Holmesian theory are not only self-evident; they completely undermine the foundations of "the theory of our Constitution." Justice Hugo Black put his finger on the essence of the matter when he said in the *Barenblatt* case (see Chapter 5): "To apply the [Supreme] Court's balancing test under such circumstances is to read the first amendment to say 'Congress shall pass no law abridging freedom of speech, press, assembly and petition, unless Congress and the Supreme Court reach the joint conclusion that on balance the interest of the Government in stifling these freedoms is greater than the interest of the people in having them exercised.' "[8] Precisely. Black's fears reflected brute fact: The first amendment is not enforced unless the Supreme Court considers that it is reasonable to do so—on "balance."

Justice Black should not have been surprised. The first amendment has never been enforced pursuant to its precise terms. Nor has any other provision of the Bill of Rights. For that matter, Black himself was far from consistent in his views about absolute freedom of expression. In *United States v. O'Brien*,[9] for example, he agreed with seven of his colleagues (only Justice William Douglas dissented) that burning a draft card in public was not a form of protected speech. The majority determined that the law against destruction of draft cards served a legitimate governmental objective—the effective operation of the Selective Service System. That meant that the Court, with Black silently concurring, "balanced" the interests of O'Brien in that form of expression and the interests of the state during the Vietnam "war." Scheingold's point was validated—the "dominant political coalition" wanted, as Professor Dean Alfange has said, "to put a stop to this particular form of antiwar protest, which they deemed extraordinarily contemptible and vicious—even treasonous—at a time when American troops were engaged in combat."[10] So much for the Holmesian idea of the first amendment and his idea that we should be vigilant against attempts to stifle expressions that we loathe. The clear lesson of American constitutional history is that freedoms of expression are indeed available (and certainly much more so than in many other countries) but only until the state considers it necessary to suppress them.

That is a lesson that Judge Skelly Wright has never publicly (or privately, to my knowledge) accepted. His is the plain and simple faith of Justice Black in *Barenblatt* (but not in *O'Brien*): Free expression means that expression shall be free. In that position, Wright runs contrary to the mainstream of judicial thought. A close friend of Justice Black and undoubtedly influenced in many of his views by Black, Wright is a first amendment purist. Furthermore, he perceives freedom of expression as both an *intermediate* and an *ultimate* goal—intermediate in the sense of enhancing the personal autonomy of individuals and ultimate in the sense that it is a process or a way for reaching other goals. It is considered by many, and Wright agrees, to be fundamental to the "democratic" way of life. The task of this chapter is to examine how Skelly Wright has achieved those two goals in the context of the first amendment.

II

Professor Thomas Emerson asserts that "the courts have been and must remain the keeper of the American conscience in upholding the rights of the individual against encroachment by the government. They should continue this role in dealing with . . . the first amendment."[11] That is a "negative" conception of the amendment, with the task of courts to eliminate restrictions on expression. The basic constitutional problem, however, goes much further: Is there an "affirmative" or "positive" dimension as well, one that requires government to enhance the opportunities for free expression? The answer, I think, is yes—and both Emerson and Wright seem to agree. Wright shares with Emerson the view that courts must play an aggressive role in strengthening both the negative and positive aspects of the amendment. Wright's views are to be found in numerous judicial decisions and in two important law journal articles.[12]

First, a general statement from a 1982 law journal article, "Money and the Pollution of Politics: Is the First Amendment an Obstacle to Political Equality?"; this is perhaps his most important expression of first amendment theory.

In the name of the very first amendment in our Bill of Rights, the present Supreme Court has put serious obstacles in the path of our society's advancement toward political equality through law. In two vitally important and, in my judgment, tragically misguided first amendment decisions, *Buckley v. Valeo* and *First National Bank v. Bellotti*, the Court has given effect to the polluting effect of money in campaigns. As a result, our political system may not use some of its most powerful defenses against electoral inequalities. Concentrated wealth . . . threatens to distort political campaigns and referenda. The voices of individual citizens are being drowned out in election campaigns—the forum for the political deliberations of our people. If the ideal of equality is trampled there, the principle of "one person, one vote," the cornerstone of our democracy, becomes a hollow mockery.[13]

What, then, were the Supreme Court decisions that caused this extraordinary outburst from a sitting judge on an inferior court that convenes in the shadow of the Supreme Court? *Buckley*[14] concerned a congressional statute limiting political contributions to $1,000 to any single candidate per election, with an overall annual limitation of $25,000 by any contributor; and also limited independent expenditures by individuals and groups, as well as personal campaign spending by candidates. There were other provisions in the statute, but those are the ones that exercised Judge Wright. The Supreme Court concluded: "We sustain the individual contribution limits, the disclosure and reporting provision, and the public financing scheme. We conclude, however, that the limitations on campaign expenditures by individuals and groups, and on expenditures by a candidate from his personal funds, are constitutionally infirm." Why? The first amendment was transgressed. Said the Court:

We find that the governmental interest in preventing corruption and the appearance of corruption is inadequate to justify [the] ceiling on independent expenditures. . . .
It is argued . . . that the ancillary governmental interest in equalizing the relative ability of individuals and groups to influence the outcome of elections serves to justify [this limitation]. But the concept that government may restrict the speech of some elements of our society in order to enhance the relative voice of others is wholly foreign to the First Amendment, which was designed "to secure 'the widest possible dissemination of information from diverse and antagonistic sources,' " and to " 'assure unfettered interchange of ideas for the bringing about of political and social changes desired by the people.' " The First Amendment's protection against governmental abridgment of free expression cannot properly be made to depend on a person's financial ability to engage in public discussion.

To that, Judge Wright says: Why not? He is correct, as he also is in his criticism of *Bellotti*.[15]

Bellotti invalidated a Massachusetts law prohibiting expenditures by corporations to influence the outcomes of referenda that had nothing to do with the corporations' business activities. Speaking for the Supreme Court majority, Justice Lewis Powell insisted that the proper question was not "whether corporations have first amendment rights and, if so, whether they are coextensive with those of natural persons." Rather, he asserted, the question must be "whether [the statute] abridges expression that the first amendment was meant to protect. We hold that it does." The reason for knocking the law down was that "the inherent worth of the speech in terms of its capacity for informing the public does not depend on the identity of its source, whether corporation, association, union, or individual." That is a nice sentiment, and if one accepts the premise that corporations are always to be equated with natural persons under the Constitution, then the decision inexorably flows as a matter of simple logic. The problem, however, is in the nature of the premise. If it is faulty—as Judge Wright believes, in electoral situations at least—then Powell's conclusion is invalid. In practical effect—Wright explicitly says this—the decision and *Buckley* undercut the principle of one person-one vote in the political arena. The reality of unequal economic rights and an unequal distribution of economic power changes the political mix. The "free speech" of a corporate giant—say, Exxon or IBM or AT&T—is obviously greater than that of any individual. A parlous situation, indeed, Orwellian in its implications: Everyone is equal before the law and under the first amendment but some—those with accumulated wealth—are more equal than others. What Wright appears to be saying is this: Justice may be blind but there is no need for the Supreme Court mindlessly to trample on the slogan deeply carved in the facade of the Marble Palace: "Equal Justice Under Law." For the Court to do so in *Buckley* and *Bellotti* is "tragically misguided."

That harsh accusation is indubitably correct. Wright's strong belief that there is a close correlation between spending and speech, and thus that the democratic process is "polluted," is difficult to gainsay. Persons, including corporations, have as a consequence a disproportionate impact upon elections. If, as McGeorge Bundy once remarked, "the fundamental function of the law is to prevent the natural unfairness of society from becoming intolerable,"[16] the Supreme Court has added to, rather than diminished, that unfairness.

The necessary inference from Judge Wright's published articles is that he believes that the first amendment has an affirmative or positive dimension, as well as being a negative limitation on government. He seems to believe that government has a duty—inchoate, to be sure—under the Constitution to help unclog the channels of communication, and thus to make the voices of the poor and powerless more effective in the political arena. The notion that the first amendment is an implicit command to public officials to do something affirmative, as compared with being prevented from doing something, to aid the workings of the system of freedom of expression is both relatively new and little recognized. Professor Emerson has lent some insight into the matter:

Traditionally, the first amendment, like other provisions of the Bill of Rights, has operated primarily as a negative force in maintaining the system of freedom of expression. It has served to prevent the government from prohibiting, harassing, or interfering with speech or other forms of communication. On the other hand, the first amendment has not been viewed as a significant factor in efforts to promote freedom of expression or to impose limits on governmental participation in the system.

There is growing concern now, however, with the affirmative side of the first amendment. Major distortions in the system—failure of the marketplace of ideas to operate according to the original plan—have not been solved by the negative approach. . . . The underlying trend of modern government toward social control by persuasion rather than by coercion . . . has enhanced greatly the government's affirmative role in the system.

. . . The development of rules for employing governmental powers to expand the system of freedom of expression, while at the same time limiting and controlling those powers, is emerging as one of the crucial problems of the future. As we move inevitably toward some form of social control over our destinies, the need to maintain a high degree of laissez-faire in the system of freedom of expression, when laissez-faire is diminishing or disappearing in the economic sphere, poses a critical dilemma. *Unless we are able to resolve this dilemma, the system of freedom of expression as we hitherto have conceived it cannot continue to exist.* (Emphasis added.)[17]

Emerson further asserts that the primary initiative for promoting freedom of expression rests with the legislative and executive branches, but the courts, too, have a role to play. Two questions, unanswered and even unasked by Professor Emerson, emerge from his analysis: First, can the judiciary mandate governmental promotion of freedom of expression? It is one thing, that is, to limit governmental impediments on expression, another to make facilities available for people to speak, and still another to undertake "a deliberate, affirmative and even aggressive effort . . . to support the system of free expression." Second, to what extent does government itself enjoy first amendment freedoms; and should there be constitutional limitations on government expression?

Judge Wright has been concerned, at least inferentially, with the first question. As for the second, neither he nor other judges, and most commentators, have even recognized the problem (Professor Mark Yudof of the University of Texas Law School is the major exception here).[18] But the questions, as with the basic idea of an affirmative thrust to the first amendment, are on the frontier of first amendment activity. They are part of the dilemma noted by Professor Emerson.

Have the courts done anything about the dilemma? Some halting beginnings may be observed. The *Buckley* case is significant. Although, as has been noted, Wright has criticized part of the Supreme Court's decision because it allowed money to pollute election campaigns, another part of the decision upheld governmental subsidies in elections through use of tax money. Rejecting an argument that the subsidies violated the first amendment, the Court held that the legislation "is a congressional effort, not to abridge, restrict or censor speech, but rather to use public money to facilitate and enlarge public discussion and participation in the electoral process, goals vital to a self-governing people." The law, therefore, "*furthers, not abridges, pertinent First Amendment values.*" (Emphasis added.) So far, so good: The Court has legitimized a congressional effort to support freedom of expression. Could it have gone further? The answer, at least to Judge Wright, is yes. When the case was before the Court of Appeals, the statute was upheld; Wright agreed with an unsigned opinion for the entire court. That opinion was in fact written by him (although issued *per curiam*—unsigned). "The statute taken as a whole affirmatively enhances First Amendment values. By reducing in good measure disparity due to wealth, the Act tends to equalize both the relative ability of all voters to affect electoral outcomes, and the opportunity of all interested citizens to become candidates for public office. This broadens the choice of candidates and the opportunity to hear a variety of voices."[19]

Clearly, therefore, Wright believes that the first amendment *permits* affirmative governmental action to further the freedoms protected by the amendment; the crucial question, as yet not directly confronted by him (or others), is whether the amendment *requires* such action. Is there, in other words, an affirmative duty on government to take action to further first amendment values; and if so, is that duty judicially cognizable? By no means has Wright addressed himself to that difficult problem (and, should he do so, it is entirely possible that the posture of judicial passivism that was noted and discussed in Chapter 4 would preclude him trying to impose a duty upon government). But he has said this: "The Supreme Court, of course, says what the law is"; but equating money with speech, as the Supreme Court did in *Buckley* and *Bellotti*, was wrong in theory and principle:

The growing impact of concentrated wealth on the political process, and the glaring inequalities in political campaign resources, threaten the very essence of political equality. The warning signs are plain for all to see. Today's threat to democracy is not the impending collapse of the structure of our democratic institutions, but their continuing erosion from within. If this erosion is not checked, the principle of one person, one vote could become nothing more than a pious fraud. Ironically, the underpinnings of our democratic system are being menaced in the name of the liberties of the first amendment.[20]

That was written in 1982. Compare a 1975 statement:

Our democracy has moved a long way from the town hall, one man, one vote conception of the Framers. Politics have become a growth industry and a way of life for millions of Americans. We have not been sufficiently vigilant; we have failed to remind ourselves, as we moved from town halls to today's Romanesque political extravaganzas, that politics is neither an end in itself nor a means for subverting the will of the people.[21]

Neither of these statements, of course, indicates that Judge Wright has translated his very real concern for the pollution of the electoral process into a notion of constitutional duty on government to take affirmative action to further first amendment values. Surely, however, that is the logical step for him to take.

Would such a step be a foray into legal *terra incognita*? The answer is no. At times, simple prohibitory orders or even agreement with what Congress has done to further constitutional values are not enough to provide the relief that is really necessary. Express constitutional provisions are not self-executing; they require a willing plaintiff who presents a "case or controversy" in the constitutional sense. Statutes, such as that in *Buckley,* are self-executing; and all courts need do is defer to the legislative judgment. But what about the values of constitutionalism, those not expressly set forth in the document? If the Holmes (and Wright) concept of the first amendment's underlying theory is accepted, does it follow that government has the duty to help create and maintain a viable marketplace of ideas? For example, Congress has enacted a "freedom of information" law under which people, under rather restricted circumstances, can get information about what government has done in the past. Should that statutory duty on government, as imperfect as it is, be constitutionalized? If Holmes was in fact correct in his theory, then imposition of such a duty is both logical and necessary. (No such duty has as yet been recognized by any court.) Should, to give another example, the "private" governments of the mass media be constitutionalized, so that they would be required to print or air all points of view on a given policy issue? (The Court has spoken resoundingly—unanimously—in the negative.[22] But that does not eliminate the problem.)

The essential problem is this: The citizenry cannot have informed opinions about public policies, past or present or projected, unless they have access to the data relevant to those policies *and* a means of making their views known. That is the dilemma to which Professor Emerson alluded. And that is implicit in Judge Wright's concerns about the inordinate power of money in electoral matters.

That courts can "command" officers in other branches of government to do something affirmatively is not a novel idea. In Chapter 3, we have seen that the Supreme Court has done precisely that in racial segregation cases. It has also done so in the cases involving one person-one vote, on the apportionment of legislatures—national, state, and local. If judicial intervention in the governing process is invoked because of congressional enactment, the assumption is that the statute contains an affirmative regulatory objective. Even if the suit is based on constitutional provisions, long regarded as restricting governmental power, there is an increasing tendency to treat them as embodying affirmative values, to be furthered by judicial action.[23] Both the legislatures and executives failed or refused to act to correct the long-suffered wrongs of black Americans. Finally, however, the courts did act, as we have seen; that action is, in retrospect, a prime example of the judiciary telling other government officers what to do. The system of American constitutionalism, including of course the first amendment, can be truly vital only insofar as it is predicated on the following rules: First, those who wield governmental power *cannot* do certain things; and second, there are certain things that they *must* do. The hard, unavoidable fact is that courts are indispensable to the achievement of both goals—the "cannot" as well as the "must."

Judge Wright seems to be edging toward such a position in first amendment matters. He fully realizes that judges are, in Justice William Brennan's words, "not mere umpires, but, in their own sphere, lawmakers—a coordinate branch of government. . . . Moreover, judges bear responsiblity for the vitally important task of construing and securing constitutional rights." And further: "Judges are obliged to be discerning, exercise judgment, and prescribe rules. Indeed, at times judges wield considerable authority to formulate legal policy in designated areas."[24] So they do, and one need not look very far to find examples. The *Cooper* and *Green* cases discussed in Chapter 3 are obviously in that category. So, too, are *Miranda v. Arizona* and the *Abortion Cases.*[25] In these and other cases, the Supreme Court has gone far beyond the specific factual situations to make legislative pronouncements. It is "an axiom of statesmanship," Henry George once observed, "that great changes can be brought about under old forms."[26] So they can, and so it is in litigation: The *form* of adjudication remains, and the judges still adhere to the adversary system, at least in theory, but the *substance* of what they are doing is undergoing major changes.

It would not take an enormous intellectual leap for judges to begin finding affirmative aspects in the first amendment, up to and including placing duties on the other branches of government. That there would be immense problems accompanying such a move is obvious. One is enforcement: Just how can judicial commands to other officers of government to do something affirmatively be enforced? As has been seen, that is one of the pervasive difficulties with the desegregation of American society. Another problem is the identification of the criteria by which judges would operate in finding affirmative duties. There is no *vade mecum* to be consulted for answers. Judges must, accordingly, do what they have done in the past and do today in constitutional matters: In the words of Chief Justice Earl Warren, follow the Constitution and their "own consciences."[27] There is no real alternative. Our constitutional system, Professor Ronald Dworkin remarks, "rests on a particular moral theory, namely, that men have moral rights against the state."[28] That it does—and the correlative is also clear: The state has moral obligations to men. And it is the task of judges to translate those rights and obligations into some sort of operational reality. Judges, of course, cannot work alone; they must have the full cooperation of the other branches of government. Woodrow Wilson said it well: "Government is not a body of blind forces; it is a body of men, with highly differentiated functions, no doubt, in our modern day of specialization but with a common task and purpose. Their cooperation is indispensable, their warfare fatal."[29]

The need, as Dworkin tells us, is for a fusion of moral philosophy and constitutional law. That, whether he has realized it or not, is what Skelly Wright is trying to do. He consistently adheres to views of equality and of the furtherance of human dignity. He has had little help in that quest. His has been and still is a lonely pilgrimage of one man trying as best he can within the constraints of his office to strike blows for the dignity and equality of the individual. Although he accepts the Holmesian view of the first amendment, he is not naive. He fully realizes the barriers to reasonably full realization of the theory. He must at times feel like Sisyphus, pushing the boulder of free expression up a hill toward the summit of actualization—only to see it roll back down again. But with tenacity and singleness of purpose, he keeps up the effort. His is a faith that people, given the right conditions, can make wise policy choices; and he sees it as the task of the law to help develop those conditions.

III

Equality is a principal aspect of Judge Wright's first amendment decisions. I now examine some of them.

I begin with a recent decision, not written by Wright but by Judge Abner Mikva. Wright concurred, with a caveat. The case is *Community for Creative Non-Violence v. Watt* (1983),[30] and its facts are relatively simple. The Community for Creative Non-Violence (CCNV) received a permit from the National Park Service (NPS) to conduct round-the-clock demonstrations on public property in Washington, D.C., for the purpose of impressing the plight of poor and homeless people upon the president, the Congress, and the general public. The NPS permitted 24-hour physical presence at the symbolic campsites that had been set up, on public land, but denied a permit to sleep at them (because NPS regulations prohibited "camping"). CCNV protested that denial, was rejected in district court, and appealed to Judge Wright's court. That court, with eleven judges sitting, held that the denial was unconstitutional as an infringement upon CCNV's first amendment rights of expression. Five judges dissented.

The case is a classic illustration of how admittedly intelligent people, learned in the law, can flounder over a simple question: Do people have a constitutional right to demonstrate peacefully on public property? CCNV made no threat of violence; nor did its members molest anyone or interfere with the rights of others. Why should not the quick and unequivocal answer be yes, that such a right does exist? The judges, however, made a complexity out of a simplicity. Engaging in tendentious debate, the eleven wrote six different opinions—four for the majority and two for the dissenters—with a total of 85 printed pages. One is puzzled at the logorrhea: What useful purpose did it serve? If a few people wanted to sleep in the dead of winter in tents on public grounds, why should they not be allowed to do so? The majority agreed, but only after considerable agonizing (typical of many other first amendment decisions). (Chief Justice Warren Burger promptly issued a stay of the court's decision, thus blocking it until the Supreme Court ruled—long after the purpose of the "expression," in winter.)

Judge Mikva held that sleeping is "expressive conduct" within the meaning of the first amendment, and went on to say:

That CCNV's conduct comes within the scope of the first amendment, however, only begins our constitutional analysis. In *United States v. O'Brien*, . . . the Supreme Court noted that "when 'speech' and 'non-speech' elements are combined in the same course of conduct, a sufficiently important governmental interest in regulating the non-speech element can justify incidental limitations on First Amendment freedoms."

. . . In short, *O'Brien* requires us to engage in a balancing of first amendment freedoms and their societal costs that is structured to place a thumb on the first amendment side of the scales.

In making that statement—which, unhappily, is standard judicial "reasoning"—Mikva quoted from a 1972 opinion of Judge Wright: "The basic issue in all such cases is how much the first amendment requires society to give up in the interests of communication—that is, what price are we willing to put on free speech."[31] Wright also said in 1972, in a case similar to CCNV's (it dealt with protests against the Vietnam "war"): "There is unmistakable symbolic significance in demonstrating close to the White House or on Capitol grounds which, while not easily quantifiable, is of undoubted importance in the constitutional balance. Although this theory has been used to justify demonstrations near state capitols as well, . . . it is in Washington—where a petition for redress of national grievances literally must be brought—that the theory has its primary application."[32]

Judge Mikva illustrated many of the shortcomings of what constitutes judicial reasoning. It is not to denigrate either his opinion or the judgment itself—for his opinion, in style, is the norm rather than the exception—to say that he displayed at least three errors of greater or lesser significance. Judge Wright, too, can be criticized for these errors, because he concurred in Mikva's opinion (with only the remark that he did not believe that sleeping would in all circumstances be equated with expression).

First, Mikva relied on the Supreme Court's decision (and opinion for the Court) in the *O'Brien* case—by any criterion one of the worst of the Warren Court's decisions (and one of Warren's least defensible opinions). The Court upheld O'Brien's conviction and sentence to jail for publicly and defiantly burning his draft card. Warren maintained that the Court could not accept "the view that an apparently limitless variety of conduct can be labeled as 'speech' whenever the person engaging in conduct intends thereby to express an idea." That, however, was not the question before the Court. No one had argued that any type of conduct could be speech. A year later, the same Supreme Court sustained a high school student wearing a black armband to protest the "war." Small wonder, therefore, that Justice John Harlan could wryly comment in 1970 that the Supreme Court "has, as yet, not established a test for determining at what point conduct becomes so intertwined with expression that it becomes necessary to weigh the state's interest in proscribing conduct against the constitutionally protected interest in freedom of expression."[33]

O'Brien illustrates, once again, how the Supreme Court oft-times is a *de facto* arm of the political branches of government. Already noted is Professor Alfange's accurate remark that Congress wanted to stop that type of protest—draft-card burning—"which they deemed extraordinarily contemptible and vicious—even treasonous—at a time when American troops were engaged in combat." The Court dutifully went along with Congress's vindictive law, in as pusillanimous a decision as the Justices ever rendered. There is no other way to view the *O'Brien* decision than to maintain that the Court is part of the governing coalition of the nation, only ostensibly (as in the myth) independent from it. Two first amendment scholars have correctly observed: "The balancing of the competing interests in *O'Brien* was essentially no balancing at all. First amendment interests were hardly considered and were casually relegated to a position subordinate to the alleged government interest underlying the draft card-burning law."[34]

If that be so, and it is, they why did the *CCNV* judges rely so much on the test purportedly applied in *O'Brien*? That decision, rather than being built for the ages and, thus, establishing solid criteria for evaluating other symbolic activity that is argued to be expression, was in fact a political decision by a political Court, with the Justices bowing to Congress and the Executive in manner supine. Even the "reason" given by Chief Justice Warren—that destroying a draft card jeopardized the effective operation of the Selective Service System—is far from "substantial," as Warren asserted. Considered by hindsight, for eight Justices to agree that it was verges on the ludicrous. Warren, to be sure, attempted to state a lasting set of principles for evaluating the extent to which conduct can be considered to be protected expression, but failed. Warren's "test" is this: "A government regulation is sufficiently justified if it is within the constitutional power of the government; if it furthers a substantial government interest; if the government interest is unrelated to the suppression of free expression; and if the incidental restriction on alleged first amendment freedoms is no greater than is essential to the furtherance of that interest." That is the type of judicial statement that sounds good on first reading. Once it is analyzed, however, it can be seen for what it is—a question-begging pronouncement that at once is in consonance with the expectations of the myth system (because it is written in language with which lawyers are familiar) and permits an enormous amount of discretion by other judges (as the operational code provides). The latter point is illustrated by the fact that both the majority judges and the dissenters in *CCNV* cited *O'Brien* as authority for their inconsistent conclusions.

Second, Judge Mikva (and thus Judge Wright) perceived their judicial role in *CCNV* as that of balancing the interests involved—on the one hand, the desires of members of CCNV to dramatize their views by sleeping in tents during winter; and on the other hand, the interest of the government (asserted to be the security of the demonstrators and keeping the tent areas clean). That is standard constitutional reasoning, but reasoning that, when carefully analyzed, cannot withstand rigorous scrutiny. The so-called balancing test is no test at all. No external standards of judgment or evaluation are applied. No matter how often or how loudly the term, "balancing test," is employed, it still does not tell a judge how to identify the competing interests accurately, how to weigh them against each other, and how to determine which set of interests should prevail. The "test" is in fact a counterpane beneath which judges can and do exercise discretion. They make decisions, as was discussed in Chapter 1, in accordance with their ideological predispositions. Each judge sees the dispute before the court through spectacles whose lenses have been beclouded by his or her entire heredity and environment. In this respect, the judging process differs little, if at all, from that of others who are authorized to make important societal decisions. In the words of three political scientists, ". . . we might summarize our comments on the nature of choice as follows: information is selectively perceived and evaluated in terms of the decision-maker's frame of reference. Choices are made on the basis of preferences which are in part situationally and in part biographically determined."[35] In sum, reason *qua* reason has a role to play in adjudication, but it is a strictly limited one. The really important matter is the nature of the premises from which judges proceed. Often those premises are not articulated. As Oliver Wendell Holmes wrote in 1881:

The very considerations which judges most rarely mention, and always with an apology, are the secret root from which the law draws all the juices of life. I mean, of course, consideration of what is expedient in the community concerned. Every important principle which is developed in litigation is in fact and at bottom the result of more or less definitely understood views of public policy; most generally, to be sure, under our practices and traditions, *the unconscious result of instinctive preferences and inarticulate convictions*, but nonetheless traceable to views of public policy in the last analysis. (Emphasis added.)[36]

Reason comes into play when conclusions are reached in given factual situations, conclusions that are logical—that is, reasoned—derivations from a judge's premises.[37]

Not that the Warren test in *O'Brien* does not serve a purpose. It does. The test gives the appearance of rationality and objectivity to the judicial process; their pre-eminent roles in constitutional interpretation is one of the most powerful myths in American law. Warren's test, and its uncritical use by judges and commentators alike, are central to an understanding of what was called earlier in this chapter the formal Constitution "of the books." Due obeisance is accorded "the rule of law"; but the harsh reality, under the operative Constitution, is the rule of men and women—in the *CCNV* case, those called upon to judge their fellow humans.

Third, Judge Mikva writes about "societal costs" in balancing interests, as if that term means something precise. It does not. Although the words, "society" and "societal costs," are often employed, they are never defined in judicial opinions. Judges routinely confuse society with government and with the state. All three terms, each of which is important to constitutional law, require exact and rigorous use of language. They are not synonymous, although they are often used as if they are. The state is a metaphysical entity larger than and superior to the arithmetical sum of the individuals in the populace; government is the apparatus of the state; and society is the congeries of individuals and groups within the geographical entity called the nation. So seen, how Mikva could write about societal costs without defining the term remains completely mysterious. In no way, furthermore, could he both identify and, more important, quantify (not necessarily in financial terms) what those costs might be. Professor K. William Kapp has demonstrated that the concept of social costs—which must be a synonym for Mikva's societal costs—is extremely complex, one not easily understood and less easily measured.[38]

On at least three scores, therefore, the Mikva opinion (and Judge Wright) can be faulted. I do not speak of the result, which I believe was correct, but of the explanation given. And I do not fault Mikva alone; others on the Court of Appeals used the same type of "reasoning." It is useful in this connection to contrast the two dissenting opinions, by Judges Malcolm Wilkey and Antonin Scalia, with Mikva's.

Wilkey acknowledged that the Supreme Court had not provided guidance "as to what conduct beyond traditional communicative activities such as marching and picketing may qualify as 'speech'," and then went on to emulate the Supreme Court (as discussed previously) in deciding matters not before the court. Asserting that the substantiality of the governmental interest "cannot be doubted," he concluded that if camping, whatever the purpose, were allowed in the public areas of Washington, "those parks would be overrun by campers during summer months." As with the Supreme Court in *Cooper* and *Miranda*, *Green* and *Roe* (see above), he made a mental leap from the specific facts of the *CCNV* case to the general facts of numerous campers despoiling parks. And as with the Supreme Court, he thereby rendered an advisory opinion even though it was not labeled as such. In theory and in practice, federal courts do not issue formal advisory opinions at the request of anyone, including the president and Congress. But the courts do so in a "backdoor" fashion when they see the facts of a given dispute having some sort of general application. That was what Wilkey did, and that, at least apparently, because of his concurring opinion, is what Judge Wright thought that Mikva did. Engaging in a great "either-or," Wilkey saw the problem as either allowing all camping (sleeping) or imposing a flat-out ban on sleeping. He had "no difficulty in sustaining this Park Service regulation permitting every type of communicative action, but drawing the line at 'camping,' i.e., actually occupying living accommodations in Lafayette Park 24 hours a day for days on end.'' He was willing to approve a lunchtime nap by someone in the park, but would not go the full mile and agree that people, lawfully in the park, could close their eyes at night and actually sleep.

Obviously, Mikva and Wilkey started from different premises and then reasoned their ways to opposite conclusions.[39] No better illustration of the myth of the rule of law can be found. Judge Scalia is no better. He believed that extending constitutional protection to affect actions "which happen to be conducted for the purpose of 'making a point' is to stretch the Constitution not only beyond its meaning but beyond reason, and beyond the capacity of the legal system to accommodate." He had no trouble in finding the NPS regulation valid, simply because he read its purpose as not that of suppressing communication. He then went on to say:

The effect of the rule I think to be the law may be to permit the prohibition of some expressive conduct that might be desirable. Perhaps symbolic campsites and symbolic fire bases are a good idea. But it is not the function of the Constitution to make such fine judgments; nor is it within the practical power of the courts to apply them. There is a gap between what the Constitution requires and what perfect governance might sometimes suggest, in the area of expression as in other fields.

Scalia concludes by maintaining that the majority makes the "great right of free speech" ridiculous and obnoxious.

That can hardly be correct. Nor was he correct in asserting that courts could not make "fine judgments." Judges do that routinely. No one, furthermore, was asking for "perfect governance," whatever that might mean. What Scalia and Wilkey would do is relegate CCNV to ineffectual modes of expression—something more than mere verbal speech, but something less than riveting the attention of the nation via the mass media upon the spectacle of people willing to sleep in tents during the dead of winter. Wilkey conceded that sleeping in tents in winter was "their most effective mode of expression," but he and Scalia (and the other dissenters) were willing to deny CCNV that way of making their point. CCNV well knew, and the judges must be considered to have known, that until the mass media, particularly television, focused on the protest, CCNV's message would have all of the impact of a snowflake floating down on the bosom of the mighty Potomac. Wilkey even conceded that the fundamental question was one of equality, and had the *chutzpah* to quote Anatole France's famous dictum: "The law in its majestic equality forbids the rich as well as the poor to sleep under bridges, to beg in the streets, and to steal bread." But he refused to confront and answer the question of how what he called the "most helpless members of our society" could make their views heard, and possibly heeded. Presumably, he and Scalia would not have permitted pouring tea into the sea or refusing to buy stamps as permissible means of expression by Americans 200 years ago; nor would they have allowed Gandhi to lead a boycott on buying salt as a means of protesting British rule in India. Theirs is a cavalier dismissal of the plight of the poor and downtrodden.

The various opinions in the *CCNV* case have been discussed at some length, even though Judge Wright did not author the opinion for the majority, for several reasons. First, Judge Mikva's opinion, written in standard first amendment language, does largely reflect Wright's views on freedom of expression. Second, the decision reveals how judges react differently to a rather simple factual situation—which means that it is not so much those facts nor law as it has been received and understood, as the personal philosophies of the different judges that are important. Third, Mikva seems to say, and Wright thus agrees, that what Wilkey called "the most helpless members" of society must be given a chance to express themselves meaningfully. If so, that is close to adherence to an affirmative dimension to the first amendment. Fourth, of larger general significance is the fact that each judge who wrote an opinion appeared to assume that the decision far transcended the immediate litigants. The court thus saw itself as a mini-"legislature," making decisions for litigants unknown and for generations yet unborn. In this, the judges resembled the Justices of the Supreme Court who at times, as has been mentioned, issue "backdoor" advisory opinions. This in itself is an interesting development: It is one thing for the Supreme Court to act "legislatively," to set norms of general applicability (although, even there, the practice is controversial); but it is quite another for a lower court to do so. The reach of the Supreme Court far exceeds that of the Court of Appeals of the District of Columbia; even though the latter set of judges may be the second most important court in the nation, its jurisdiction is limited (as are all other courts of appeals).

What the High Court began in *Cooper v. Aaron* (see Chapter 3) has therefore been extended at least to the Court of Appeals in Washington. That makes for real difficulties in deciding cases. If the judges on that court perceive their role as a legislative one, then they will be inclined to evaluate the facts of specific cases much differently from the way they would were they to confine their scrutiny solely to the litigants before the bar of the court. All that Judge Wright and colleagues were authorized to do, under the statutes and the Constitution, was to decide the immediate issue before them—and nothing more. Had they seen their duty in that way, it seems possible, although one cannot say for certain, that the case would have been summarily decided without the judges going through the lucubrations necessary to produce six different opinions. The point, I suppose, is this: The Court of Appeals, perhaps because it sits in Washington in the shadow of the Supreme Court, considers itself to be a *de facto* branch of the High

Court. But that, quite obviously, is not true. The *CCNV* case was emphatically not a sort of informal class action, in which the litigants sought to speak not only for themselves, but for all others similarly situated. Whatever may be the case for the Supreme Court, the writ of the Court of Appeals runs only to the parties before the bench. It has no power, although the judges apparently think (and act) otherwise, to issue general norms.

IV

J. Skelly Wright believes that political equality is the cornerstone of our democracy. That belief is based on a faith that in turn would have to be predicated upon certain assumptions about the nature of the American polity and the American experience. Wright agrees, in whole or part, with all except the penultimate assumption. They include:

—The United States is in fact a democracy
—Wise, or at least better, decisions will come from government if the channels of communication are unclogged
—People in general want to know, and have the capacity to learn, in sufficient detail the intricacies of proposed public policies
—The representatives of the people will both listen to and heed what the people say
—In a bureaucratized nation, secrecy is aberrational
—Government, and other groups wielding significant power, does not engage in propaganda designed to influence the popular mind
—More then formal equality is necessary, because equality before the law is inconsistent with unequal property rights (wealth)[40]

Except for the last, each of those assumptions is demonstrably faulty. It is important to understand why, and thus to understand that Wright, by publicly adhering to the final assumption, is in process of evolving a first amendment theory that goes beyond the simplisms of Justice Holmes. As recently as 1980, a prominent lawyer in the course of an encomium published about Judge Wright, stated that Wright has a "short and simple gospel, the faith that free speech means that speech shall be free."[41] If that was true in 1980, as perhaps it appeared to be from reading Wright's publications, then by 1982 he had begun to develop a much more sophisticated theory of the first amendment. In 1971, as the headnote to this chapter shows, Wright based his theory of free speech on the notion that people will indeed make proper choices if they have all the facts. The lawyer's tribute to Wright, mentioned above, calls this an example of "cockeyed optimism," a "fragment of the belief that evolution is ever upward, without retrograde mutation." "I do not know," the writer continued, "that Wright has ever dealt with Mill's observation of the 'idle sentimentality that truth, merely as truth, has any inherent power denied to error.' "

That judgment, whatever its validity in 1980, is overly harsh today. Indeed, as early as 1976, Judge Wright had begun to question Mill's "idle sentimentality," not expressly, to be sure, for he still adhered to the idea that a kind of community process lies at the heart of the first amendment—"a process wherein ideas and candidates prevail because of their inherent worth, not because prestigious or wealthy people line up in favor, and not because one side puts on a more elaborate show of support."[42] That statement, published in the *Yale Law Journal*, stoutly denied that "money is speech"—as Wright said the Supreme Court held in *Buckley v. Valeo.* The article is a turning point in Wright's thinking; for the first time he publicly began to state how economic inequalities polluted the electoral process. Those 1976 seeds of thought bore fruit in his 1982 article in the *Columbia Law Review.*

The same lawyer who could call Wright a "cockeyed optimist" in 1980 also concluded that he is pre-eminent among contemporary judges for his first amendment decisions; he "has seen farther, and covered more new territory, than any other legal professional of our time."

That's a large claim. Is it justified? Does Wright outshine Justice Hugo Black and William Douglas in furtherance of first amendment values? Has he done as much as Justice William Brennan? Has he outshone his colleague, Judge David Bazelon? Comparisons, we are told, are odious, and that they are. Furthermore, I know of no way by which to measure comparatively Skelly Wright's contributions to those of other judges. What can be said is this:

—He has done as much as any other judge to enhance first amendment values
—However, no truly consistent thread is discernible, one that ties together in a unifying theory his views on the first amendment
—He has not fully given up on his belief in Holmes's simplisms
—He candidly acknowledges, as has been mentioned before, that:
  • "If I want to do something, I can find a way to do it"
  • "My emotional reactions are visceral, but they are checked against approved principles"
  •"I can always find a way to go"

Indeed he can.

Consider some of his best-known opinions. In *Capital Broadcasting Co. v. Mitchell* (1971),[43] the court majority, against a Wright dissent, upheld a statute that prohibited cigarette advertising on the air. Wright called the cigarette companies "seductive merchants of death," but concluded that the first amendment "does not protect only speech that is healthy or harmless." The case involved the so-called commercial speech doctrine. Wright maintained that "when commercial speech has involved matters of public controversy, or artistic expression, or deeply held personal beliefs, the courts have not hesitated to accord it full first amendment protection." Early Supreme Court decisions (dating from 1942) had denied constitutional protection to commercial speech—that uttered for the purpose of furthering commercial interests as distinguished from the speech of citizen critics of government. Since 1942 that form of speech has received greater protection,[44] although the Supreme Court has not gone so far as to embrace Wright's views in *Capital Broadcasting*. The Justices still consider electronic advertising to be different from that appearing in the print media.

Judge Wright's views about constitutionally protected cigarette advertising should be compared with his opinion in *Warner-Lambert Co. v. Federal Trade Commission* (1977),[45] in which he held that the FTC could prohibit the makers of Listerine from asserting medicinal values of a product that was in fact not very beneficial. Here he saw the issue as one of false and misleading advertising. He went even further and upheld a FTC requirement that the company would have to publish corrective advertising. According to Wright, the governmental interest in prevention of consumer deception necessitated a corrective remedy, because, absent such a correction, previously deceived consumers would continue to use Listerine to cure colds and sore throats.

Are the two Wright decisions consistent? On the one hand, he would allow an admittedly harmful product to be advertised; but on the other, he would not only prohibit advertising of a harmless but not very helpful product, but would require corrective advertising in future appeals to the public. There is an apparent inconsistency, but the decisions can be reconciled when viewed as examples of Judge Wright's deep-felt fear of corporate power. Although neither decision expressly speaks in those terms, it is of interest to note that in the *Mitchell* case the court majority, against Wright's dissent, actually upheld what the tobacco companies wanted—the elimination of the requirement, sustained in *Banzhaf v. Federal Communications Commission* (1968),[46] that the FCC's "fairness doctrine" required the electronic media to "present a fair number of anti-smoking messages." The success of those ads, said Wright, "frightened the cigarette industry into calling on Congress to silence the debate." (Congress complaisantly did so—and the court majority went along.) Wright, thus, was more interested in curbing excess corporate power (as he saw it) than in furthering the first amendment. He cut through the legalisms to show what really was at stake. I have already noted his distrust of corporate power, as revealed in his law journal articles. In effect, he said in *Mitchell* that silencing the national debate (on radio and television) about smoking resulted in promotion of more smoking. He, thus, was willing to authorize more cigarette advertising by "seductive merchants of death." Seen that way, his Listerine opinion is consistent. It, too, dealt with corporate power, and the relative impotence of the individual in a bureaucratized nation.

It is this sensitivity to the excesses of corporate power that makes Judge Wright, if not unique among federal judges, then certainly a rarity. It truly sets him apart from the others on the federal bench, those who, speaking generally, are all too willing to rule in favor of the instruments of corporate capitalism. In this respect, today's federal judges are little different from those of the past, those who protected property throughout American history through use of such doctrines as "vested rights" and "substantive due process." We will see in Chapter 8 that Skelly Wright carries his fear and dislike of corporate power into the criminal law area. Although not minimizing the nature of consequences of predatory crime, he is convinced that Americans suffer more from "white collar"—corporate—crime, even though the impact is usually indirect.

In the Listerine case, Judge Wright saw the facts as verging on misrepresentation—perhaps actual misrepresentation—by the company. He views such behavior with particular repugnance. Consider, in this respect, *Brandywine Main-Line Radio, Inc. v. Federal Communications Commission* (1972),[47] in which he approved denial of renewal of a radio license to a fundamentalist preacher (Carl McIntire) on the grounds of misrepresentation. That case is one of the few times that he differed from Judge David Bazelon, who would have granted the renewal on first amendment grounds. *Brandywine* should be compared to *Rodriguez v. Seamans* (1972),[48] in which Wright dissented from a majority holding that a false statement on an official form concerning Communist affiliations should subject a federal employee to discharge. The employee, said Wright, "used the only means available to protect himself against an unconstitutional exercise of government power." He maintained that government had no "need to know" in the first place, and, therefore, it had no "constitutionally legitimate interest in a correct answer." Acknowledging that Rodriquez would have been better advised to challenge the questions asked him and stand on his constitutional rights, Wright went on to say: "We need a Constitution because there are . . . ordinary people in this country who, while more easily intimidated [than the courageous], are still entitled to political freedom." That shows a deep concern for the lone individual, the relatively powerless person who is confronted by a massive federal bureaucracy. But it also shows that misrepresentation—falsehood—does invoke Wright's displeasure. The *Rodriguez* opinion of Judge Wright should also be compared to the *Himmaugh* case that he prosecuted as United States Attorney in New Orleans. In *Himmaugh*, he came down hard upon a false statement about Communist affiliations.

Skelly Wright's concern for the poor and powerless may be seen in *Edwards v. Habib* (1968),[49] in which he found a constitutional basis for protecting a tenant who had been evicted for reporting housing code violations—even though the District of Columbia law allowed evictions of month-to-month tenants "for any reason or no reason at all." No other member of the panel agreed with what Judge Carl McGowan called Wright's "constitutional speculations"; Wright, however, prevailed as a matter of statutory construction. Displaying innovation in writing an opinion, Wright held that for the D.C. courts to favor the landlord would not only violate the first amendment, but also the equal protection clause (again, Wright's concern for equality). He rhetorically asked: May a court "consistently with the Constitution prefer the interests of an absentee landlord in evicting a tenant solely because she has reported violations of the housing code to those of a tenant in improving her housing by resort to her rights to petition the government and to report violations of laws designed for her protection?" He went on to say that it would be both unreasonable and unconstitutional to hold for the landlord in such circumstances. Yes, indeed, Wright can "always find a way to go" if he wants to do something. He views the Constitution not as a mere lawyers' document, but as a charter for the achievement of social justice.

Edwards, and perhaps *Rodriguez*, illustrates an important point. For a variety of reasons, most people for most of the time do not act to exercise their rights. (That is so despite the well-known explosion of litigation in recent years.) Whether it is for lack of knowledge, courage, money, determination, hope, faith, or whatever, most persons are legally passive and quiescent. Furthermore, the degree of legal activity or efficacy seems to be directly related to socioeconomic class. The rich and the affluent are much more apt to use the courts; and when they do, they are much more likely to prevail. Therefore, it seems all the more important that, when dealing with "ordinary" or "poor" persons, as in *Rodriguez* and *Edwards*, efforts be made to minimize the costs or obstacles associated with the exercise of legal rights. This Judge Wright strives to do. Retaliation of one kind or another by the opposing side is a potent factor in intimidating many of the poor and the powerless from exercising their rights. It is in this sense that Wright's opinions in *Edwards* and *Rodriguez* are a valiant, if futile in the sense of being alone in his views, effort to construe constitutional protections broadly so as to minimize those retaliations. That is no small matter. It is further evidence that he is a *rara avis* among the judiciary, an unusual and extraordinary person with an instinct for "goodness"—apparently his word for social justice—and incorporating it into the Constitution.

That observation may be verified by two cases that arose out of the public controversy over the Vietnam "war": *Women's Strike for Peace v. Morton* (1972)[50] and *Business Executives Move for Vietnam Peace v. Federal Communications Commission* (1971).[51] In the former, an antiwar group (WSP) wanted to erect a temporary shelter and display it on the Ellipse—federally owned property near the White House—protesting the war. A panel of three judges all agreed that the permit should be granted, but could not agree on the reasons. Wright's opinion is a direct predecessor to his views, discussed above, in the *CCNV* case. Noting that the Ellipse was being used with government permission for an annual Christmas pageant, he maintained that the "First Amendment was not designed to protect the voice of government or government-approved speech. The First Amendment in this country protects the voice of the people even against government." So it does, and it is relevant to wonder why that simple proposition was not so self-evident as not to require restatement. In a long opinion, Wright went on to say that "we pay a price for the right to speak—a price which can be measured in the hard currency of rage, instability and inconvenience. But the wisest men are sometimes those who gladly pay the piper. The full cost of repression and uniformity would be far greater and, ultimately, would be more than any of us would like to bear." Again, that is self-evident; and the mystery is why Judges Harold Leventhal and Roger Robb, also on the panel, did not fully agree with such standard constitutional argumentation. They found the denial of a permit discriminatory and refused to follow Wright into the first amendment battleground. Wright in the *WSP* case, furthermore, speaks in terms of an affirmative obligation on government to make public lands available for freedom of expression purposes: "The parties . . . join hands on the extent to which the government is obligated to turn over use of public park land to private parties seeking to engage in First Amendment conduct." And further: "A right of access to public places for expression of views" is "part of our constitutional jurisprudence."

Since a right in its legal sense carries with it, under standard legal theory, a correlative duty on someone to fulfill that right—in other words, rights and duties are two sides of the same medal—no large mental leap is required to say that Wright in the *WSP* case was in fact asserting that government had a constitutional duty to make public places available for people to express their views. I have noted above that recognition of such a duty is the direction in which first amendment theory is heading. Judge Wright clearly is in the vanguard of judicial thought about the nature of freedom of expression under the Constitution.

The *Business Executives* case differs from *WSP*. A group that wished to buy air time to speak on controversial issues was denied its request by the FCC. The group appealed to Judge Wright's court, which held that a flat ban on paid public issue announcements by television and radio licensees violated the first amendment. Wright wrote the opinion for the court, saying that such a ban could not be justified when other paid announcements (commercials) were being accepted. He saw the case as "one of fundamental importance: it concerns the people's right to engage in and to hear vigorous public debate on the broadcast media." Wright was careful to acknowledge the licensee's right to exercise control and judgment of the medium. "All we do is forbid an extreme form of control which totally excludes controversial public debate from broadcast advertising time." He concluded:

In the end, it may unsettle some of us to see an antiwar message or a political party message in the accustomed place of a soap or beer commerical. But we must not equate what is habitual with what is right—or what is constitutional. A society already so saturated with commercialism can well afford another outlet for speech on public issues. All that we may lose is some of our apathy. For as the Supreme Court has said, a function of free speech under our system of government is to invite dispute. It may indeed serve its high purpose when it induces a condition of unrest, creates dissatisfaction with conditions as they are, or even stirs people to anger.

That is a latter-day affirmation of the Holmesian theory of expression. It is a faith by which Skelly Wright lives and decides.

To Wright, all of the presumptions "must run in favor of free speech, not against it"—thus making it extremely difficult for suppressions of expression to survive. His language in the *Pentagon Papers Case* (1971), in which he dissented from a three-judge panel's decision to permit an injunction against publication of the papers "for the shortest possible period" to let the government substantiate its position that the papers should not be published, shows the passion with which he views the first amendment:

This is a sad day for America. Today, for the first time in the two hundred years of our history, the executive department has succeeded in stopping the presses. It has enlisted the judiciary in the suppression of our most precious freedom. As if the long and sordid war in Southeast Asia had not already done enough harm to our people, it now is used to cut out the heart of our free institutions and system of government. I decline to follow my colleagues down this road and I must forcefully state my dissent.[52]

Wright's views, of course, ultimately prevailed in the Supreme Court, but the victory there was far from complete.

V

This has been an impressionistic survey of Judge Wright and freedom of expression. I have discussed only a handful of the many opinions he has written and the even greater number of decisions in which he has participated. Enough has been shown to reveal his basic pattern: Freedom of expression means that expression should be free. He is a first amendment purist. As with all of his other decisions, he accords great care and attention to his opinions. In this area, he is much more the innovator than he was in racial segregation issues—where he had to apply the mandate of the Supreme Court as best he could to a tumultuous New Orleans. In the first amendment area, he does not hesitate to advance into legal *terra incognita*. Few other judges follow him, but that does not bother him; he is accustomed to being the sole advocate of what he believes the Constitution requires. One writer has described him in this way:

One follows this lonely scholar in his journey with the respect and awe Keats felt in considering Chapman's Homer:

> Then I felt like some watcher of the skies
> When a new planet swims into his ken;
> Or like stout Cortez when with eagle eyes
> He star'd at the Pacific—and all his men
> Look'd at each other with a wild surmise—
> Silent, upon a peak in Darien.[53]

That is really not quite correct: Skelly Wright is less the scholar than the explorer of new reaches of constitutionalism, including freedom of expression. He sees the Constitution as a means by which people, given the chance, can help create a better society. His is a fervent belief that the truth can make us free. As such, he stands in direct line with Justice Louis Brandeis, who wrote in 1927:

Those who won our independence believed that the final end of the state was to make men free to develop their faculties: and that in its government the deliberative forces should prevail over the arbitrary. *They valued liberty both as an end and as a means.* . . . They recognized the risks to which all human institutions are subject. But they knew that order cannot be secured merely through fear of punishment for its infraction. . . . Believing in the power of reason as applied through public discussion, they eschewed silence coerced by law. (Emphasis added.)[54]

Judge Wright would agree with that statement. And he also would agree with Brandeis in the latter's fear of corporate power. Skelly Wright is the Brandeis of the present day.

There are several reasons for calling Wright the modern successor to Brandeis. Both exemplify the following: carefully crafted and structured opinions; a willingness to buck the tides of the day; a recognition of the realities of private power in the polity; the respect and admiration (though perhaps grudging at times) of their peers; a belief in the validity of the Holmesian theory of freedom of expression; cognizance of the fact that judges at times must act in a "political " way (as Wright did in New Orleans); a fierce honesty and integrity; a basic decency toward others; and belief systems that seem to be characteristic of the Progressive Age. There are, indeed, many resemblances between the Kentuckian who became a wealthy Bostonian who graced the Supreme Court for many years and the far-from-wealthy Southerner who should have been named to the High Court. I do not, of course, suggest that the parallel is exact—but it is close enough to merit consideration. Wright's conscious role model, however, likely was his good friend, Justice Hugo Black of the Supreme Court; and certainly their backgrounds and careers are in many respects similar. Nevertheless, Skelly Wright is as much a successor to Louis Dembitz Brandeis as he is to Hugo Lafayette Black.

7

Judge Wright and
Personal Autonomy

*A life hung in the balance. There was no time for research and
reflection. Death could have mooted the cause in a matter of minutes, if
action were not taken to preserve the status quo. To refuse to act, only
to find later that the law required action, was a risk I was unwilling to
accept. I determined to act on the side of life.*

—J. Skelly Wright (1964)[1]

I

Of all the problems of law and of constitutionalism, none is quite so
complex, so difficult for judges to resolve, as that of the sovereignty of the
self—the idea of personal autonomy. The basic question is relatively easy to
explicate: To what extent can the state, speaking for the collectivity called
society, intervene so as to limit a person's capacity to govern himself? Are
there moral boundaries that protect the self from intrusion? People are not
Robinson Crusoes; they are units of society, receiving protection from and
owing duties to society. Are there correlative duties that society owes to the
individual? Behind those simple questions are concepts and principles that
cut to the core of American constitutionalism.

Instances are easily identified where the state has long had, and continues
to have, an overriding interest before which the person—the self—must give
way. Protection of children and of those considered to be mental defectives
comes to mind. The state routinely intrudes upon a person's autonomy
when antisocial acts (crimes) are committed; even suicide has been made a
crime in several states. Despite the constitutional prohibition against
involuntary servitude, jury duty is compulsory, and men can be forced to
fight, and even to die, for their country. Motorcyclists can be required to
wear protective helmets, and seatbelts in automobiles probably could be
made compulsory. One's luggage can be searched before boarding an
airplane; when a person returns from abroad, not only his luggage, but his
body can be searched—all without a warrant. Use and sale of some drugs is
punishable. To top it off, government may, if it wishes, sterilize alleged

mental defectives against their will in order to protect "society"—a major extension of the analogous right of the state to require vaccination against contagious diseases.

This list does not exhaust the category of permissible state interventions into the domain of the sovereign self. The list is lengthy, but it is not endless. At some point, the self may invoke rights of self-determination and autonomy that the state, under the Constitution, must recognize and upon which it may not intrude. The line between what the state can do and what it cannot do is by no means bright and sharp. Two separate categories are identifiable. On the one hand, there are the actions of the National Security State (see Chapter 5), some of which impinge upon personal liberties, as well as what will later be called the activities of the paternalistic state. This category exalts either the societal good (national security), or the good of the individual over what that person considers to be his right. On the other hand, there are a growing number of specific actions or desires of the self that are receiving constitutional protection—often under the rubric of the right to privacy. One is the right of adults in command of their faculties to refuse medical treatment. This chapter is concerned with one of Judge Skelly Wright's most controversial decisions, *Application of the President and Directors of Georgetown College, Inc., A Body Corporate* (1963).[2] None of Wright's hundreds of decisions, many of which have been hotly disputed, has so perturbed some of the professoriate as his authorizing Georgetown Hospital to administer a Jehovah's Witness blood transfusions against her expressed will. Twenty years later, he still draws sharp criticism from those who believe that he exceeded the bounds of judicial propriety and also unduly intruded upon the patient's self. Why that is so is the burden of this chapter. I have concluded that the case is a close one, but that the critics are basically wrong. The problem, however, is far from an easy one.

I begin with a general examination of the concept of personal autonomy, as a means of providing a background for the ruling. "Personal autonomy involves," Professor Joel Feinberg observes, "the idea of having a domain or territory to which the self is sovereign," much like the autonomous nation-state.[3] Unlike that of the state, however, the boundaries of the sovereignty of the self are far from clear. I have listed above some interventions into self-sovereignty that are lawful and generally accepted. The question is when one may cry *haro*! and compel the state—paradoxically using an organ of the state, the judiciary, for that purpose—to stop and not proceed further. (*Haro*! was a cry used in medieval Europe, even against the sovereign, of persons who believed they had been wronged by the state.) Says Feinberg: "We do speak of an inviolable right which is infringed whenever another person inflicts a harmful or offensive contact on one's body without one's consent—an unwanted caress, a slap, a punch in the nose, *a surgical operation*, or even a threatening move that provides the reasonable apprehension of such contacts." (Emphasis added.) He further says, in language relevant here, "my bodily integrity [is] violated by a surgical operation ('invasion') imposed on me against my will."[4]

Personal autonomy as self-sovereignty means, to use the medical example, that one cannot be treated in certain ways against one's will. (But, as the vaccination and sterilization examples noted above reveal, personal autonomy in medical matters is not an absolute.) More, the consent to treatment must be voluntarily given, with full cognizance of the relevant facts. Unless and until one is an actual danger to someone else, or intrudes unduly upon the rights of others, the self is sovereign. The most fundamental of all autonomous rights is the right to determine how one is to live one's life. "No man is an island, entire of itself," but some activities of persons indeed are "islands"—and must be if the self is to be protected. At the same time, since the person—the self—lives in a community, there are certain obligations owed to the collectivity.[5]

Legal paternalism is the polar opposite of personal autonomy—the idea that it is morally legitimate for the state to intervene upon a person's bodily integrity solely to prevent that person from harming or risking harm to himself. No third party interests need be involved. Under paternalism, a person's *right* is subordinated by the state to what the state perceives to be the person's own *good*. That theory underlies, for example, legislation mandating helmets for motorcyclists. Rather like a parent telling a child to take medicine because "it is good for you," the state orders the motorcyclist to wear a helmet. Obviously, this order impinges upon the cyclist's autonomy. The meaning, of course, is that paternalism at times outweighs personal autonomy in the constitutional order. John Stuart Mill, in *On Liberty*, argued against such a notion. He believed that even if a wholly nondespotic state were to impose its view of an adult's own good on that adult, it would almost certainly be self-defeating. To Mill, an adult's own good is "best provided for by allowing him to take his own means of pursuing it."[6] There is still another, and perhaps better, way of considering the right-good dichotomy: Even if a person is not fully able to make decisions to achieve his own good, the state should not intrude simply because self-autonomy is—at least, may be—far more important to the person than his own good (his personal well-being). "The life that a person threatens by his own rashness is after all *his* life; it *belongs* to him and to no one else. For that reason alone, he must be the one to decide—for better or worse—what is to be done with it in that private realm where the interests of others are not directly involved."[7] According to that view, legal paternalism is rejected. A person choosing an alternative that may in fact be bad for him does not do it because he believes that, ultimately, the consequence will be bad. Rather, the choice is made because other factors outweigh even the known bad consequences that may flow from a given decision. (But how many "private realms" exist in fact? Everyone intersects, more or less directly, with others.)

The Supreme Court has located somewhat in the spirit of the Bill of Rights (and the fourteenth amendment) a moral and, thus, a legal right to privacy. Feinberg maintains that if privacy means anything in a constitutional sense, and insofar as philosophers are concerned, it means personal autonomy or self-determination. The latter-day discovery by the Justices of a constitutional right to privacy, of course, adds to the express provisions of the Constitution. It is a prime example of judicial constitution-making abhorred by some and applauded by others. (Judge Wright's judicial role model, Justice Hugo Black, adamantly refused to follow his colleagues in that venture of informal amendment of the fundamental law.)

Privacy has no precise constitutional boundaries. As with other constitutional precepts, such as due process of law and equal protection of the laws (both of which are express commands of the fundamental law), privacy can only be identified by discrete examples of whether given governmental conduct falls within or without its legal parameters. Thus, today we know that privacy extends to the intimacies of the marital relation; to decisions about whom to marry; family planning (i.e., contraception and abortion); heterosexual conduct generally; to types of family living; to what Professor Kenneth Karst has called "the right of intimate association"; and to the use of pornography in one's home. Outside of the bounds of privacy, by either Supreme Court decree or refusal of the Court to rule, are homosexual relations, even among consenting adults; certain types of drug-taking, even in one's home; not voluntarily watching obscene movies in places of public accommodation; and, as seen in Chapter 5, interception of one's overseas messages for purported national security reasons. The Supreme Court has yet to recognize a constitutional right of a competent adult to refuse medical treatment, although other courts, particularly at the state level, have done so. "From the first," Professor Thomas C. Grey (a former law clerk of Judge Wright) maintains, "the [Supreme] Court has suggested to philosophically minded commentators the possible elevation to constitutional status of Mill's principle of liberty."[8] The Justices, however, have not fulfilled the original promise. They still struggle with the metes and bounds of the concept of privacy. Perhaps this is because, as Professor Stuart Scheingold has asserted, law has two faces. First, there are the obvious familiar, formal rules and institutions. But second, there is the "ideological" existence of the law, which leads to what Scheingold calls "the myth of rights," a myth that leads Americans to believe that law and legal processes play a significant *independent* role in America.[9] That, however, is simply not true. Law and politics are closely interconnected, with politics being dominant. Rights such as privacy receive recognition when it is politically feasible to do so. All of the activities that have been judicially drawn within the ambit of constitutional privacy are those that the dominant political coalition considers desirable. So, too, for actions outside of protection of privacy: They are those that the governing elites simply consider not useful to recognize.

Privacy, moreover, as personal autonomy has had to travel piggyback on express constitutional terms, such as due process of law and, of greater present importance, the free exercise of religion; or has been found by some Justices to be a "penumbral" right lurking somewhere in the spirit of the Bill of Rights. (After two centuries of operation, federal judges are still reluctant to clothe their opinions in anything other than language familiar to lawyers. Hence, the usual practice of tying privacy to an express constitutional term, even though all knowledgeable observers know that, in fact, the judges are creating the right out of the whole cloth.) Privacy is really one of the great silences of the fundamental law, created in recent years, perhaps as a reaction to the growth of a bureaucratized society. As with all such rights, it has both a *manifest* and a *latent* function—manifest in the protection given to the individual and his self-sovereignty, latent in that it gives the *appearance* of social justice—something quite important in itself—while simultaneously helping to socialize the people by leading them to believe not only that ours is a government of laws rather than of men, but that their privacy is in fact protected. (The cruel fact is that, as a lawyer-director of a large West Coast bank once said, "privacy is dead in America."[10])

When privacy piggybacks on the free-exercise-of-religion clause of the first amendment, as was true in the *Georgetown Hospital Case*, it is important to recognize that the amendment does not mean what it says. First, it does not mean that "Congress shall make no law . . prohibiting the free exercise" of religion; that really means that Congress and the states may make *some* laws about the exercise of religion. Second, a distinction has long been made between religious *beliefs*, which are protected almost absolutely, and religious *practices*, which may be regulated. Thus it is that the Supreme Court considers polygamy to be a practice of religion and punishable criminally, as can the handling of poisonous snakes; furthermore, everyone can be vaccinated to prevent the spread of disease. All of that is true even though in each instance some sect claims the practice to be a tenet—a belief—of its religion. Mill's liberty does not extend that far, although it is difficult to perceive how anyone is harmed by, say, a Mormon male who wishes to marry several women at the same time. How, for example, can it be rationally said that multiple wives are forbidden, and an argument that "eating blood" by a Jehovah's Witness, even though death may occur because of a refusal to receive a blood transfusion, is generally protected? The state tells the Mormon that if he wishes plural wives, he must marry them in succession—carefully getting a divorce before marrying the next one—but often tells the Jehovah's Witness that her life is her own to sacrifice.

II

We come, thus, to Judge Wright's decision in the *Georgetown Hospital Case*, the facts of which will help flesh out some of the terse abstractions set forth above. The questions Wright faced were multiple: informed consent in the doctor-patient relationship; the right of physicians to invoke the authority of the state when a person refuses treatment; whether religious freedom extends to refusal of medical treatment; whether a person asserting religious freedoms owes a concomitant, and perhaps overriding, obligation to an infant child; whether the person's privacy would be invaded by a court-ordered blood transfusion; and whether, in the first place, the case was suitable for judicial intervention. Moreover, precisely what law was Judge Wright to apply in the case, if he heeded or rejected the patient's wishes?

The episode began for Judge Wright when Edward Bennett Williams, a well-known lawyer, rushed unannounced into Wright's office at 4:00 P.M. on September 17, 1963. Williams was seeking judicial permission for the hospital to administer blood transfusions to an emergency patient, Mrs. Jessie Jones. Williams had first gone to District Judge Edward Tamm with his application, but was summarily turned down. He therefore had to know that he was doing something extraordinary in requesting that Judge Wright hear and decide the case. The document Williams presented to Wright read:

In re: Application of the President and Directors of Georgetown College, Inc., a
    Body Corporate

This cause having come on to be heard upon application of The President and Directors of Georgetown College, Inc., a body corporate, owning and operating Georgetown University Hospital, and it being represented by counsel for the applicant that a Mrs. Jesse [*sic*] E. Jones is presently a patient at Georgetown University Hospital and that she is in extremis and it being further represented that the physician in attendance, the chief resident at Georgetown University Hospital, Edwin Westura, is of the opinion that blood transfusions are necessary immediately in order to save her life and it being further represented by the applicant that consent to the administration thereof can be obtained neither from the patient nor her husband: it is therefore

Ordered that the applicant acting through its duly accredited and licensed physicians in attendance may administer such transfusions as are in the opinion of the physicians in attendance necessary to save her life.[11]

One hour and twenty minutes later, at 5:20 P.M., Judge Wright signed the order in Mrs. Jones's hospital room, he having gone there with Williams and Wright's law clerk. In eighty minutes, he had listened to Williams, telephoned the hospital, motored several miles to the hospital, conferred with both Mr. and Mrs. Jones as well as the hospital staff, and made his decision. Wright's memorandum order reads:

The applicant having appeared before me for the issuance of a writ permitting the applicant to administer such transfusions as are in the opinion of the physicians in attendance necessary to save the life of Mrs. Jesse [*sic*] E. Jones and it appearing that on September 17, 1963, the District Court denied such application; and a hearing having been conducted before me at which all the interested parties were present and upon due consideration had thereon, I signed, pursuant to the provisions of Section 1651, Title 28, United States Code, the attached order granting such relief which counsel had presented to the District Court Judge and which had been denied by him, is it therefore

Ordered that the Clerk of this court is hereby directed to file this memorandum order and attachment.[12]

Enveloped in those two brief documents is one of the great dramas of Skelly Wright's career. Whether he was wrong is the queston. To answer it, one must know the facts of the entire episode.

Mrs. Jessie Jones had been taken to the hospital by her husband for emergency care, "having lost," Wright wrote, "two-thirds of her body's blood from a ruptured ulcer." She had no personal physician. She was 25 years old, the mother of a seven-month-old child, and she and her husband were Jehovah's Witnesses. That sect's teachings prohibit "eating" blood, basing its interpretation upon the Bible. In *Leviticus 17:10*, it is said: "I [the Lord] shall certainly set my face against the soul that is eating the blood, and I shall indeed cut him off from his people"; and *Leviticus 17:14* reads: "For the soul of every sort of flesh is its blood by the soul of it. Consequently, I say to the sons of Israel: 'You must not eat the blood of any sort of flesh, because the soul of every sort of flesh is its blood. Anyone eating it will be cut off'." Mrs. Jones refused to permit transfusions, even though the doctors told her that she would die without them. The doctors also argued that a transfusion was different from "eating" blood. To no avail. Death without the injection of blood was imminent, at least in the opinion of the doctors; the hospital retained Williams to get the permission of the state to transfuse. They and Williams simply believed that, whatever rights Mrs. Jones had, they knew what was good for her—and were determined to make their will prevail. When Judge Tamm denied the application, Wright was the only Court of Appeals judge in the courthouse (the court was not then in session). Two other judges were unavailable.

After listening to Williams's oral request, and reading the application, Wright telephoned the hospital, which confirmed Williams's representations. Why did he hear Williams out and then proceed on the course that he did, even knowing that Judge Tamm had summarily denied the application? His answer, given in 1983, is straight and simple: "Because there was an emergency."[13]

Judge Wright then went to the hospital, where he spoke to Mr. Jones, who told him that because of religious convictions he would not approve the transfusions. Jones, however, told Wright that if the court ordered a transfusion, the responsibility was not his. He also said that Mrs. Jones was the fervent believer in the tenets of the sect; and that she had gotten him to join it. Wright advised Jones to obtain a lawyer. Jones then telephoned members of his sect, only to return a few minutes later to tell Wright that he did not want counsel. The case thus devolved down to a desperately ill Mrs. Jones versus the hospital; Mr. Jones was, for all practical purposes, a mere spectator.

After conferring with several doctors, all of whom asserted that Mrs. Jones would die without a transfusion and that she had only a 50 percent chance of living with one, Judge Wright then went to Mrs. Jones's bedside. He tried to speak to her, telling her what the doctors had said. Her only audible statement was: "Against my will." Wright interpreted this as meaning that if the court ordered a transfusion, the responsibility would not be hers. Five months later, he wrote in his opinion filed in February 1964:

I was reluctant to press her because of the seriousness of her condition and because I felt that to suggest repeatedly the imminence of death without blood might place a strain on her religious convictions. I asked her if she would oppose the blood transfusion if the court allowed it. She indicated, as best as I could make out, that it would not then be her responsibility.[14]

Judge Wright believed that it was "obvious that the woman was not in a mental condition to make a decision."[15]

He then went outside Mrs. Jones's room, where the doctors and Father Bunn, the president of Georgetown, were trying without success to get Mr. Jones's approval. Wright would have accepted (gladly) Mr. Jones's consent to the transfusions, but would not take his disapproval. He thereupon "signed the order allowing the hospital to administer such transfusions as the doctors should determine were necessary to save her life." So Mrs. Jones was transfused—and lived. Less then a month later, she filed a petition for rehearing before the entire court. She wanted Wright's decision overruled as a matter of law. She could not get justice, as she understood justice, but wanted official vindication of her position. The petition was denied. She then sought review by the Supreme Court, and was again denied.

Several observations are relevant about Judge Wright's action. First, he took the doctors' opinion at face value, without any apparent attempt to question them or to get another opinion. Next, he himself decided that Mrs. Jones was not mentally able to make a decision, although there can be no question that she had made her wishes known before Wright's arrival. Her subsequent efforts to get his decision overturned evidence her dislike of his decision. This, then, appears to be a clear instance of an unwanted intrusion, authorized by the state, into the self-sovereignty of a person. Was it morally and constitutionally proper for Judge Wright to decide as he did?

The question asks much. My analysis begins with a quotation from a heretofore unpublished memorandum signed by Judge Wright two days after the transfusions were authorized:

> Mrs. Jones had been brought to the Hospital for emergency care, having lost two-thirds of her body's blood supply from a ruptured ulcer. She had no personal physician. She relied solely on the Hospital staff. She was a total Hospital responsibility. When death without blood became imminent, the Hospital was faced with the choice of turning the patient out of the Hospital for failure to accept medical treatment, which of course was impossible because of her condition, letting her die in bed, with whatever responsibility that would entail, or administering the blood. In their dilemma the Hospital authorities sought the advise of their counsel, who applied to the court in the name of the Hospital for permission to administer the blood. This court at the time of the application was unaware of any precise legal precedent for its action. It was advised of similar cases respecting children. But here the patient was a 25-year-old adult. Because of the demonstrated imminence of death from loss of blood, this court decided to sign the order to save the patient's life, in the event that subsequent research supported its authority to do so. The court was also comforted by the apparent assurance from the patient herself as well as from the husband that if the court undertook the responsibility for authorizing the transfusion, they themselves would not be in violation of their religious beliefs.

> /s/ *J. Skelly Wright*
> UNITED STATES CIRCUIT JUDGE

September 19, 1963[16]

Twenty years later, Judge Wright said, when asked about the decision, that his was an "instinctive reaction," and the "chances are that several factors went into the decision."[17]

When in 1964 he wrote an opinion explaining and justifying his decision, he gave several reasons for it. After noting that Mrs. Jones was voluntarily in the hospital, he analogized her condition to sick children, saying that "because Mrs. Jones was *in extremis* and hardly *compos mentis* at the time in question, she was as little able to decide for herself as any child would be." He further maintained that were she to die after refusing treatment, it would be tantamount to a voluntary abandonment of her infant child. "The patient," he said, "had a responsibility to care for her infant. Thus the people had an interest in preserving the life of the mother." Moreover, he dismissed the argument that Mrs. Jones had a right to die in defense of her religious beliefs—that is, to commit suicide—in two ways. First, Wright said, her voluntary presence in the hospital testified to her desire to live; death, rather than being "a religiously-commanded goal, [was] an unwanted side effect of a religious scruple." A Jehovah's Witness was not the same as a Buddhist monk voluntarily immolating himself by fire in furtherance of his religious beliefs. Second, the hospital might have been either civilly or criminally liable had it stood aside and not done everything possible to save her life. Convinced that Mrs. Jones's life "hung in the balance," and with no time for "research and reflection," Judge Wright chose life.[18]

It was Judge Wright acting as a Good Samaritan. He would not—he could not—turn aside and allow a young woman to die. With his characteristic honesty and total unwillingness to dredge up reasons that might help make his decision more palatable to his critics, he forthrightly admits that it was instinctively made and that it is "hard to pinpoint reasons for making the decision." His 1964 opinion failed to convince some of his colleagues on the Court of Appeals. Judge Wilbur Miller said in dissent that there was really no case—in legal parlance, no justiciable controversy—before Judge Wright. There were no adverse parties, and no one argued for the patient. Conceding that Wright was "impelled by humanitarian impulses and doubtless was himself under considerable strain," Miller concluded that he "should not have been asked to act in the circumstances." That, however, was less an argument against Wright—after all, he had been asked to act—than against the hospital authorities and their attorney.

Judge Warren Burger (now Chief Justice Burger) raised a second objection:

This episode presents on the one hand an example of a grave dilemma which confronts those who engage in the healing arts and on the other hand some very basic and fundamental issues on the nature and scope of the judicial power. We can sympathize with the one but we cannot safely or appropriately temporize with the other. . . .

Since it is not disputed that the patient and her husband volunteered to sign a waiver to relieve the hospital of any liability for the consequences of failure to effect a transfusion, any claim to a protected right in the economic sphere would appear to be unsupportable.

In short, said Burger, some matters are beyond the judicial power; and contrary to Wright, the hospital would not have been liable for not transfusing Mrs. Jones. He quoted Justice Louis Brandeis's well-known statement about "the right to be let alone—the most comprehensive of rights and the right most valued by civilized man." He asserted that judges are not knights errant, roaming at will in pursuit of their own ideals of beauty or goodness.

III

Judge Wright's decision and opinion may be evaluated in many ways. One is to follow Judges Miller and Burger and view the problem as mainly one of legalisms. The late Professor Alexander Bickel, Wright's most formidable academic critic, was of the same mind. As Professor Thomas Grey has written, his professors at the Yale Law School often ridiculed Wright:

My Yale professors warned me about Judge Wright before I went to work for him in 1968. I remember best the late Alexander Bickel's portrayal. In one case, the Judge had held a hearing at a patient's bedside on a hospital's request that he order a blood transfusion. To Professor Bickel, this symbolized Warren-era judicial activism—a judge "bursting" from his courtroom, "rushing" to the hospital "with robes flapping." On another occasion, I recall Professor Bickel analogizing Judge Wright's judicial intervention into the District of Columbia schools to a coup by a Latin American junta.

These bits of Bickelian hyperbole were only colorful expressions of view put less memorably by others among my teachers.[19]

Bickel was a friend and disciple of Justice Felix Frankfurter, whose views on "judicial self-restraint" have been widely influential (those views, as was seen in Chapter 2, led him into condemning Willie Francis to death). There is an aridity and sterility about the Miller-Burger-Bickel position. Is our legal system so impotent that it cannot act in emergency situations? Must judges stand by and invoke the nebulous canons of judicial propriety while a persons's life ebbs away? For Judge Tamm and the Miller-Burger-Bickel trio, the clear answer to those questions is yes.

The basic question is not as they would have it. Rather, it is whether one's self-sovereignty should prevail in the circumstances of Mrs. Jones's case. There are times, and this to Judge Wright was clearly one of them, when legalistic niceties must give way to action that is immediate and relies more on the judge's instinct for the proper end rather than worries excessively over the means. As he said in his 1964 opinion, "he who wills the end wills the means"; Mrs. Jones had entered the hospital on her own volition and the end she wished was to regain her health. In these circumstances, some language of Theodore Roosevelt (a statement that James Meredith carried in his wallet when he, a black man, integrated the public University of Mississippi) is apposite:

It is not the critic who counts, not the man who points out how the strong man stumbles, where the doer of deeds could have done them better. The credit belongs to the man who is actually in the arena; whose face is marred by dust and sweat and blood; who strives valiantly; who errs and comes short again and again; who knows the great enthusiasm, the great devotion, and spends himself in a worthy cause; who, at the best, knows in the end the triumph of high achievement; and who, at the worst, if he fails, at least fails while daring greatly, so that his place shall never be with those cold and timid souls who know neither victory nor defeat.[20]

Skelly Wright was quite aware of the risks of disapproval he was facing when he agreed to go to the hospital. He dared greatly. He accepted the risk and proceeded. He was a "doer of deeds . . . actually in the arena." Today, he makes no apology for his decision and maintains that he would do it again were the situation to present itself. It ill behooves one not confronted with Mrs. Jones's case to sneer at his willingness to save a life.

The crucial question is this: What would Judge Wright have done had Mrs. Jones been lucid and able to make an informed consent? I asked him that question in July 1983. He could have fudged his reply, citing the reasons given in his 1964 opinion, with emphasis upon the infant's need for his mother's presence. But he did not. With typical honesty and candor, he said that had Mrs. Jones been lucid, it would have "given a lot of pause"; and "I might have stopped dead in my tracks." Even more directly: "If I had been convinced of her lucidity, I would probably not have" authorized the transfusions.[21] I said that his reply largely undermined his main articulated reason (in his opinion) for the decision—the child's welfare—but again he came back honestly and candidly: "I don't know what part the child had in the decision." With a situation where literally minutes could make a difference between life and death, he made an "instinctive reaction."[22] When I gently suggested that he had undercut the arguments in his opinion, his reaction was again typical of Skelly Wright, the man and the judge: It was a problem that "cannot be sliced up in neat legal categories."[23] His capacious mind saw beyond the arid legalisms of the Miller-Burger-Bickel trio.

Another way to evaluate Wright's decision is to inquire into the propriety of the hospital authorities seeking to invoke the power of the state so as to work their will upon Mrs. Jones. With overweening arrogance, they knew what was best for her. They determined her *good* as against her expressed willingness to follow the dictates of her conscience—her *right* of personal autonomy. Judge Wilbur Miller was quite right: The courts should not have been asked to act. But asked they were. What is it about the medical profession that leads so many physicians to play God with others' lives? Judge Wright uncritically accepted the medical opinion of the hospital's doctors, four of whom filed affidavits after the fact that the transfusions were necessary to save Mrs. Jones's life. He thus can be said to have put into effect one of John Stuart Mill's principles. Mill maintained that "over himself, over his own body and mind, the individual is sovereign," but went on to say in *On Liberty*:

It is, perhaps, hardly necessary to say that this doctrine is meant to apply only to human beings in the maturity of their faculties. We are not speaking of children, or of young persons below the age which the law may fix as that of manhood or womanhood. *Those, who are still in a state to require being taken care of by others, must be protected against their own actions as well as against external injury.* (Emphasis added.)[24]

That is the principle, and that is, as has been seen, what Judge Wright saw himself as doing—taking care of a person not able to make mature decisions. (He was not, as he argued in 1964, trying to preserve the status quo, for there was simply no way, under the circumstances, that the status quo could be preserved.)

The third, and the most telling, argument against Judge Wright's decision is that he gave too much credence to the state's right to intervene and too little to Mrs. Jones's right of self-sovereignty. That, however, can be met. The child and, indeed, the husband have to loom large in that equation. No matter how much one may agree that a mature person is sovereign over his body and mind—a position with which Judge Wright would agree—that person is nonetheless part of a community, a community that includes the family relationship. This in turn means that a member (unit) of a community (large or small; in this case, a family) has reciprocal rights *and* duties. One of those duties Mrs. Jones clearly owed to her child (and, although Wright did not mention it, to her husband). Just as an adult cannot invoke religious freedom arguments to prevent his child from being vaccinated against contagious disease, an adult cannot be said to have a right to deprive an infant of his mother's care. The self-sovereignty of the child, thus, is as important as that of Mrs. Jones, and the state—speaking through Judge Wright—acted as an umpire in the resolution of those conflicting rights. Mrs. Jones, in net, was not a discrete entity, an atomistic individual standing alone by herself.[25] I readily admit that this analysis does not jibe with Judge Wright's candid remarks in July 1983—but he himself is not entirely consistent in his position on the question (as will be shown in a moment).

In the summer of 1982, Judge Wright took part in a seminar conducted by the Aspen Institute. During one of the meetings, he was belabored by the participants for intervening into the situation and allowing the desires of the Georgetown Hospital doctors to prevail. A major objection raised was that of nonjusticiability and of judges going far beyond their judicial role—the same criticism leveled by the Miller-Burger-Bickel trio of faultfinders. As is his wont, Wright listened patiently and replied courteously to the critics. Finally, however, he leaned back and posed a question himself: "How much would you bet," he quietly asked, "that Mrs. Jones and her child are glad today for the decision?" The answer he received: complete silence from those who objected. As usual, he had cut through the niggling legalisms to the core question—the human element that was involved in the case.[26] J. Skelly Wright could not, as a man—and as a judge—stand idly by and allow a person to die. That would have gone against his entire biography and personal philosophy.

In a public address in 1980, in which he discussed his decision, Wright identified three important state interests that had to be weighed: the value attached to lives of the citizenry, the state's obligation to ensure that the hospital was not liable for failure to act, and, of most importance, "safeguarding children from abandonment by their parents."[27] The state had a "strong and compelling interest in seeing that mothers met their financial, emotional, and material commitments to their infants." He recognized the right of Mrs. Jones to make a choice. But "with a life hanging in the balance, a judge must shift his inquiry from the particular to the general, from the question of whether this person is competent to make this choice to the question of what kind of choices do sane and competent people normally make in similar circumstances." People who are capable of active, healthy lives, he continued, "normally choose life over death and they normally choose to accept such medical treatment as is necessary to preserve life." Such a conclusion was applicable to Mrs. Jones because she was voluntarily in the hospital for treatment—and, thus, had willed the end that Wright afforded her. The meaning is that while she had self-sovereignty, she had a duty to her family and had to comply—as all do—with societal norms.

Admittedly, the *Georgetown Hospital Case* is a tough and hard question. It is, however, no answer to say with Judge Wilbur Miller that "hard cases make bad law." Judge Wright would not extend the principle he invoked to situations in which new technologies permit the prolongation of life for a time. "I see," he says, "an enormous difference between life-prolonging and life-saving treatment," noting that the difference is not always recognized.

IV

"The chief end of the law," Judge Wright has said, "is to respect the dignity of human life."[28] There can be no question that Judge Wright acted in a paternalistic way in the ruling that saved Mrs. Jones's life. His views have had influence upon other judges, who are called upon to decide similar issues. There are several things that may be said in conclusion, including:

1. Judge Wright carefully limited the reach of his decision to the particular facts of the case he decided. He placed great emphasis upon the fact that he considered Mrs. Jones to be both *in extremis* and *non compos mentis*.
2. Wright's decision is only one milestone on a never-ending journey that seeks to find a unifying principle to reconcile the interests of the state and those of the self.
3. Only those who see legal disputes in an "either-or" manner, those, that is, who begin with a premise and readily come to a conclusion, can consider this case to be an easy one.

4. It would be far better for the law to be settled sufficiently, so that judges need not be called upon to make hasty life-or-death decisions. That, however, is less the function of judges than it is of legislatures, which must be held to have failed dismally thus far to deal with the problem Wright faced.

5. Finally, however judges might rule and whatever legislatures might say, those official actions will do little to change the deep beliefs of members of religious sects. Some Mormons still practice polygamy in the mountains of Utah and Arizona—a century after it had been outlawed. And Jehovah's Witnesses still adhere to the proscription against "eating blood."

8

Judge Wright and Crime

The preservation of the integrity of the judicial process . . . is a task for which the judiciary has a special competence and a special responsibility. It is only by seeing the criminal process as it functions in actual cases that the areas where constitutional rights are threatened, and the remedies required to vindicate them, become evident.

—J. Skelly Wright (1968)[1]

I

That crime is a problem in the United States cannot be doubted. That it is far from a new problem, one solely characteristic of the present-day, should be self-evident, but it is not. Many people view the past roseately, indulging consciously or subconsciously in the myth of the golden age—not only generally, but particularly about crime. The notion that any polity, including the United States, should be relatively crime-free is a modern idea. Crime is today, and was in the past, at least endemic and perhaps epidemic or even pandemic in human society—at least in the Western world. What is new in recent years is the growth of predatory crime—against person and property—that has escalated in the United States.

Historical examples of crime are easily found. Thucydides begins his classic *History of the Peloponnesian War* with an account of rampant crime in ancient Greece. In "ancient times" (for which he gave no date), he observed: "Piracy became a common profession both among the Hellenes and among the barbarians and in the islands. . . . The same system of armed robbery prevailed by land; and even up to the present day [*circa* 400 B.C.] much of Hellas still follows the old way of life."[2] In his masterful *Whigs and Hunters*, British historian E. P. Thompson remarks: "The British state, all eighteenth-century legislators agreed, existed to preserve the property and, incidentally, the lives and liberties of the propertied." In other words, there was much crime, for few of the citizenry were in fact "propertied."[3] Thompson echoed Adam Smith, who in 1776 maintained that "civil government, so far as it is instituted for the security of property, is in reality instituted for the defense of the rich against the poor, or of those who have some property against those who have none at all."[4] Again, crime was widespread. "Civil government," of course, secures or defends property through law—most law, but ultimately the criminal law. So, too, with John Locke, the putative "father" of the American Constitution: "Government has no other end but the preservation of property"[5]—through the state, which has a monopoly on the legitimate use of violence. As for the United States, there can be no question that corruption is as American as apple pie, and there there has always been some predatory crime.

This chapter develops Judge Skelly Wright's approach to the problem of crime in modern America, which he has dealt with both as a United States Attorney and as a judge. Some generalized statements will help set the crime problem in a larger context. At least two propositions are apposite.

First, it is necessary to distinguish, once again, the Constitution "of the books" from the Constitution "in operation" or, more precisely, the myth system of the social and political order from the operational code of the nation. The myth system is a more or less clearly stated set of rules of behavior that purportedly guide human conduct; the operational code is a private or at least largely unpublicized set of rules that in fact govern behavior. The former travels under the name of law; the latter has no commonly accepted label. Thus, under the myth system, the United States has a written fundamental law that both structures and, of greater present importance, ostensibly limits governmental power. The correlative to limitations is that the citizenry have certain rights against the state, set forth mainly in the Bill of Rights and the fourteenth amendment. That is the formal law, the law of the books. But, as has been discussed in previous chapters, a gap always exists between the pretense and the reality, between the formal law and the operational code. One student of crime, James Q. Wilson, expresses the point in this manner:

As I studied, first the police and then crime itself, I was struck with how remote from the reality was the rhetoric I heard. Demands that the police "get tough" and "crack down" on crime seemed incongruous given what I knew . . . about what the police actually spent their time doing. Public entertainments in which the climax of the mystery story was the arrest of the guilty party bewildered me because, in the real world, an arrest rarely ends anything. The arrested person is usually released within a few hours, will probably not come to trial for months, and, even if his guilt is determined, has an excellent chance of being returned to society promptly without any penalty at all. Most of those charged with offenses can be divided into two groups: those for whom arrest is an embarrassment and those for whom it is a mere inconvenience.[6]

My point is that, contrary to Judge Wright (in the headnote to this chapter), it is not the criminal process in "actual cases" that is really significant.

Rather, it is what goes on in the "real world"—the station house, the cop on the beat, and so forth. Wilson continues:

The intense debate over the evidentiary rules governing search and seizure, police interrogations, and the taking of confessions, while it illuminated some interesting legal and philosophic issues, had a hollow ring when recalled in the context of what actually happens in a police station house.

What, one must therefore ask, is *the* law in criminal matters—that laid down by legislatures and judges or that which takes place in the police station house? The short answer, based on a modification of Eugen Ehrlich's sociology of law, is that "the law" is what governmental officers actually do, not what they are theoretically supposed to do and not what they say they do.[7] The "formal" law, thus, often differs from the "living" law.

Of the two, by far the more important for the individual is the second, that is, what actually happens (the living law). The police have much more discretion in their day-to-day operations than would appear from reading the formal law—or from reading Supreme Court opinions (and, as Wilson says, watching public entertainments on television). To that wide range of police discretionary actions may be added the practically unlimited amount of prosecutorial discretion. Prosecutors are public employees with a mission to help safeguard society. They are largely autonomous, answerable only to themselves. Who is prosecuted and for what dereliction is usually left to the judgment of the prosecutor, who in many states does not even have to consult a grand jury. When he does, he is in fact, although not in theory, in control of what that jury does. Plea bargains—a form of crude barter economics traveling under the banner of law—have, accordingly, become the principal way of dealing with those suspected criminals who are brought to trial (which is only a tiny percentage of those detained or arrested).[8] Indeed, the "criminal justice" system could not operate without suspects being able, through their lawyers, to negotiate with prosecutors over the charges to be brought and the penalities assessed. There are simply not enough courts and judges to handle the number of criminal trials, with everyone being given a full-dress hearing by judge and jury. That situation has led the Supreme Court to approve plea bargaining, which means that it is primitive economics, often under mental and emotional duress, rather than law that is the controlling factor.

As a consequence, an aura of aridity and sterility characterizes what appellate judges say about criminals. That includes Judge Wright's court. His own work, as well as that of this colleagues, has largely dealt with the lofty concepts of constitutional principles applied to a few police officers. Wright articulates the "law of the books." No way exists under present practice for judicial scrutiny of what happens in fact to the *mass* of suspected and actual criminals. Appellate judges are confined to blind guesses about their status. That, in and of itself, would not necessarily be unsatisfactory were it not for one fact—federal appellate judges, particularly Supreme Court Justices, but also those on the courts of appeals, view their specific decisions about an individual or group as statements of general norms. They see themselves as legislating not only for the person in a given case, but for an untold number of others. That shift in emphasis from the individual to the group, from the particular to the general, creates jurisprudential problems that cut to the core of the adversary system of adjudication.[9]

Moreover, Judge Wright and other judges have dealt far more with predatory street crime than with so-called white-collar or corporate crime or with "victimless" crimes. For whatever reason, prosecutors pay little attention to corporate crimes. This reflects the view of the general public, and of legislators and other governmental officers, that predatory crime against person and property is by far the more serious matter. Professor Wilson agrees; he maintains that predatory crime "makes difficult or impossible the maintenance of meaningful human communities."[10] The fabric of society is being torn apart by fears engendered by muggers and rapists and burglars.

Second, surely both types of crime are socially significant—what might be called the economic crimes of bribery, embezzlement, consumer fraud, antitrust violations, and the like, and the predatory crimes such as robbery, burglary, homicide, rape, and mugging. To be sure, the latter are much more evident; they affect many people directly and contribute to a pervasive climate of fear (the loss of community that Wilson mentions). On a monetary basis and to the extent that measurements are possible, which is not very much, the overall social costs of economic crimes likely are far heavier, but their impact upon people is largely indirect. Judge Wright has not yet spelled out his views about the comparative impact of the two types of crimes and has dealt mainly with predatory crime in his decisions. He recognizes, however, the importance of economic crimes.

Economic crimes are significant not because they result in a loss of community, but because their existence contributes to a growing cynicism about government. With the spread of mass education and the advent of at least intermittent media attention, people increasingly despair of those in positions of authority and power. Which is more dangerous—the loss of community or the growing cynicism—cannot be measured. It is enough to say that neither is desirable; both pose dangers to the viability of the social structure.

Some students of crime go even further. For example, Frank Browning and John Gerassi, in *The American Way of Crime*, maintain (although they do not use the term) that crime is part of the operational code of the nation:

Lost in the uproar over muggers, gangsters, and dope addicts, is [the fact] that crime has become an inherent ingredient of the American system. It is a means of making money, regulating business, supporting the poor. And, as burglaries, fraud, frame-ups, illegal spying, and drug experimentation on unsuspecting victims by the FBI and CIA made clear during the Watergate aftermath, it is often a way of running the government. According to a 1976 congressional study, street crime, the crisis issue that breeds fear and sells newspapers, costs society at most only one-tenth as much as does the respectable crimes of corporate price-fixing, computer embezzlement, and tax fraud. Yet neither the politicians nor the press like to acknowledge such a fact. Instead, they focus on the street. Because it is visible and immediate, such crime is considered more real than all the rest. To individual Americans, it represents a triumph of brute force over law and civilization, and becomes a major cause of their fear and insecurity.[11]

So it does. And it is that type of crime that receives the bulk of attention from those who administer the criminal justice system. Browning and Gerassi maintain that a *sixth estate* has emerged in the United States, namely, "the complex world of professional and organized crime." (The other "estates" are the traditional powers in government—historically, the nobility, the clergy, and the "commons," by which was meant only those with means and property. The fourth estate is the press, and the fifth is the military-intelligence combine.) That sixth estate exerts enormous power on "government, economics, laws, police, value system, tastes, mores, and habits." Browning and Gerassi maintain that the nation could not function without it, for it cuts across traditional class and political lines, and acts almost as a state within a state. "The sixth estate is an independent force that both permeates and opposes the others and has become endemic to every element of modern life."[12]

If they are correct, then much of the administration of American criminal law touches only a small segment of a much larger whole. That larger whole penetrates all of society. No governmental institution has been immune. Richard Nixon's crimes precipitated his resignation and subsequent pardon by President Gerald Ford. Vice President Spiro Agnew was allowed to plea bargain an escape from jail for his crimes. The so-called ABSCAM episode implicated a number of prominent members of Congress. The judiciary at times is culpable: witness Judge Otto Kerner of the Sixth Circuit Court of Appeals. Corporate crime is rampant, as Marshall Clinard and Peter Yeager have demonstrated.[13] Some unions, notably the Teamsters, are notoriously crime-ridden. Seemingly, there is no institution, public or private, that is free from some people at some time getting caught doing something illegal. The emphasis there is upon "getting caught": No one knows, or possibly could know, the full extent of actual criminal activities in the nation. Even the statistics on known crime, compiled by the FBI, tend to be quite unreliable.

To think systematically and adequately about crime requires at the outset some views about the nature of man. "Political theory which does not start from a theory of man . . . is quite worthless."[14] The criminal law and its administration involve not only a theory of society, but ultimately a theory of man. There are, of course, no easy or quick answers to those questions; indeed, there is far from a consensus on them. Professor Wilson maintains that "man is refractory enough to be unchangeable but reasonable enough to be adaptable. The institutions of governance created by man reflect his nature."[15] That is far from satisfactory. What *is* "his nature"? The late Erich Fromm, in his monumental *The Anatomy of Human Destructiveness*, confronted the problem and concluded:

> In this study, I have tried to demonstrate that prehistorical man, living in bands as hunter and food gatherer, was characterized by a minimum of destructiveness and an optimum of cooperation and sharing, and that only with the increasing productivity and division of labor, the formation of a large surplus, and the building of states with hierarchies and elites, large scale destructiveness and cruelty came into existence and grew as civilization and the role of power grew.
>
> Has this study contributed valid arguments in favor of the thesis that aggression and destructiveness can once again assume a minimal role in the fabric of human motivations? I believe it has.[16]

We have seen in Chapter 6 that Skelly Wright has a faith in the essential goodness of humans, one that has helped to motivate his first amendment decisions. Can the same faith be discerned when he is confronted with questions of crime? Does he agree with Fromm that human aggression and destructiveness can be reduced?

II

The short answer to those questions is "yes." He perceives the biggest problem about crime today as that of poverty, accompanied by a lack of education.[17] Accordingly, Judge Wright considers the human being to be basically good and sufficiently malleable as to be able to lead a socially acceptable life, provided he is given the right opportunity. A committed egalitarian, he thinks that all people should have equality of opportunity. Government, he maintains, should see to it that everyone has equality of opportunity "to maintain his status or improve it." Implicit in that belief is that everyone—at least, most people—want to become a part of conventional mainstream America. Perhaps that would make Wright in agreement with Professor Daniel Bell who has asserted that "organized crime is merely another technique for the lower classes to achieve upward mobility."[18]

I shall return to the question of whether crime is a way of life for a growing number of people later in this chapter. First, it is necessary to explicate how Judge Wright has dealt with criminal law cases. Contrary to many of his administrative law decisions, Wright is a committed judicial activist in criminal matters. He agrees with his colleague, Judge David Bazelon, who once remarked: "I continue to believe that it is the function of the courts to bring to the surface problems that other institutions in society have ignored."[19] Wright has said of Bazelon that he, Wright, is "probably the only judge on any federal court of appeals who can call Judge David L. Bazelon conservative"[20]—which may well be accurate. During the 1960s, at a time when the Court of Appeals still had jurisdiction over local crime in the District of Columbia—a situation now changed by statute—the two acted as a duo. They perceived many constitutional violations by the police and worked together—so much so that their names almost became merged into one (Bazelon-Wright or Wright-Bazelon)—to help those least able to defend themselves. They wanted the police to respect the law and not take shortcuts in enforcement of the criminal laws. They were successful, in the long run at least. Today, the police department in Washington, D.C., is far better than it was in the 1960s. It is no longer a racist institution, one with the apparent primary goal of repressing the black populace. Their courage drew sharp criticism from the police officers and others in Washington, aided by congressional committees headed by racist members of Congress. One of the then critics is Professor Gerald Caplan, who at the time was general counsel to the police department. He acknowledges today that he and others saw Wright and Bazelon as two judges who seemed to "enjoy socking it to the police." Reflecting on the period today, Caplan considers that Wright and Bazelon were two courageous judges who, in no small part, were great men in their times. He is able now to see what they were trying to do—and to appreciate and approve of it. Caplan now believes that by tempering police activity, the judges were helping to benefit society.[21] And that, says Skelly Wright today, is precisely what he was trying to do. I have previously maintained that Judge Wright has often acted pursuant to the Principle of Reason-Directed Societal Self-Interest. His decisions in criminal law matters are additional examples of the operation of that principle. By helping some lone and powerless individual, he was helping to siphon off simmering social discontent. The winners, so far as there were winners, were both the individuals and society.

Interaction with Judge Bazelon may be seen in another area. In 1954, Bazelon issued a controversial ruling on insanity pleas in criminal cases. He maintained, in *Durham v. United States*,[22] that "an accused is not criminally responsible if his unlawful act was the product of a mental disease or mental defect," thereby throwing out the time-honored test—the so-called *McNaghten* rule—which asked only if the suspect knew the difference between right and wrong. Although *Durham* was overruled in 1972, the Court of Appeals adopted a definition of mental disease that was independent of any psychiatric definition: "Any abnormal condition of the mind which substantially affects mental or emotional processes and substantially impairs behavior controls." Judge Wright was one of the chief architects of that definition. He remarked in 1974:

When I first joined the Court of Appeals, it was deeply divided over an attempt to elaborate a definition of mental disease, as that term is used in the insanity defense. As a newcomer to the court, I was cast to some extent in the role of a mediator. I worked individually with each of the eight other judges on the court, and ultimately we forged a resolution of the problem, to which each judge contributed. In working on that case, line by line and word by word, I had my introduction to the problem [of insanity].[23]

John Hinckley, the man who attempted to assassinate President Reagan, is in a mental institution today, rather than prison, because of changing definitions of insanity to which Wright (and Bazelon) contributed so much. This is not to say that the problem of insanity in criminal matters has been solved. My only point is that Judge Wright has had a major role in developing the standards to be applied when the insanity defense is raised.

III

Analysis and discussion of Wright's decisions in the criminal area will be helped by reference to what the late Professor Herbert Packer called "two models of the criminal process"—the Crime Control Model and the Due Process Model. "The value system that underlies the Crime Control Model," Packer said, "is based on the proposition that the repression of criminal conduct is by far the most important function to be performed by the criminal process."[24] The claim is that the model is a positive guarantor of social freedom. It operates under a presumption of guilt and aims toward efficiency, and may be likened to an assembly line.

The Due Process Model is not necessarily the polar opposite of the Crime Control Model. It resembles an obstacle course and does not make efficiency a primary goal. It does not deny the social desirability of repressing crime. It seeks to ensure accuracy, to prevent and eliminate errors to the maximum extent possible. Shortcuts in the criminal process are rejected. It "resembles a factory that has to devote a substantial part of its input to quality control. This necessarily reduces quantitative output." It operates under a presumption of innocence, which means that the state must prove with clear and convincing evidence that an accused is in fact guilty of a crime.

That attenuated description of Packer's two models leaves much to be desired, but there is no present need to expand upon them. Skelly Wright, as United States Attorney, tended to follow the Crime Control Model and had much to do with cleaning up fraud and corruption in New Orleans during his tenure. As a judge on the Court of Appeals, he obviously has adhered to the Due Process Model, as a discussion of a representative number of his decisions will demonstrate.

I begin, not with Skelly Wright as judge or even as prosecutor, but with his second appearance before the Supreme Court as an advocate. It will be recalled that Wright lost his first case before that Court, and that the hapless Willie Francis walked a second, and final, time to the execution chamber in Louisiana. Soon thereafter, Wright handled the case of Ann Johnson, who had been convicted in Seattle of possession of opium and other narcotics.[25] (He got the case from a friend in Seattle who was unable to come to Washington. Wright, contrary to the *Francis* case for which he received no fee whatsoever, got $300 for arguing the *Johnson* case.) Police had found the narcotics in Johnson's apartment. When the officers arrived at her apartment, they were admitted even though they had no warrant. On smelling burning opium, they placed her under arrest, searched the apartment, and found a still warm opium pipe containing opium. At her trial, she invoked the fourth amendment's prohibition against unreasonable searches and seizures, which also requires that warrants can be issued only on probable cause shown. (It will be noted that her lawyer at the trial had the good sense and ability to raise the constitutional question, whereas, as we have seen, the attorneys for Willie Francis made no defense at all.)

The Supreme Court again split 5 to 4 in *Johnson*. This time Wright won, and Johnson's conviction was reversed. The line-up of the Justices shows shifts in position from the *Francis* decision. Justices Robert Jackson and Felix Frankfurter, who had voted against Willie Francis, joined with William Douglas, Frank Murphy, and Wiley Rutledge to make up the majority. But as was his wont, Justice Harold Burton sustained the government's position; he was joined by three members of the *Francis* majority—Fred Vinson, Hugo Black, and Stanley Reed. It is at least difficult and probably impossible to reconcile the divergent positions of Burton, Frankfurter, and Jackson in *Francis* and *Johnson*. The latter two were willing to let Francis go to his death, even though they opposed capital punishment; their self-imposed philosophy of deference to state authorities, however, did not prove to be a barrier for Ann Johnson. She went free because the constable stumbled. Willie Francis was killed even though state officers had acted recklessly. (So goes the rule of law at the Supreme Court level.)

The point, however, is not to try to untangle the threads of the two cases, but to show the ability of a young Skelly Wright in being able to convince five Justices that Ann Johnson had been treated indecently. Wright persuaded the Court majority to set standards that still make up the *formal* law about the proper limits on police searches. Said Jackson for the majority:

The point of the Fourth Amendment, which often is not grasped by zealous officers, is not that it denies law enforcement the support of the usual inferences which reasonable men draw from evidence. Its protection consists in requiring that those inferences be drawn by a neutral and detached magistrate instead of being judged by the officer engaged in the often competitive enterprise of ferreting out crime. . . . When the right of privacy must reasonably yield to the right of search is, as a rule, to be decided by a judicial officer, not by a policeman or government enforcement agent.

The persistence of that "rule" was seen in Chapter 5, in the establishment of a special court to authorize national security searches. As was noted there, the formal law and the living law tend to be at odds. Warrants are relatively easy to get from complaisant judges. What Jackson was saying, at Wright's bidding, and what Wright was to say in the 1960s, is that the police should not take shortcuts. Searches can be made, but proper procedures must be followed.

Procedural propriety is something that sounds good, but, in practice, does not necessarily govern. What judges say in their opinions quite likely will be far from reflections of the realities of police procedure. Not only are warrants easily obtained from judges, warrantless searches still occur; they are probably far more common than searches with warrants. The judges propose, but the police (and others) dispose. How does Judge Wright stand on the question of searches? *United States v. Robinson* (1972)[26] provides insight. A car driven by Willie Robinson was stopped for a "routine spot check" by police, who found that his driver's license had been revoked. A few days later the same officer saw Robinson driving the same car and arrested him for operating an automobile after revocation of his permit to drive. Under District of Columbia police regulations, suspects so arrested must be thoroughly searched. The officer did so and found a package of heroin in Robinson's pocket. At the trial for possession of narcotics, Robinson's attorney moved to suppress evidence of the narcotics; he argued that an unconstitutional search had been made. The question before the Court of Appeals was whether such a search could be made of motorists without a warrant. A plurality of the court found it unconstitutional; Judge Wright wrote the opinion for the plurality.

Drawing on Justice Jackson's opinion in the *Johnson* case (quoted above), Wright maintained that the "cardinal rule" was that warrants are the rule and searches without warrants the exception. He went on to say that searching Robinson was itself lawful, as was the removal of the package (containing heroin) from Robinson's pocket. But the search *within* the package was not lawful. The searches of the car and of Robinson were permissible because, Wright said, there may be a "need to seize weapons and other things which might be used to assault an officer or effect an escape, as well as by the need to prevent the destruction of evidence of the crime." But, once having located the (cigarette) package, opening and examining it was an intrusion on Robinson's privacy that "should be permitted only if necessary to achieve substantial governmental interests." Wright found none in the circumstances of the case; the search of the package was, for instance, not necessary to protect the officer's life. He rejected the argument that such searches were necessary to deal effectively with crime by concluding that the risk of injury to an officer in such circumstances is "remote."

Judge Wright's adherence to a full Due Process Model in the *Robinson* case did not get complete support from his colleagues on the Court of Appeals sitting *en banc*. Nor did the Supreme Court agree with him; in 1973, it reversed his ruling and authorized a thorough search in all custodial arrests, even for traffic offenses. Writing for the Court, Justice William Rehnquist said the "fact of the lawful arrest" by itself "establishes the authority to search."[27] Justice Lewis Powell, concurring, declared that it is the arrest, not the search, that is "the significant intrusion of state power into the privacy" of the person. Once arrested, said Powell, the person "retains no significant Fourth Amendment interest." Clearly, the Supreme Court today had adopted the Crime Control Model of the criminal process. The Justices continue to do so; little by little they are chipping away and undermining gains in criminal procedure that were made during the tenure of the Supreme Court under Earl Warren.

Skelly Wright remains fully committed to the Due Process Model. He wishes to channel police action within lawful bounds, and make officers obey the law. He is not so much logical in his opinions as he is a judge who is trying to be right and fair. His decisions closely parallel those of the Warren Court in criminal procedure, as well as elsewhere. The police of Washington, of course, saw him differently; they viewed him as uncompromising, uninformed, and as a judge who simply did not like the police. Says Professor Caplan: "The police believed, rightly or wrongly, that the Court of Appeals, led by Wright and Bazelon, were anti-police."[28] The police were aided by the District Committee of the House of Representatives, headed by white southerners who helped generate an anticourt feeling. The white business community of Washington worked with and encouraged that Committee. Judge Wright and such others on his court as Judges Bazelon and Spottswood Robinson got little or no support from the community leaders. But that did not deter Skelly Wright. Professor Martin Levine, a former Wright law clerk, has summarized his criminal procedure decisions:

A number of principles seem exemplified in . . . Judge Wright's criminal procedure cases. . . . As a prerequisite to affirmance of conviction and punishment, several factors must concur. Some of them look backwards to rights, rules, and morality, and other look forward to consequences.

The guilty should be punished, and only the guilty. Affirmance should be based on a factually accurate account as to what happened at trial and during the offense; no unnecessary factual presumptions on ambiguous data should be indulged against the accused and his act; acquittal is in order if they deem him either legally or morally innocent. The police, prosecutor and court must observe the accused's constitutional rights. The government may morally condemn the accused only if it has acted morally toward him in the transaction between them.

The court may properly consider the effect of its decision on the immediate parties; an affirmance of conviction is no abstract philosophical judgment, but may result in long imprisonment. The court may also properly consider the effect of its decisions on others, that is, both deterrence of criminality and deterrence of police abuse. The court has a responsibility to reconsider old principles of law, and has a variety of bases of legal authority by which to develop the law.[29]

As a former United States Attorney and as a district judge, Skelly Wright had close, firsthand experience with the operation of the criminal justice system. He knew, thus, that the state possesses a violent potential, and he has worked mightily to curb it.

Needless to say, Judge Wright has not always been able to prevail in his criminal law decisions. When he was on a panel (in the 1960s) with Judges Bazelon and Robinson or today with Judges Patricia Wald or Abner Mikva, he does gather allies to his views. Quite often, however, he runs into the mentality of judges who adhere to the Crime Control Model of criminal procedure. Thus, Judge Malcolm Wilkey could, in 1978, call one of Wright's opinions "patently frivolous." Wilkey, still on the Court of Appeals, frequently dissents from Wright's decisions. So did Judge (now Chief Justice) Warren Burger, who once accused Wright of going to "ridiculous lengths." And Judge Wilbur Miller wrote of the same Wright decision: It is "another example of what I think is this court's tendency unduly to emphasize technicalities which protect criminals and hamper law enforcement. . . . It is shocking to me that upon such tortured grounds the court reverses the conviction of this man who has confessed to a bizarre and brutal murder. . . . In our concern for criminals, we should not forget that nice people have some rights, too." In 1978, Wilkey accused Wright of "legerdemain"; Wilkey asserted that "my colleagues are apparently prepared to labor mightily to exculpate the defendants," and that "the majority attempts to construct a new haven for escaped criminals."

If such criticisms bother Judge Wright, he does not mention it. If anything, perhaps they make him solidify his own views, views on criminal procedure that have changed little if at all during the time he has been an appeals judge. He is also fully aware of the fulminations of some academics about what they consider to be his perfervid judicial activism. The late Alexander Bickel was mentioned in Chapter 7. Another harsh academic critic is Professor Philip Kurland of the University of Chicago Law School, another votary in the cult of Frankfurter worship that has invaded the law schools. He believes that Wright furthers his own personal values without regard to the law—which is erroneous (Wright does not)—and he attacks Wright's activism, which he condemns as exalting "autocracy over democracy, . . . faction over society, equality over liberty, the mass and the class over the individual, and even mindlessness over reason."[30] Kurland knows better. His broadside against Judge Wright and others he considers to be judicial activists is merely a restatement of his mentor and idol (he is a former Frankfurter law clerk), who was himself—despite his fervent protestations to the contrary—also an activist and a result-oriented judge. Professor Kurland knows full well that all judges pursue their own philosophies (values). He is merely seeking to change the thrust of what Wright is doing—the decisions themselves.

Members of Congress have also castigated judicial activists such as Judge Wright. Speaking in 1969, for instance, Senator Sam J. Ervin criticized judicial activists as

judges who undertake to amend the Constitution or the laws while professing to interpret them. In so doing, they actually substitute their personal notions for constitutional principles and rules of law. . . .

Judicial activists labor under the delusion that there was little, if any, wisdom on earth before their arrival. As a consequence, they lay the flattering unction to their souls that the amendments they usurp the power to make improve the Constitution and the laws. For this reason, they believe the ends they have in view excuse the unjustified means they employ to accomplish them.[31]

As with Bickel and Kurland, Ervin should have known better than to issue unctuous hyperbole. The bottom line about such criticisms is that it is the results Wright reaches, rather than the means taken to attain them, that so exercises other judges, academics, and members of Congress.

The fundamental core about Judge Wright's criminal procedure decisions is, as has been suggested, that in helping a few of the poor and powerless—by making the police turn square corners when dealing with criminal suspects—he is also helping to siphon off social discontent. His decisions, thus, serve a societal as well as individual interest. Contrary to Professor Kurland, he is interested in the individual—and the individual's right to have the police themselves respect the laws they are sworn to enforce. Wright strives to follow the law, and indeed does follow it; but, as he put it in 1983, "the law is sufficiently flexible to enable me to find a way to go"; and further, "the law can be interpreted to avoid injustice."[32] That, in a nutshell, is what Judge Wright's criminal law decisions are about—the avoidance of injustice.

IV

That Skelly Wright has had much to do with the development of the formal law of criminal procedure is obvious. His decisions as a judge were one of several forces that coalesced in recent years to transform police practices. Speaking generally, we have better police departments today because courageous judges like Wright were willing to further the ideals of constitutional limitations even in the face of bitter criticism. There is, of course, much yet to be done—as Professor Wilson has pointed out. The living or operative law of police practice often differs widely and markedly from that of the formal law. The problem of crime is far from solved; and, indeed, there is a high probability that it never will be. That, I think, points up a failure of the constitutional order itself. "In many respects," Professor Larry Berg and Associates have said, "the emergence of immorality in American politics reflected the failure of the framers of the Constitution to construct governmental institutions that would eliminate or minimize corruption. In *The Federalist* and other writings, the principal architects of the American political system explicitly stated that this system was designed to protect the public from avarice and scandals."[33] Although Berg was discussing corruption in the political order, his observations appear to be generally applicable.

The function of the criminal law process is to protect members of society from predatory and economic crimes. This is accomplished by the state establishing a system by which criminal guilt can be, in theory at least, determined and a penalty imposed. The ideal of the process is far from the reality. Although he does not label it as such, Professor Lloyd Weinreb has caught the essential *constitutional* nature of that gap in these words:

It is a dangerous self-deception to attribute the deficiencies of criminal process simply to lack of resources or inevitable human failings, as we commonly do. The social resources now committed to it are not used nearly as productively as they might be; and we are not in any event likely to spend much more in the future. Public officials and professional people who are responsible for investigation and prosecution perform their duties ably. *The irrational procedures that we employ are not irregularities of an otherwise sound process; they constitute the process itself.* (Emphasis added.)[34]

Whether or not Weinreb so intended it, that is a statement of a constitutional problem—namely, the criminal process itself is inadequate to the need. Our institutions do not protect us from crime; and those caught up in the administration of the criminal law—the criminals, actual or suspected—often are not accorded fundamental constitutional protections.

Weinreb again says it well; he maintains that the deficiencies of the criminal process have a common thread running through them, and echoes Professor Wilson by saying : "Notwithstanding our preoccupation with law and order and the rights of the individual, our thinking about criminal justice is dominated by an abstract model which has little relation to what actually happens." Despite a plethora of rhetoric about criminal justice and much tinkering with detail, particularly by the courts, the underlying framework of the system has never been challenged or even noticed. Weinreb maintains that the adversary system itself is unsound. And so it may be. Criminal trials are often latter-day versions of trial by combat, verbal joustings that more often than not are battles of wits. And plea bargains are a confession of failure of the system, in which, as has been said, not law but crude barter economics is the means by which guilt is assessed. It is, furthermore, a gamble by the suspect, who probably will be faced with a more severe sentence if he elects to go to trial; but by so electing, he gambles for an acquittal. Plea bargains usually eliminate the risk of extra severity in sentencing—but the person pleads guilty to something he did not do.

All of this illustrates that the ways in which such judges as Skelly Wright deal with crime do not confront the truly important questions about criminal process. Wright's reforms, such as they are, deal with individual instances of shortcomings by police officers. They do not, because they cannot, reconstitute the system itself. If that type of comprehensive reform is to come, it must be by the legislature. Judges can point out specific examples of improprieties, but can do little more. The meaning is that legislatures have failed to grapple with systemic reconstruction of the criminal justice process. So, too, has the American Bar Association.

Another dimension exists to the constitutional dimension of crime adumbrated by Professor Berg and Associates. If Browning and Gerassi are correct—and I believe that in large part they are—then crime permeates all of society. To repeat: "Crime has become an inherent ingredient of the American system. It is a means of making money, regulating business, supporting the poor. And . . . it is often a way of running the government." The dirty little secret of America is the pervasive corruption of its institutions. American society is essentially schizoid. We pretend both that we are law-abiding citizens and that crime is aberrational. The reality is otherwise. In many respects, this is illustrative of the dark side of capitalism and of a competitive society that rewards the person willing to take risks, even when those risks skirt or trench upon the law. There is little that the police can really do. Says Robert di Grazia, former chief of police of Boston and St Louis: "We are not letting the public in on our era's dirty little secret." That secret, he said, "is that there is little the police can do."[35]

Di Grazia could have gone further; he could have said that there is little that the present criminal justice system can do—thus echoing Professor Weinreb. We do not even know what causes crime, although Judge Wright echoes former Attorney General Ramsey Clark in asserting that it is "poverty and lack of education" that lie behind most crime. Says Clark: "The motives of most crimes are economic. Seven of eight known serious crimes involves property. . . . Their main purpose is to obtain money or property."[36] But, says Professor Caplan: "There is no more fruitless inquiry than searching for the causes of crime. Everyone has a pet theory. And such is the state of our knowledge that none are demonstrably false. Indeed, you have a point no matter whom you blame: the Supreme Court, narcotics traffickers, permissive parents, the economy. You can select without fear of contradiction. And without fear of having reached a solution."[37] The essential problem, I maintain, is constitutional—namely, how government, how the political economy is constituted within the nation. This problem is not constitutional in the sense of specific clauses or provisions of the fundamental law, but, rather, in the sense of the basic structure of society. An economic system has evolved in America, say Browning and Gerassi, that is the primary means of support for millions of persons who live on the fringes of what ordinarily is considered to be "legitimate" society.

If Judge Wright has ever considered these larger questions about crime and criminals and the constitutional order, he has not announced his conclusions publicly. Deep down, he knows that, as Professor Jerold Auerbach has remarked: "In the United States justice has been distributed according to race, ethnicity, and wealth, rather than need."[38] Moreover, Judge Wright strives within the constrictions of the judicial process to do something about that disparity in treatment. Wright views crime not as a plague that is epidemic in American society, but as a series of individual episodes. He, furthermore, has not thought about the propensity of Americans to reduce many social issues to problems of crime. Thus it is that "crime in the streets" is, in many respects, a code term for racism. (Dissent, in general, has been treated as criminal behavior.) But street crime is much more; it has always played a large part in American society, as witness an 1842 statement of the Board of Aldermen of New York City:

Thronged as our city is, men are robbed in the streets. Thousands, that are arrested, go unpunished, and the defenseless and the beautiful are ravished in the day time, and no trace of the criminals is found. The man of business, in his lawful calling, at the most public corner of our city, is slaughtered in the sunshine and packed up and sent away.[39]

That, of course, is an all too familiar complaint about the threat of street crime today. The United States has never been crime-free, but as Charles Silberman has shown in his thorough review of the proliferation of street crime, *Criminal Violence, Criminal Justice*,[40] that threat has worsened in recent years.

Where Judge Wright errs—if, indeed, it is an error—is in what might be termed his excessive attachment to the plight of the underdog and his apparent inability to fully appreciate the difficulties and motives of the Establishment (wherever located) in criminal matters. Power does not necessarily always corrupt, as Wright's career bears impressive testimony. Furthermore, the fact that crime is as American as apple pie and as old as recorded history fails to come to grips with the heavy toll that it visits upon so many people today. Crime reduces us as human beings, diminishes our sense of community and thus lowers the quality of life (often substantially), and unduly intrudes upon one's sense of self. Not only do most criminals go unpunished, even uncaught, but society has yet to develop means by which it can intervene *before* crimes are committed. The police forces of the nation are forever playing "catch-up"; and not doing a good job at it. The growth of predatory crime against person and property is a well-documented fact of life in most cities.

Judge Wright's criminal law rulings spring from his concern for the plight of the poor and underprivileged; they are examples of his deepfelt interest in promoting equality in America. He is not trying, in those decisions, to restructure society—to raise, that is, the fundamental constitutional question—but he does seek to bring to a few individuals a better shake of the legal dice, dice that through most of American history have been loaded against the poor and disadvantaged. He deals with constitutional questions, but as details of the fundamental law, rather than that law itself. That, no doubt, is as much as a judge can do, hemmed in as he is by the constraints of tradition and precedent and notions of judicial propriety. Wright has no wish to reorganize society, but merely to ameliorate some of its more obvious excrescences. Even in his controversial criminal decisions, therefore, he remains very much the Establishmentarian. Where he differs, as has been seen, is in his intuitive knowledge that by helping a few, he also aids society itself. That is no small accomplishment.

9

Judge Wright in Perspective

Being a judge gives me the opportunity to do some good.
—J. Skelly Wright (1983)[1]

I

How, then, can one evaluate the professional career of James Skelly Wright?

My answer is that of President John F. Kennedy: He is "one of the great judges of America."[2] If ever a person deserved to be on the Supreme Court, it is Skelly Wright. Had he been named to the High Bench, he doubtless would have joined Justices Hugo Black and William Douglas, as well as Chief Justice Warren and Wright's good friend, Justice William Brennan, in making up a solid bloc of "liberals." But that was not to be. His chances vanished when Kennedy was assassinated. Nevertheless, his work as an appeals judge has placed him in the forefront of all federal judges. As Justice Brennan said on the occasion of Wright's thirtieth anniversary as a judge: "Judge Wright is a quiet modest man, more embarrassed than happy with praise. That makes only the more fitting the dedication of this issue of the Hastings Constitutional Law Quarterly in his honor, in Learned Hand's words to "Acclaim one who—all unaware of his deserts—has so richly earned our gratitude.' "[3] Or as Judge Elbert P. Tuttle has said of him: "The mind and heart of this dauntless judge enhances the great tradition of the federal judiciary."[4]

Judge Wright, with the possible exception of Judge Frank M. Johnson of Alabama (now on the Eleventh Circuit Court of Appeals),[5] has endured more calumny and actual danger to his life than any other judge in American history. His ordeal in "the second battle of New Orleans" was a trial by fire, in which, as I have noted, he stared down the entire state of Louisiana in one of the most dramatic confrontations between law and mob rule the nation has ever witnessed. That travail, added to his inherent sense of decency, has led him to further, whenever he can, the ideal of equality under the law. He could have been weakened by his New Orleans experience, but he was not. And he could have given up, succumbed to the numbing pressures of friend and foe alike, in trying to bring equality to the black citizens of New Orleans. (I asked him in 1983 if he had ever thought of that; and his answer came back quickly and firmly: "Oh, no, no, no, never.")[6] He seeks within the law, as he knows it, to protect the weak and powerless. He does this because he possesses a sense of quiet outrage. Abraham Sofaer, Wright's law clerk in 1965-1966 (and now a federal district judge in New York), has said about Wright:

I had worked my way through college and law school and on the law review, and when I graduated from law school I was tired. Then I came to Wright. He was in his fifties, but he gave me energy. He was a young man in his idealism, vigor, and most of all his capacity for outrage.[7]

The same can be said of Skelly Wright today. As a man in his early seventies, he has an instinct for goodness, and a large capacity for instilling in his law clerks that sense of wanting to do good.

Judge Wright relies heavily on his clerks. They work as a team in drafting opinions. Quite often, he will insert large chunks of the memoranda his clerks produce in his opinions. This by no means is exceptional. Rather, reliance upon law clerks has become typical of the judiciary. But Wright is the one, and the only one, who makes the decisions. Sometimes, it seems, Wright places too much reliance on his clerks. Some of his opinions, as well as his nonjudicial writings, have all the appearance of articles in legal periodicals—a clear indication that the clerks have had much of their language taken over and accepted by Wright. (I recall a conversation in 1975 with Judge Wright, concerning his opinion in *Zweibon v. Mitchell*, discussed in Chapter 5, in which I teased him for using the word "paradigmatic" three times. I said that I did not think he had ever used the word before and asked why he had employed it. He answered by laughing and saying, "My law clerk liked the word.") Wright, however, has a gift for eloquent language and is able to state in a few words what his clerks take pages of turgid prose to enunciate. Consider his 1956 opinion in the *Bush* case (Chapter 3). He wrote, as has been mentioned, the following on the back of a program for a Mardi Gras Ball:

The problem of changing a people's mores, particularly those with an emotional overlay, is not be taken lightly. It is a problem which will require the utmost patience, understanding, generosity and forbearance and from all of us of whatever race.

But the magnitude of the problem may not nullify the principle. And that principle is that we are, all of us, free-born Americans with a right to make our way unfettered by sanctions imposed by man because of the work of God.[8]

He wrote that for a purpose—to try to get to the religious people of New Orleans. That language, enclosed in clear plastic, now sits on his desk in his chambers in Washington. And in his 1962 *Bush* opinion, the following language appears—word for word from a handwritten, in pencil, scrawl on a slip of paper that may now be found in Judge Wright's district court papers in the Library of Congress:

> Generations of Negroes have already been denied their rights under the separate but equal doctrine of *Plessy v. Ferguson, . . .* and, at the present pace in New Orleans, generations of Negroes yet unborn will suffer a similar fate with respect to their rights under *Brown* unless desegregation and equal protection are secured for them by this court.
>
> The School Board here occupies an unenviable position. Its members, elected to serve without pay, have sought conscientiously, albeit reluctantly, to comply with the law on order of this court. Their reward for this service has been economic reprisal and personal recrimination from many of their constituents who have allowed hate to overcome their better judgment. But the plight of the Board cannot affect the rights of school children whose skin color is no choice of their own. These children have a right to accept the constitutional promise of equality before the law, the equality we profess to all the world.[9]

There can be no question that Wright has a knack for eloquence that far surpasses what he has written (or approved) in many of his lengthier opinions. Just as his quick mind enables him to penetrate through legalisms to the core of the cases that come before him, so it is when he writes personally (and not with the collective help of his law clerks).

What makes J. Skelly Wright run? What makes him the workaholic that he is, the man who seldom takes a vacation, the judge who works the summer through in the fetid air of Washington? I asked him that question in July 1983. His reply, as always, was quick and direct: "I enjoy my work. Being a judge gives the opportunity to do some good."[10] That is the credo by which Wright lives—and works. He has no plans to retire. He still takes the bus on most days from his home in Maryland to near the courthouse, where he gets off and walks; on entering the building, he forgoes the elevators and literally runs—at least, jogs—the five flights of steps to his chambers.

The fact that he is able to devote full time to professional matters, and can accomplish so much as a judge, is in no small measure attributable to the gracious Helen Patton Wright, who understands the importance of his work and provides a harmonious sanctuary where he can replenish his energy for the next day's struggles "to do some good." She does not make him "run," but her quiet strength is of great importance to Judge Wright.

Wright is a judge who is proud of his ability to attract some of the best law clerks in the nation, often the top law students from elite law schools, and takes great pride in the fact that many go on to become clerks to Supreme Court Justices. That, of course, also is a reflection of the confidence that several Justices have in his ability to inculcate high standards in the clerks; an apprenticeship with Wright makes them wholly ready to undertake the task of being a clerk in the Supreme Court. (Two of his 1982-83 clerks went on to become clerks to Justice Sandra Day O'Connor, who by no means is on the same philosophical wavelength as Wright, but who knows that a year with Wright is about as good a training as any law clerk can get.) The judge presides over the activities of three law clerks and the invaluable Martha Scallon, who has been his secretary and assistant since 1959. More than once he has said that she is indispensable to him, that he "couldn't operate without her." She fits his needs perfectly, going about her work quietly and efficiently. Further, she has an excellent memory, and is able to recall details of her association with him with clarity and precision. Skelly Wright is a "clean desk" man, and Martha Scallon helps to keep him that way.

I have suggested previously that Justice Hugo Black was Judge Wright's judicial role model, and I believe that in large part this is an accurate assessment. Certainly, they were close friends; and certainly they saw many of the constitutional issues that confronted them similarly. Black, however, changed during his last years on the Supreme Court—a period that coincides in time with his marriage to his second wife—so that he became much more "conservative." That cannot be said of Skelly Wright. He remains a judge who has a passion for excellence, who works mightily to further the ideal of equality in the constitutional order, whose opinions remain essentially the same today as they were previously. He does not regret his decisions in the *Bush* or *Hobson* or *Georgetown Hospital* cases, and would rule the same today were he to be faced with like situations. He is aware of the criticisms that some of his decision have engendered, but shrugs them off. His critics have not changed his mind. When, however, their shafts become unduly sharp, he can fight back in a gentlemanly way. Thus, in 1971, he demolished his strongest academic critic, the late Professor Alexander Bickel, in an article in the *Harvard Law Review*.[11]

Wright believes that it is "unfortunate that judges are forced into managerial roles"—as in the *Bush* case—and that "any good judge would try to avoid that." "However," he says, "there are times when there is no alternative."[12] What he did in New Orleans was to "manage" the school system. Freely admitting that it was "not really proper judicial action," it was necessary because he was "trying to get the job done." That job, as has been noted, was the delegation from the Supreme Court to the "58 lonely men" in the South to put the decision in *Brown v. Board of Education* into operation "with all deliberate speed." Those 1983 statements by Judge Wright go far, in my judgment, to show that he is very much Establishment-oriented. Although he is willing to do some things that other judges scurry from, he nonetheless is uneasy about allowing the judiciary that much power. That attitude may be traced to his faith in the democratic process, a faith that, as was suggested in Chapter 6, is similar to that enunciated by Justice Louis Brandeis, a faith in the essential goodness of people and their ability to govern themselves. He is, accordingly, both a *d*emocrat and a *D*emocrat. In more ways than one, he is the Brandeis of the present era, the judge who sees the dangers in government spying, who tries to further free and open expression, and who perceives the threat that concentrated wealth can bring to the political process. Wright, like Brandeis, is far from naive. He readily sees through the pomposities of politicians; and he knows how politics really operates. After all, his uncle, Joseph Skelly, was a politician in New Orleans—and the man who got Skelly Wright his first job as Assistant United States Attorney. Wright saw, firsthand, the grimy politics of Louisiana, and seems to believe that politics in Washington is merely Louisiana on a national scale. But his faith in the people abides. He will not permit himself to become cynical, and, as the saying goes, would rather light one candle (of goodness) than stand aside and curse the darkness.

II

Throughout this volume, I have suggested that Judge Wright is also motivated by the Principle of Reason-Directed Societal Self-Interest. He is interested in helping the individual person, "no matter how small,"[13] but believes that in so doing he is also helping people generally. That, of course, makes him an "activist"—and even more, a "result-oriented activist." No one should cringe at the label. As was adumbrated in Chapter 1, all judges—indeed, all people—are result-oriented. In many respects, the same may be said of Wright as has been said of Chief Justice Earl Warren: "Warren cast legal controversies in ethical terms, identified instances of injustice, and sought to use the powers of his office to provide a remedy."[14] (There are many resemblances between Wright and Warren. Wright's penchant for "goodness" as the goal of judicial action is akin to Warren's oft-stated desire for "fairness.") Wright, however, recognizes that people will act from self-interest, and further believes that it is a principal task of society to create a social milieu in which self-interest will wish to be enlightened. He acknowledges that the courts have limited powers in such a situation. But within the ambit of their powers, there is much that judges can do.

Skelly Wright, like Warren, gets his ethical premises, not from a grand schema of moral philosophy but intuitively—from his well-tuned sense of right and wrong, from his "sense of injustice." He is also a "pragmatic instrumentalist." All of this raises the question about the role of reason in adjudication. If Wright adheres to views of social justice, as was suggested in Chapter 2, he knows and quite candidly concedes that those views are personal to himself—as, indeed, they are to all persons. Judges are no exception, although under the myth system they are supposedly exceptional beings who can divorce themselves from the facts of specific cases and impartially and uniformly apply the law. The facts are otherwise. Judge

Wright is not different from other judges in that respect. Where he differs is in his willingness to speak candidly and openly about how he makes decisions. He knows, as Nobel Laureate Herbert A. Simon recently stated, that "reason, taken by itself, is instrumental. It can't select out final goals, nor can it mediate for us in pure conflicts over what final goal to pursue—we have to settle these issues in some other way. All reason can do is help us reach agreed-on goals more efficiently."[15] How Wright goes about making decisions may be determined by excerpts from a letter (to me) dated October 9, 1963 (I asked him in 1982 if he still adhered to what he said there, and he answered affirmatively):

> I have now read your articles, "An Affirmative Thrust to Due Process of Law" and "Notes on the Concept of the Living Constitution." The first time I just skimmed them, as I do everything that comes across my desk. I want to say that I think your articles make a definite contribution to the dialogue between judicial activists and those addicted to judicial restraint—and on the right side. I believe that it is the duty of those of us who feel that the judiciary has a greater role to play to speak out in defense of those opinions of the Supreme Court which advance the role of judicial activism.
>
> I also agree with you that criticism of court opinions because they have not been "reasoned" or because they fail to expound the principles on which they rely and show how the principles lead to the result should be answered. In my judgment, a court opinion is not a mechanical thing producible by computer. *Intellectual honesty requires an admission that most opinions are result-oriented—initially, at least, visceral reactions to a given set of facts. Whether the initial reaction becomes the final result depends on a subsequent check of the legal authorities which support it. And if the initial reaction is strong enough, it will tend to overcome precedents which stand in the way.*
>
> As far as expounding the principles which underlie decisions is concerned, I believe that this function can largely be left to the law teachers and text writers, whose work can be used by subsequent courts in determining whether or not prior cases should be accorded value as precedents.[16] (Emphasis added.)

Obviously, Judge Wright and Professor Simon perceive the nature of reason in decision making similarly.

A need exists for legal scholars, as Judge Wright implied in his letter, to develop an accurate theory of judicial review in a nation that calls itself a democracy. Far too many scholars—the bulk of them, in fact—still adhere to outmoded notions of how judges should act. I do not wish at this time to repeat what was said in Chapter 2, but do suggest that the invisible chains that bind judges are not what there was called the "middle way" of "reasoned" or "principled" decisions. Rather, it is the extent to which the operations of the political process will permit judges to go. There are, of course, no set boundaries or limits; judges must intuit those limitations. Although they can, as Wright has said, be the "conscience of a sovereign people," and thus able to erect standards toward which the people might reasonably be expected to aspire, by no means can they be too far out in front. There *are* limits to what law can do; and as has been previously noted, Professor Martin Shapiro has suggested:

> If judges . . . are inevitably lawmakers, what happens to our prototype of independence, preexisting legal rules, adversary proceedings, and dichotomous solutions, and more particularly, what happens to the substitution of legislation for legal rules consented to by the parties? In the first place, lawmaking and judicial independence are fundamentally incompatible. No regime is likely to allow significant political power to be wielded by an isolated judicial corps free of political restraints. To the extent that courts make law, judges will be incorporated into the governing coalition, the ruling elite, the responsible representatives of the people, or however else the political regime may be expressed.[17]

The meaning is clear; the ties that bind judges are less "the law," for the law that comes to appellate courts usually exhibits the operation of the Principle of Doctrinal Polarity, than "politics." I do not, of course, use the word *politics* in a deprecatory or invidious manner. In constitutional and probably other questions, the storied Rule of Law is in fact the Rule of Politics.

Only by an indefensible fiction can it be said that constitutional decisions are either logical derivations from the sacred text of the Document of 1787 or latter-day discoveries of the intentions of those who wrote that instrument of governance. Those who exercise governing authority in the United States are limited mainly by the political process. This includes the judiciary. Despite the myth system, decision makers can in general do whatever politics permits. Some learned professors, such as Owen Fiss of the Yale Law School, do not like that; they call it "nihilism."[18] Like it or not, power rather than law is supreme—always has been and likely always will be. We may not approve of that, but it is something with which we have to live. It is not interdictory law, but politics, that determines the thrust and measure of significant governmental action. The decisions may be couched in familiar legal forms—statutes, judicial decisions, executive orders—but that is merely a counterpane under which politics operate.

If that, speaking generally, sets out what the judicial process essentially amounts to, it is quite obvious that an immense gap exists between pretense and reality. (That chasm characterizes legal education.) Judge Wright is fully aware of that differentiation, but nonetheless manages to walk a tightrope between the two opposites. He is at once a judicial craftsman, admired for the rigor of his opinions (even by those who dislike his conclusions), and a person with an instinct for "what's right." A political scientist who interviewed Wright in 1969 came away with the following impressions:

Despite time limits, a solid interview. Wright answered by deep furrowing of brows, closing eyes tight as if it hurt, then after a pause gave succinct replies. The interview took less time than others, but little time was lost. I got the impression that he was a man of quiet effectiveness, of controlled feeling and intense conviction, who probably did not antagonize others . . . because of his personal manner, courtesy, and (as suggested by another judge) the feeling that he was diligent in his homework and opinions. These traits are discernible in the interview; they became much sharper as other judges mentioned Wright.[19]

So it is today. Not for nothing did Chief Justice Burger, who dissented so vehemently from some of Judge Wright's criminal law decisions as well as the *Georgetown Hospital Case*, select Wright to be Chief Judge of the Emergency Court of Appeals (a position he holds today). Burger well knew that Wright has an enormous capacity for work, is well organized, is fair-minded, and would administer that court as well as or better than any other judge.

I do not imply that Judge Wright would agree with the outline above that it is the rule of politics, not the rule of law, that controls. If he has ever thought deeply and comprehensively about the subject, I am not aware of it. Nonetheless, to those who follow and study the judicial process, there is perhaps a tacit opinion that Wright believes in the pre-eminence of politics. Consider the following statements; the first comes from a law professor who does not know Wright, and the second comes from a law professor who was a law clerk of his.

I believe that Judge Wright has no superior in his contribution as a judge over the last three decades. His attention to manifestations of injustice—particularly his awareness of the ways in which injustice is uniquely potent when not readily apparent—is, to me, Judge Wright's outstanding contribution. . . .

You asked about Judge Wright's shortcomings. I do not know of any on a first-hand basis. I have never appeared before him as a lawyer. I would say of his judicial opinions that he has failed to resolve the dilemma of how paternalistic a judge may or should be. Of course, none of the rest of us has had much success with that problem either. . . . I would characterize Judge Wright's judicial philosophy as an approach which serves as a prime example of judicial creativity in playing the role of advanced judicial activism. By this I mean in particular Judge Wright's capacity for identifying, and identifying with, the victims of societal injustice.

It is in this context that I believe his decision in *Hobson v. Hansen* was a major contribution. I am well aware of the implementation difficulties. Nevertheless, I believe Judge Wright was breaking important new ground with the realism he introduced beneath the legalism of the day. Further, had the trend he pioneered continued, and become more rather than less popular, even the overwhelming implementation problems might have been somewhat manageable. Finally, constitutional law is and must be largely symbolic, and Judge Wright understands this well. I do not believe that difficulties in enforcement should entirely foreclose recognition of vital constitutional rights.

I have no first-hand knowledge of Judge Wright's performance as a federal district judge in New Orleans. I do know by reputation his record as an extraordinarily courageous judge. For this, of course, he must be counted as unusual and admirable. . . .

To summarize my views about Judge Wright, I would say that his judicial career has been a paradigm of the way in which judges should be aware of those excluded from society's benefits. His most outstanding opinions, and his non-judicial writing, generally seem to me to be a lonely, but vital, call to narrow the gap between law and justice.[20]

That statement well summarizes one view of Judge Wright. (As has been noted, other professors—mainly those who are votaries in the cult of Frankfurter worship—entertain different views.) The last sentence of the quotation, furthermore, appears to be another way of saying that Wright has been motivated by the Principle of Reason-Directed Societal Self-Interest. If so, then it is a perception of Judge Wright that he (Wright) realizes that in the last analysis the judges will not have the final say in vital questions of American governance. This seems to be the opinion of his former clerk, who is now a professor of law.

I have met several famous men in my life. Most of them . . . had lost their sense of proportion. Down deep I knew they felt they were better, more valuable, than those who achieved less. Not so Judge Wright. He is a true populist. He has little use for the perquisites which attract others who may have left-wing views because they believe it their heritage, or because they believe it a way to make their mark, or because they have so made their mark and now have expectations to fulfill. Judge Wright clearly came to his views not because it was the course of least resistance to adopt them, but because he knew right from wrong and he refused to let the mumbo-jumbo of the law obscure human injustice.

Judge Wright can be labeled a judicial activist and a judicial realist. He knows that judges inevitably have a certain power in our system and he uses the power to try to help people who need help in our unjust society. Justice may have little to do with precedent. Yet the impact of a ruling on the development of the law will turn on the respect it gives to precedent. Judge Wright understands this well. His impact derives from his great sense of justice (or if you prefer, equity), his willingness, desire, and ability to work with his clerks to support justice or equity somehow with the legal precedent, and his unwillingness to accept the facile rationalization of the law.

His greatest decisions were his early District Court anti-segregation decisions because those had the most immediate and the most lasting impact. Few social problems can be as readily addressed by the court as de jure segregation. *Hobson v. Hansen* was correct even if it did hasten an inevitable, unfortunate process. I cannot fault men like Judge Wright for believing that this country might do something about the effects of white flight and metropolitan residential segregation. It all is a question of political will. *Milliken v. Bradley* was decided by judges who were also judicial activists and realists. But like most judges, and unlike your subject [Judge Wright], their activism and realism is for the powerful and the rich with whom they number themselves. That really is the only difference. Some judges realize they are activists; then they are realists as well. . . .

Judge Wright loves politics; he loves people. He has the Catholic (albeit fallen) appreciation of the imperfection within us all. But he is truly willing to trust the democratic process when it functions fairly. He simply can smell when it does not. Judge Wright's hope, I think, is that some of what he can do judicially will strike a legislative and executive spark. He believes, I think, that *Brown v. Board of Education* and its progeny served this function, and helped bring us the great Acts of 1964 and 1965. He wants to do his part, but he has no illusions about courts being able to replace legislatures.

. . . By now you know that I think the judge is a humble man who was able to rise to the opportunity of history because he refused to identify with an establishment which he could perceive was responsible for flagrant injustices. He stands as a hero for young idealists, and as a model for responsible, aging activists. A man could do worse.[21]

Indeed, a man could. Judge Wright is not only trying in his decisions to catch the consciences of the politicians; he also is a role model for others. Consider in this connection the following assessment by the former dean of the Tulane Law School:

Judge Wright has been one of the noteworthy judges of America during his career. His career has been marked by unusual courage and the willingness to do what he thinks is right regardless of the personal consequences to his family and himself. He has been an activist nonpareil—though in late years his success has encouraged competition, not only in his own court, but in such courts as the Supreme Court of California. At one time, I thought he might become the intellectual heir of Justice Hugo Black and attain membership on the Supreme Court. His impact has been substantial, not only in the decisions he has rendered but also in the example which he has set among law students and professors. Many of them regard him as a model of what a judge should be. He not only has a set of values which are firm and clear, but he also produces opinions which are technically of good quality. He is a good speaker. His wife, Helen, is entitled to credit and consideration, also, in an appraisal of his career. She is an intelligent, attractive, articulate woman, with high ideals and staunch commitments. . . .

Judge Wright and Helen are very friendly and open people—no stuffed shirts there. While I would not want to bill this as a second coming, I will say that they are unusually good human beings who have really tried to help humanity. I am glad it has worked out so well. . . .

[Skelly Wright is] brave, bold and able. Those qualities have made him famous. In ordinary times and places he might have gone unnoticed.[22]

"Brave, bold and able"—that is James Skelly Wright.

It will not do to maintain that Judge Wright has been successful in his efforts to goad other governmental officers—and, indeed, the people themselves—into actions designed to further the interests of everyone in the

collectivity we call the United States of America. True it is that he has the
Progressives' faith in the malleability of human nature, as well as in the
essential goodness of human beings, but his victories have generally come in
the formal law rather than in the attitudes and behavior patterns of people.
He has not, because he cannot, altered the "living" law. No judge has that
much power. But that does not deter him. Nor should it. He continues to
erect standards toward which Americans can and should aspire. Law is
indispensable in the achievement of a better society. Wright sticks to his
last, keeping the hope and the faith that change will come, secure in the
knowledge that he has the respect and admiration of the people who are
important to him. His adherence to the Principle of Reason-Directed
Societal Self-Interest is an example of the judicial process at its best. He is
indeed the "conscience of a sovereign people," a jurist who has been "the
foremost explorer of what is new in every reach of the Constitution"; he has
"seen farther, and covered more new territory, than any other legal
professional of our time."[23] His is the vision of a free and sovereign people
equal in dignity to each other. The fault is not his, but ours, if we do not
hark to the cues of social justice that run through his hundreds of opinions
and several dozen nonjudicial writings.

Notes

Chapter 1

1. Interview with Judge Wright, Feb., 1983.

2. Grey, *J. Skelly Wright*, 7 Hastings Constitutional Law Quarterly 873 (1980).

3. A. Miller (ed.), On Courts and Democracy: Selected Nonjudicial Writings of J. Skelly Wright (1984).

4. Newsweek, Dec. 17, 1979, at p. 99, as quoted in Brennan, *Chief Judge J. Skelly Wright,* 7 Hastings Constitutional Law Quarterly 859 (1980).

5. 329 United States Reports 459 (1947).

6. Bazelon, *A Colleague's Tribute to Chief Judge J. Skelly Wright*, 7 Hastings Constitutional Law Quarterly 864 (1980).

7. Quoted in Bernick, *The Unusual Odyssey of J. Skelly Wright*, 7 Hastings Constitutional Law Quarterly 971 (1980).

8. Interview with Judge Wright, Feb., 1983.

9. See Rochin v. California, 342 United States Reports 165 (1952).

10. Kurland is quoted in Oster & Doane, *The Power of Our Judges*, U.S. News & World Report, Jan. 19, 1976, at p. 29.

11. Wright, *The Role of the Courts in Expanding Freedom: The Conscience of a Sovereign People*, The Reporter, Sept. 26, 1963.

12. Wright, *Professor Bickel, the Scholarly Tradition, and the Supreme Court*, 84 Harvard Law Review 769 (1971).

13. Letter from Judge Wright to present author, dated Sept. 12, 1980. The text from which the quotation comes reads: "In the Bickel piece I did I used the word 'goodness' as a test on which a judge's work may be judged. I used the word in its philosophical sense, which was intended to include considerations of whatever constraints are placed on judges by their oaths of office." In an interview with Judge Wright in June, 1983, he equated "goodness" with "justice."

14. Quoted in M. Mayer, The Lawyers 490 (1967; paperback ed. 1968).

15. W. Wilson, Congressional Government 30 (1885).

16. D. Miller, Social Justice 27 (1976).

17. P. Rhinelander, Is Man Incomprehensible to Man? 97 (1973).

18. R. Summers, Instrumentalism and American Legal Theory (1982).

19. See A. Bickel, The Supreme Court and the Idea of Progress (1970), criticized by Judge Wright, supra note 12.

20. Quoted in M. Cohen, American Thought: A Critical Sketch 163 (1954).

21. T. Arnold, The Symbols of Government 5 (1935).

22. 347 United States Reports 483 (1954).

23. 339 United States Reports 629 (1950).

24. Goldberg, *A Tribute to Chief Judge J. Skelly Wright,* 7 Hastings Constitutional Law Quarterly 862 (1980).

Chapter 2

1. Wright, *Professor Bickel, the Scholarly Tradition, and the Supreme Court*, 84 Harvard Law Review 769 (1971).

2. 384 United States Reports 436 (1966).

3. Richmond Newspapers, Inc. v. Virginia, 448 United States Reports 555 (1980).

4. See J. Peltason, Fifty-Eight Lonely Men: Southern Federal Judges and School Desegregation (1961).

5. 347 United States Reports 483 (1954).

6. 329 United States Reports 459 (1947).

7. See R. Merton, Social Theory and Social Structure 115-22 (rev. ed. 1968).

8. W. Blackstone, Commentaries * 69.

9. See, for example, Mishkin, *The High Court, The Great Writ, and the Due Process of Time and Law*, 79 Harvard Law Review 58 (1965).

10. F. Frankfurter, Law and Politics 62 (1939).

11. See Miller, *Toward A Definition of "The" Constitution*, 8 University of Dayton Law Review 633 (1983).

12. Quoted in M. Mayer, The Lawyers 490 (1967; paperback ed.).

13. Tushnet, *Truth, Justice, and the American Way: An Interpretation of Public Law Scholarship in the Seventies*, 57 Texas Law Review 1307 (1979).

14. G. Gilmore, The Ages of American Law (1977).

15. J. Ely, Democracy and Distrust 54-55 (1980).

16. R. Funston, Constitutional Counter-revolution? 29 (1977).

17. Saphire, *The Search for Legitimacy in Constitutional Theory: What Price Purity?* 42 Ohio State Law Journal 335 (1981).

18. R. Neely, How Courts Govern America (1981).

19. W. Galston, Justice and the Human Good (1980).

20. For a fuller discussion of the Francis case, see Miller & Bowman, *"Slow Dance on the Killing Ground": The Willie Francis Case Revisited*, 32 DePaul Law Review 1 (1983). This article contains citations to the details of the case that are set forth in Section II of Chapter 2. For that reason, only a few parts of Section II are referenced.

21. Interview with Judge Wright, Aug., 1982.

22. Ibid.

23. A complete, documented account of the Francis case is now being written by the present author and Jeffrey H. Bowman, with the tentative title of Death by Installments: The Ordeal of Willie Francis.

24. See Miller & Bowman, supra note 20.

25. A. Bentley, The Process of Government: A Study of Social Pressure 295 (1908).

26. See Wright, supra note 1.

27. Linde, *Due Process of Lawmaking*, 55 Nebraska Law Review 197 (1976).

28. Y. Simon, Philosophy of Democratic Government 123 (1951).

29. Frankfurter, *The Judicial Process and the Supreme Court*, in F. Frankfurter, Of Law and Men 35 (P. Elman ed., 1956; paperback ed.).

30. Wright, supra note 1.

31. L. Hand, The Spirit of Liberty 81 (I. Dilliard ed., 1953; paperback ed.).

32. D. Miller, Social Justice 20 (1976).

33. Ibid.

34. Ibid., quoting H. Sidgwick, The Methods of Ethics, Book III, c. 5 (1907).

35. Raphael, *Conservative and Prosthetic Justice*, 12 Political Studies 154 (1964).

36. Miller, supra note 32, at 26.

37. Corwin, *The Basic Doctrine of American Constitutional Law*, 12 Michigan Law Review 247 (1914).

38. Davies, *The Development of Individuals and the Development of Politics*, in R. Fitzgerald (ed.), Human Needs and Politics 74 (1977).

39. Maslow, *A Theory of Human Motivation*, 50 Psychological Review 394 (1943).

40. Bay, *Needs, Wants and Political Legitimacy*, 1 Canadian Journal of Political Science 241 (1968).

41. Galston, supra note 19.

42. Miller, Social Justice, supra note 32.

43. McCloskey, *Human Needs, Rights and Political Values*, 13 American Philosophical Quarterly 1 (1976).

44. Wright, *Judicial Review and the Equal Protection Clause*, 15 Harvard Civil Rights-Civil Liberties Law Review 1 (1980).

45. J. Pole, The Pursuit of Equality in American History 193 (1978; paperback ed.).

46. 95 United States Reports 485 (1878).

47. Pole, supra note 45, at 193.

48. Buck v. Bell, 274 United States Reports 200 (1927).

49. See, for discussion, A. Miller, Toward Increased Judicial Activism: The Political Role of the Supreme Court c. 4 (1982).

50. See ibid.

51. Miller, supra note 32, at 175.

52. Cf. H. Simon, Reason in Human Affairs c. 3 (1983).

53. Quoted in Hitchens, *Anthony Wedgwood Benn: Can He Put England Together Again?* Mother Jones, Nov., 1981, p. 14.

54. A. de Tocqueville, Democracy in America, quoted in Pole, supra note 45, at 131.

55. A. de Tocqueville, Democracy in America, as quoted in L. Berg, H. Hahn, & J. Schmidhauser, Corruption in the American Political System 11 (1976).

56. Bernstein, *The New Deal: The Conservative Achievements of Liberal Reform*, in B. Bernstein (ed.), Towards A New Past 264-65 (1963).

57. C. Macpherson, The Real World of Democracy 14 (1966).

58. C. Friedrich, The Pathology of Politics (1973).

59. Wright, supra note 44.

Chapter 3

1. Wright, *Public School Desegregation: Legal Remedies for De Facto Segregation*, 40 New York University Law Review 285 (1965).

2. For Jefferson's statement, see F. Brodie, Thomas Jefferson: An Intimate History 110 (1974; paperback ed.). To the same effect, Brodie quotes John Dickinson, Joseph Quincy, and George Washington; ibid.

3. Ibid., at 109.

4. Ibid., at 376.

5. 1 M. Farrand (ed.), Records of the Federal Convention (1935).

6. M. Jensen, The New Nation 178 (1950). See also Parenti, *The Constitution as an Elitist Document*, in R. Goldwin & W. Schambra (eds.), How Democratic Is the Constitution? 29 (1980).

7. J. Pole, The Pursuit of Equality in American History *xi* (1978); paperback ed.). and authorities cited therein.

8. See L. Bennett, Confrontation:Black and White (1965); Patterson, infra, note 86.

9. C. McGowan, The Organization of the Judicial Power in the United States 16-17 (1969).

10. See Miller & Bowman, *Toward an Interstate Standard of Equal Protection of the Laws: A Speculative Essay*, 1981 Brigham Young University Law Review 275, and authorities cited therein.

11. For a good introduction, see Pole, supra note 7.

12. 347 United States Reports 497 (1954).

13. Report of the National Advisory Commission on Civil Disorders 1 (1968: commonly called the Kerner Commission, named after its chairman).

14. Wicker, *Introduction* to ibid., at p. *vii.*

15. Ibid.

16. 163 United States Reports 537 (1896).

17. Cumming v. Richmond County Board of Education, 175 United States Reports 528 (1899).

18. Wright, *Color-Blind Theories and Color-Conscious Remedies*, 47 University of Chicago Law Review 213 (1980).

19. A. Bickel, The Supreme Court and the Idea of Progress 7 (1970).

20. See A. Miller, Toward Increased Judicial Activism: The Political Role of the Supreme Court (1982).

21. The Hobson case was in fact a series of decisions, the principal one being Hobson v. Hansen, 269 Federal Supplement 401 (1967). Critical commentary about that decision has been plentiful. See, in particular, D. Horowitz, The Courts and Social Policy c. 4 (1977). Horowitz asserts that Judge Wright "had apparently tried . . . to be relieved of his designated assignment." Ibid., at 119. Asked about that assertion in an interview in June, 1983, Judge Wright called it an "absolutely erroneous statement."

22. The statement about Judge Wright "ruining" the schools is by a Washington, D.C., law professor, who asked to remain anonymous.

23. See I. Jenkins, Social Order and the Limits of Law (1980).

24. 446 United States Reports 55 (1980).

25. Soifer, *Complacency and Constitutional Law,* 42 Ohio State Law Journal 383 (1981).

26. 101 Supreme Court Reporter 1584 (1981).

27. Judge Wright considered the late Professor Alexander Bickel to be his foremost critic. See A. Bickel, The Supreme Court and the Idea of Progress (1970). Wright's devastating response to Bickel is Wright, *Professor Bickel, the Scholarly Tradition, and the Supreme Court*, 84 Harvard Law Review 769 (1971).

28. See G. Garvey, Constitutional Bricolage *passim* (1971).

29. San Antonio Independent School District v. Rodriguez, 411 United States Reports 1 (1973).

30. Interview with Judge Wright, June, 1983.

31. Justice Douglas's observations were made in Chandler v. Judicial Council of the Tenth Circuit of the United States, 398 United States Reports 74 (1970).

32. Wright, *Are the Courts Abandoning the Cities?* 4 Journal of Law & Education 218 (1975). See Chemerinsky, *Ending the Dual System of American Public Education: The Urgent Need for a Legislative Action*, 32 DePaul Law Review 77 (1982).

33. Chayes, *Public Law Litigation and the Burger Court*, 96 Harvard Law Review 4 (1982).

34. Bickel, *Skelly Wright's Sweeping Decision*, New Republic, July 8, 1967, at p. 11.

35. Sherrer v. Sherrer, 334 United States Reports 343 (1948; dissenting opinion).

36. D. Horowitz, The Courts and Social Policy, supra note 21, at 273.

37. Chayes, *The Role of the Judge in Public Law Litigation*, 89 Harvard Law Review 1281 (1976).

38. Johnson, *In Defense of Judicial Activism*, 28 Emory Law Journal 901 (1979).

39. R. Summers, Instrumentalism and American Legal Theory 29 (1982).

40. O. Holmes, The Common Law 41 (1881).

41. In his dissenting opinion in Abrams v. United States, 250 United States Reports 616 (1919).

42. Cook, *Scientific Method and the Law*, 13 American Bar Association Journal 303 (1927).

43. Interview with Judge Wright, Feb., 1983.

44. Ibid.

45. W. Douglas, The Court Years 8 (1980).

46. Quoted in Lash, *A Brahmin of the Law*, in J. Lash (ed.), From the Diaries of Felix Frankfurter 3 (1975).

47. Pound, *The Philosophy of Law in America*, in Vol. 7 Archiv fur Rechts und Wirtschaftsphilosophie, as quoted in Summers, supra note 39, at 45.

48. A. Smith, The Wealth of Nations (1776).

49. Green v. School Board, 391 United States Reports 430 (1968).

50. Swann v. Charlotte-Mecklenburg Board of Education, 402 United States Reports 1 (1971).

51. J. Wilkinson, From *Brown* to *Bakke* 147 (1979).

52. Editorial, Los Angeles Times, April 22, 1971. The editorial went on to state: "The process is going to be difficult; the problems, multitudinous." Yet, said the Times, the Swann decision finally had demonstrated to the nation "what it truly is, and what it must become."

53. L. Graglia, Disaster by Decree: The Supreme Court Decisions on Race and the Schools 140 (1976).

54. See Milliken v. Bradley, 418 United States Reports 717 (1974).

55. I. Jenkins, Social Order and the Limits of Law 107 (1980).

56. Ibid., at 370.

57. Summers, supra note 39, at 29.

58. 21 United States Law Week 3165 (December 1952).

59. Quoted in J. Peltason, Fifty-eight Lonely Men 7-8 (1961).

60. J. Bass, Unlikely Heroes 112-113 (1981).

61. Aristotle, Nicomachean Ethics, in The Basic Works of Artistotle (McKeon ed., 1941).

62. E. Cahn, The Sense of Injustice (1949).

63. Bush v. Orleans Parish School Board, 138 Federal Supplement 337 (1956).

64. Peltason, supra note 59, at 3.

65. Y. Simon, Philosophy of Democratic Government 123 (1951).

66. See R. Crain, The Politics of School Desegregation 223-328 (1968); Bass, supra note 60, at 112-136; Peltason, supra note 64, at 221-51; F. Read & L. McGough, Let Them Be Judged: The Judicial Integration of the Deep South (1978).

67. S. Scheingold, The Politics of Rights 5 (1974).

68. Ibid., at 218.

69. There were several Bush decisions, the first coming in 1956 and the last in 1962. See the books cited in note 66, supra.

70. Crain, supra note 66, at 245.

71. Ibid., at 237-91.

72. J. Steinbeck, Travels With Charley: In Search of America 255-56 (1963).

73. Crain, supra note 66, at 295.

74. R. Michels, Political Parties (1911).

75. Bass, supra note 64, at 119.

76. 358 United States Reports 1 (1958).

77. Bass, supra note 60, at 112-36.

78. Ibid., at 123-24.

79. Ibid., at 128.

80. New York Times, Nov. 28, 1960, p. 34.

81. Bass, supra note 60, at 135.

82. M. Taylor, Community, Anarchy and Liberty 95 (1982).

83. Ibid., at 28.

84. Quoted in Bass, supra note 60, at 133.

85. Scheingold, supra note 67, at 204.

86. Patterson, *The Black Community: Is There a Future?*, in S. Lipset (ed.), The Third Century: America as a Post-Industrial Society 244 (1979).

87. Dowd, *A Comparative Analysis of Economic Development in the American West and South*, in H. Woodman (ed.), Slavery and the Southern Economy 244 (1966).

88. Patterson, supra note 86, at 269.

89. R. Freeman, Black Elite (1976).

90. Reid, The Ramification of Bakke and the Destiny of Affirmative Action, in C. Smith (ed.), Advancing Equality of Opportunity 53 (1977).

91. Jencks, *The Future of American Education*, in Patterson, supra note 86, at 279.

Chapter 4

1. Wright, *Beyond Discretionary Justice*, 81 Yale Law Journal 575 (1972).

2. Wright, *Judicial Review and the Equal Protection Clause*, 15 Harvard Civil Rights-Civil Liberties Law Review 1 (1980).

3. Schmitter, *Still the Century of Corporatism?* 36 Review of Politics 85 (1974). See also R. Harrison, Pluralism and Corporatism: The Political Evolution of Modern Democracies (1980).

4. Wiarda, *The Latin Americanization of the United States,* 7 New Scholar 51 (1979).

5. Schmitter, supra note 3, at 85.

6. Keynes, *Am I a Liberal?* in J. Keynes, Essays on Persuasion 331 (1931; reprint of speech delivered in 1925).

7. A Shonfield, Modern Capitalism: The Changing Balance of Public and Private Power 231 (1965).

8. Discussion of the impact of the Great Discoveries on the constitutional order and the imminent closure of an "ecological trap" may be found in two essays, which, when revised, will become a chapter of a book I am now writing (working title: "Getting There from Here: Constitutional Changes for a Sustainable Society"): Miller, *The End of a 400-Year Boom*, 24 Technological Forecasting and Social Change 255 (1983); Miller, *The End of a Four-Hundred Year Boom: The Need for Major Constitutional Change*, 8 Nova Law Journal 1 (1983). The essays suggest that such institutions as representative democracy and private-enterprise capitalism would not have arisen had it not been for the Great Discoveries that began with Columbus. Furthermore, the impact of those discoveries has now run its course, so that humankind finds itself back in an ecological trap not dissimilar from what was the norm before the Discoveries. The consequence is that inordinate strains are being placed upon the American constitutional order.

9. See D. Cater, Power in Washington (1964); Heclo, *Issue Networks and the Executive Establishment*, in A. King (ed.), The New American Political System 87 (1978).

10. G. McConnell, Private Power and American Democracy 361 (1966).

11. See Phillips, *Status and Freedom in American Constitutional Law,* 29 Emory Law Journal 3 (1980).

12. O. Gierke, Natural Law and the Theory of Society, 1500-1800, at *xxix* (E. Barker trans., 1933; paperback ed.).

13. Barker, *Introduction*, to ibid., at *lxxxv*.

14. J. Griffith, The Politics of the Judiciary 213 (1977). See Miller, *The Politics of the American Judiciary*, 49 Political Quarterly 200 (1978).

15. G. Lodge, The New American Ideology c. 6 (1975).

16. W. Mommsen, The Age of Bureaucracy: Perspectives on the Political Sociology of Max Weber 99 (1974).

17. J. Ellul, The Technological Society 305 (J. Wilkinson trans., 1964; paperback ed.).

18. J. Benda, The Treason of the Intellectuals (1927; R. Adlington trans., 1969; paperback ed.).

19. V. Ferkiss, Technological Man: The Myth and the Reality 140 (1969).

20. M. Baritz, The Servants of Power: A History of the Use of Social Science in American Industry 209 (1960).

21. M. Shapiro, Courts: A Comparative and Political Analysis 34 (1981).

22. F. Neumann, The Democratic and the Authoritarian State 8 (1957). See A. Miller, Democratic Dictatorship: The Emergent Constitution of Control (1981).

23. Wright, supra note 1, at 586.

24. Wright, supra note 2, at 4.

25. Greater Boston Television Corp. v. Federal Communications Commission, 444 F.2d 841 (D.C. Circuit 1970).

26. 5 United States Code Sections 551-59 (1976).

27. Wright, *The Courts and the Rulemaking Process: The Limits of Judicial Review*, 59 Cornell Law Review 375 (1974).

28. Ibid.

29. 514 F.2d 809 (D.C. Circuit 1975).

30. 478 F.2d 615 (D.C. Circuit 1973); and 483 F.2d 1238 (D.C. Circuit 1973).

31. Wright, supra note 27.

32. 431 F.2d 615 (D.C. Circuit 1973).

33. Wright, supra note 27.

34. 483 F.2d 1238 (D.C. Circuit 1973).

35. Wright, supra note 27.

36. Ibid.

37. Ibid.

38. Ibid.

39. Ibid.

40. Ibid.

41. Ibid.

42. 541 F.2d 1 (D.C. Circuit 1975).

43. 567 F.2d 9 (1977).

44. 435 United States Reports 519 (1978). See Yellin, *High Technology and the Courts: Nuclear Power and the Need for Institutional Reform*, 94 Harvard Law Review 489 (1981).

45. See B. Schwartz, Administrative Law Sec. 7 (1976).

46. National Labor Relations Board v. Seven-Up Bottling Co., 344 United States Reports 344 (1953).

47. Ethyl Corp. v. Environmental Protection Agency, 541 F.2d 1 (D.C. Circuit 1975).

48. H. Kariel, The Decline of American Pluralism (1961); G. McConnell, Private Power and American Democracy (1966); T. Lowi, The End of Liberalism (rev. ed., 1979); R. Dahl, Dilemmas of Pluralist Democracy (1982).

49. See Schwartz, *Legal Restriction of Competition in the Regulated Industries: An Abdication of Judicial Responsibility*, 67 Harvard Law Review 436 (1954).

50. Wright, supra note 1, at 583-87.

51. Ibid.

52. As Professor Kenneth Davis has said, "Lawyers who try to win cases by arguing that congressional delegations are unconstitutional almost invariably do more harm than good to their clients' interests." K. Davis, Administrative Law in the Seventies Sec. 2.01 (1976).

53. 538 F.2d 349 (D.C. Circuit 1976).

54. 333 Federal Supplement 582 (1971), affirmed without opinion, Capital Broadcasting Co. v. Acting Attorney General, 405 United States Reports 1000 (1972).

55. 473 F.2d 16 (D.C. Circuit 1972).

56. In the Vermont Yankee case, supra note 44.

57. 449 F.2d 1109 (D.C. Circuit 1971).

58. 479 F.2d 842 (D.C. Circuit 1973).

59. 371 Federal Supplement 1291 (1971; three-judge court).

60. 514 F.2d 856 (D.C. Circuit 1975).

61. 678 F.2d 222 (D.C. Circuit 1982).

62. 103 Supreme Court Reporter 1556 (1983).

63. N. Machiavelli, The Discourses, Book II, Sec. 2.

64. 501 F.2d 722 (D.C. Circuit 1974).

65. Ibid.

66. R. Summers, Instrumentalism and American Legal Theory (1982).

67. Sundquist, *The Crisis of Competence in Government*, in J. Pechman (ed.), Setting National Priorities: Agenda for the 1980s 531 (1980).

68. President Kennedy's statement may be found in the New York Times, March 8, 1962, at 14; President Carter's is in The Miami Herald, Jan. 15, 1981, at 17A.

69. Chadha v. Immigration and Naturalization Service, 103 Supreme Court Reporter 2764 (1983).

70. K. Kapp, The Social Costs of Private Enterprise 13 (1971; paperback ed.).

71. F. Cohen, Ethical Systems and Legal Ideals 261 (1933; paperback ed.).

72. Feinberg, *Autonomy, Sovereignty, and Privacy: Moral Ideals in the Constitution?* 58 Notre Dame Law Review 445 (1983).

73. A. Bentley, The Process of Government 268 (1908).

74. J. Davis, Corporations 268 (1897).

75. Drucker, *The Meaning of Mass Production*, 57 Commonweal 547 (1953).

76. Miller, *"Constitutionalizing" the Corporation,* 22 Technological Forecasting & Social Change 95 (1982) is a discussion of the idea that corporations are *de facto* governments.

77. D. Ewing, Freedom Inside the Organization (1977).

78. See Miller, *On Politics, Democracy, and the First Amendment: A Comment on First National Bank v. Bellotti,* 38 Washington & Lee Law Review 21 (1981).

79. Brest, *State Action and Liberal Theory: A Casenote on Flagg Brothers v. Brooks*, 130 University of Pennsylvania Law Review 1296 (1982).

Chapter 5

1. Zweibon v. Mitchell, 516 F2d 594 (1975).

2. H. Lasswell, The Analysis of Political Behavior 146 (1948; reprint of an essay written in 1937); Lasswell, *The Garrison-State Hypothesis Today*, in F. Trager & P. Kronenberg (eds.), National Security and American Society 431 (1973).

3. See R. Dugger, The Politician: The Life and Times of Lyndon Johnson (1982).

4. R. Nixon, The Real War (1980), quoted in ibid.

5. Wolfers, *"National Security" as an Ambiguous Symbol*, 67 Political Science Quarterly 481 (1952).

6. Trager & Simonie, *An Introduction to the Study of National Security*, in Trager & Kronenberg (eds.), supra note 2, at 35.

7. Ibid.

8. N. Machiavelli, The Discourses, Book II, Sec. 2.

9. F. Neumann, The Democratic and the Authoritarian State 8 (1957).

10. C. Friedrich, Constitutional Reason of State 4-5 (1957).

11. J. Locke, The Second Treatise of Civil Government par. 160 (J. Gough ed., 1966). See Hurtgen, *The Case for Presidential Prerogative*, 7 University of Toledo Law Review 59 (1975).

12. Zweibon v. Mitchell, 516 F.2d 594 (1975); Halkin v. Helms, 598 F.2d 1 (1978). Both cases have several different opinions; the citations are to the first, and principal, ones.

13. The Halperin case may be found at 606 F.2d 1192 (1979); and the American Security Council case at 607 F.2d 438 (1979).

14. United States Strategic Bombing Survey, Japan's Struggle to End the War 13 (July 1, 1946). See G. Alperovitz, Atomic Diplomacy: Hiroshima and Potsdam 236-42 (1965); Baldwin, *The Atomic Bomb—The Penalty of Expediency*, in E. Fogelman (ed.), Hiroshima: The Decision to Use the A-Bomb 95 (1964); Weston, *Nuclear Weapons versus International Law: A Contextual Reassessment*, in A. Miller & M. Feinrider, eds.), Nuclear Weapons and Law (forthcoming in 1984).

15. Goldman, *Playing Global Chicken*, 4 The Dial No. 2, at 9 (1983).

16. Quoted in C. Rossiter, Constitutional Dictatorship: Crisis Government in the Modern Democracies 3 (1948).

17. Wolfers, supra note 5, at 481.

18. In the American Security Council case, supra note 13.

19. For discussion of the rise of the National Security State, see Raskin, *Democracy Versus the National Security State*, 40 Law & Contemporary Problems No. 3, at 189 (Summer, 1976).

20. See A. Miller, Democratic Dictatorship: The Emergent Constitution of Control (1981); Miller, *Reason of State and the Emergent Constitution of Control,* 64 Minnesota Law Review 585 (1980).

21. See Bernick, *The Unusual Odyssey of J. Skelly Wright*, 7 Hastings Constitutional Law Quarterly 971 (1980), citing the New Orleans Times-Picayune, Mar. 30, 1949, at p. 1, where the quote in the text appears.

22. Interview with Judge Wright, June, 1983.

23. Dennis v. United States, 341 United States Reports 494 (1951).

24. Interview with Judge Wright, June, 1983.

25. 391 United States Reports 367 (1968).

26. 360 United States Reports 109 (1959).

27. Supra note 23.

28. In Knauff v. Shaughnessy, 338 United States Reports 537 (1950; dissenting opinion).

29. J. Bamford, The Puzzle Palace (1982).

30. 691 F.2d 272 (6th Circuit 1982).

31. J. Bamford, The Puzzle Palace, supra note 29.

32. The Olmstead case may be found at 277 United States Reports 438 (1928).

33. Quoted in Bamford, supra note 29.

34. The Pentagon Papers Case is New York Times Co. v. United States, 403 United States Reports 713 (1971).

35. That judges, particularly those on the Supreme Court, consider they are promulgating general as well as specific norms is well known. The overt practice began with Cooper v. Aaron, 358 United States Reports 1 (1958). But it is now a general rule. Certainly, Judge Wright believes that when he makes a decision, it is for more than the immediate litigants, as in a freedom of expression case discussed extensively in Chapter 6 of this volume. On the general question, see A. Miller, Toward Increased Judicial Activism: The Political Role of the Supreme Court c. 5 (1982); Miller, *Constitutional Decisions as De Facto Class Actions: A Comment on the Implications of Cooper v. Aaron*, 58 University of Detroit Journal of Urban Law 573 (1981).

36. See testimony of Floyd Abrams, April 21, 1983, before joint hearings of the House Judiciary Subcommittee on Civil and Constitutional Rights and Post Office and Civil Service Subcommittee on Civil Service, reprinted in 8 First Principles No. 5, at 6 (May/June, 1983).

37. L. Hand, The Bill of Rights (1958).

38. See the book and article cited in note 20, supra.

39. 494 F.2d 493 (Third Circuit 1974).

40. 4 Wallace 2 (1866).

41. 317 United States Reports 1 (1942).

42. M. Shapiro, Courts: A Comparative and Political Analysis 34 (1981).

43. J. Griffith, The Politics of the Judiciary 213 (1977).

44. Vagts, *Introduction*, to C. Beard, The Idea of National Interest (1934; 1966 paperback ed.).

45. 606 F.2d 1183 (D.C. Circuit 1979).

Chapter 6

1. This statement appears in Judge Wright's dissenting opinion in Capital Broadcasting Co. v. Mitchell, 333 Federal Supplement 582 (1971).

2. T. Emerson, Toward a General Theory of the First Amendment 3 (1966).

3. Abrams v. United States, 250 United States Reports 616 (1919).

4. Manoff, *Covering the Bomb: The Nuclear Story and the News*, 10 Working Papers Magazine No. 3, at 18 (May/June, 1983).

5. Geertz, *Ideology as a Cultural System*, in D. Apter (ed.), Ideology and Discontent 65 (1964).

6. Ibid., at 63.

7. S. Scheingold, The Politics of Rights: Lawyers, Public Policy, and Social Change 203-204 (1974).

8. 360 United States Reports 109 (1959). See Emerson, supra note 2, at 53-56.

9. 391 United States Reports 367 (1968).

10. Alfange, *Free Speech and Symbolic Conduct: The Draft-Card Burning Case*, 1968 Supreme Court Review 115.

11. Emerson, *The Affirmative Side of the First Amendment*, 15 Georgia Law Review 795 (1981).

12. Wright, *Money and the Pollution of Politics: Is the First Amendment an Obstacle to Political Equality?* 82 Columbia Law Review 609 (1982); Wright, *Politics and the Constitution: Is Money Speech?* 85 Yale Law Journal 1001 (1976).

13. The Columbia Law Review article, supra note 12.

14. Buckley v. Valeo, 424 United States Reports 1 (1976).

15. First National Bank v. Bellotti, 435 United States Reports 765 (1978). See Miller, *On Politics, Democracy, and the First Amendment: A Comment on First National Bank v. Bellotti*, 38 Washington & Lee Law Review 21 (1981).

16. Quoted in M. Mayer, The Lawyers 516 (1967; paperback ed.).

17. Emerson, supra note 11, at 795.

18. See Yudof, *When Governments Speak: Toward a Theory of Government Expression and the First Amendment,* 57 Texas Law Review 863 (1979). See also Ziegler, *Government Speech and the Constitution: The Limits of Official Partisanship*, 21 Boston College Law Review 578 (1980).

19. 519 F.2d 821 (D.C. Circuit 1975). Judge Wright discloses in his 1982 Columbia Law Review article, supra note 12, that he authored that language.

20. The Columbia Law Review article, supra note 12.

21. Buckley v. Valeo, 519 F.2d 821 (D.C. Circuit 1975).

22. Miami Herald Publishing Co. v. Tornillo, 418 United States Reports 241 (1974).

23. Compare, on this point, Miller, *Toward a Concept of Constitutional Duty*, 1968 Supreme Court Review 299, with Emerson, supra note 11.

24. Richmond Newspapers, Inc. v. Virginia, 448 United States Reports 555 (1980).

25. Miranda v. Arizona, 384 United States Reports 436 (1966); the Abortion Cases may be found at 410 United States Reports 113 (1973).

26. H. George, Progress and Poverty 404-5 (1879).

27. 395 United States Reports *x-xii* (1969; valedictory of Chief Justice Warren).

28. R. Dworkin, Taking Rights Seriously (1977).

29. W. Wilson, Constitutional Government in the United States (1908).

30. 703 F.2d 586 (D.C. Circuit 1983).

31. Women Strike for Peace v. Morton, 472 F.2d 1273 (D.C. Circuit).

32. Ibid.

33. Cowgill v. California, 396 United States Reports 371 (1970).

34. J. Barron & C. Dienes, Handbook of Free Speech and Free Press 198 (1979).

35. R. Snyder, H. Bruck, & B. Sapin, Decision-making as an Approach to the Study of International Politics 120 (1954).

36. O. Holmes, The Common Law 35-36 (1881).

37. See the recent book by Nobel Laureate Herbert A. Simon, Reason in Human Affairs (1983).

38. K. Kapp, The Social Costs of Private Enterprise (1971; paperback ed.).

39. For discussion of the general point, see Miller, *On the Choice of Major Premises in Supreme Court Opinions*, 14 Journal of Public Law 251 (1965), reprinted in A. Miller, The Supreme Court: Myth and Reality c. 5 (1978).

40. Interview with Judge Wright, July, 1983.

41. Frank, *Judge Wright and the First Amendment*, 7 Hastings Constitutional Law Quarterly 879 (1980).

42. Wright, *Politics and the Constitution: Is Money Speech?* 85 Yale Law Journal 1001 (1976).

43. 333 Federal Supplement 582 (1971).
44. See Barron & Dienes, supra note 34, at c. 4.
45. 562 F.2d 749 (D.C. Circuit 1977).
46. 405 F.2d 1082 (D.C. Circuit 1968).
47. 473 F.2d 16 (D.C. Circuit 1972).
48. 463 F.2d 837 (D.C. Circuit 1972).
49. 397 F.2d 687 (D.C. Circuit 1968).
50. 472 F.2d 1273 (D.C. Circuit 1972).
51. 450 F.2d 642 (D.C. Circuit 1971).
52. United States v. Washington Post Co., 446 F.2d 1322 (D.C. Circuit 1971).
53. Frank, supra note 41, at 905.
54. Whitney v. California, 274 United States Reports 357 (1927).

Chapter 7

1. Application of the President and Directors of Georgetown College, Inc., A Body Corporate, 331 F.2d 1000 (D.C. Circuit 1964).
2. Ibid. Judge Wright rendered his decision in 1963; the several opinions were published in February, 1964.
3. Feinberg, *Autonomy, Sovereignty, and Privacy: Moral Ideals in the Constitution?* 58 Notre Dame Law Review 445 (1983).
4. Ibid.
5. See M. Phillips, The Dilemmas of Individualism: Status, Liberty, and American Constitutional Law (1983).
6. J. Mill, On Liberty 125 (1956 ed.; originally published in 1859).
7. Feinberg, supra note 3, at 460.
8. T. Grey, The Legal Enforcement of Morality (1983).
9. S. Scheingold, The Politics of Rights (1974).
10. Told to the present author in a personal conversation by a man who wishes to remain anonymous.
11. Set forth in 331 F.2d 1000 (D.C. Circuit 1964).
12. Ibid.
13. Interview with Judge Wright, July, 1983.
14. 331 F.2d 1000 (D.C. Circuit 1964).
15. Ibid.
16. This memorandum came from Judge Wright's files in his chambers in the Court of Appeals, a copy of which he gave to me.
17. Interview, supra note 13.
18. 331 F.2d 1000 (D.C. Circuit 1964).
19. Grey, *J. Skelly Wright*, 7 Hastings Constitutional Law Quarterly 873 (1980).
20. Quoted in F. Read & L. McGough, Let Them Be Judged: The Judicial Integration of the Deep South 207 (1978).
21. Interview, supra note 13.
22. Ibid.
23. Ibid.
24. Mill, supra note 6.
25. Whether or not he realized it—he probably did not—Judge Wright was following the spirit and perhaps the letter of the teachings of the English Idealist

philosopher, Thomas Hill Green. See the discussion in Phillips, supra note 5, at c. 1 and *passim*. Professor Phillips traces the idea to Hegel. Ibid.

26. Interview with Judge Wright, August, 1982.

27. Address in 1980 before the Eleventh Annual Meeting of the Academy of Psychiatry and the Law (typescript received from Professor Dennis Koson, Nova University Law Center).

28. Ibid.

Chapter 8

1. Wright, *The Role of the Supreme Court in a Democratic Society—Judicial Activism or Restraint*, 54 Cornell Law Review 1 (1968).

2. Thucydides, History of the Peloponnesian War 15 (R. Warner trans., 1954; paperback ed.).

3. E. Thompson, Whigs and Hunters: The Origins of the Black Act (1966; paperback ed.).

4. Quoted in A. Miller, Toward Increased Judicial Activism: The Political Role of the Supreme Court 201 (1982).

5. Ibid.

6. J. Wilson, Thinking About Crime (1975).

7. E. Ehrlich, The Fundamental Principles of the Sociology of Law (W. Moll trans., 1936).

8. See C. Silberman, Criminal Violence, Criminal Justice, c. 8 (1978).

9. See Miller, supra note 4, at c. 11 and *passim*.

10. J. Wilson, supra note 6, at *xix*.

11. F. Browning & J. Gerassi, The American Way of Crime 470-71. (1980).

12. Ibid.

13. M. Clinard & P. Yeager, Corporate Crime (1980). See also Silberman, supra note 8.

14. P. Rhinelander, Is Man Incomprehensible to Man? 1 (1973).

15. J. Wilson, supra note 6, at *xvi*.

16. E. Fromm, The Anatomy of Human Destructiveness 435 (1973).

17. Interview with Judge Wright, July, 1983.

18. Browning & Gerassi, supra note 11, at 452.

19. Bazelon, *A Colleague's Tribute to Chief Judge J. Skelly Wright*, 7 Hastings Constitutional Law Quarterly 864 (1980).

20. Wright, *A Colleague's Tribute to Judge David L. Bazelon, On the Twenty-fifth Anniversary of His Appointment*, 123 University of Pennsylvania Law Review 250 (1974).

21. Interview with Professor Caplan, July, 1983.

22. 214 F.2d 862 (D.C. Circuit 1954).

23. Wright, supra note 20, at 252.

24. Packer, *Two Models of the Criminal Process*, 113 University of Pennsylvania Law Review 1 (1964). See also H. Packer, Limits of the Criminal Sanction (1968).

25. Johnson v. United States, 333 United States Reports 10 (1948).

26. 447 F.2d 1215 (D.C. Circuit 1971), reversed on rehearing, 471 F.2d 1082 (D.C. Circuit 1972).

27. 414 United States Reports 218 (1973).

28. Interview, supra note 21.

29. Levine, *"The Great Executive Hand of Criminal Justice"*: *The Crime Problem and the Activist Judge*, 7 Hastings Constitutional Law Quarterly 907 (1980).

30. Kurland, *Government by Judiciary*, 2 University of Arkansas at Little Rock Law Journal 307 (1979).

31. 115 Congressional Record 33,033 (daily ed., Nov. 5, 1969; remarks of Senator Ervin).

32. Interview with Judge Wright, July, 1983.

33. L. Berg, H. Hahn, & J. Schmidhauser, Corruption in the American Political System 12 (1976; paperback ed.).

34. L. Weinreb, Denial of Justice 3 (1977).

35. Di Grazia, *Police Leadership: Challenging Old Assumptions*, Washington Post, Nov. 10, 1976.

36. R. Clark, Crime in America 39 (1970).

37. Caplan, *Another Crime Report*, New York Times, June 15, 1981.

38. J. Auerbach, Unequal Justice (1976).

39. Quoted in Browning & Gerassi, supra note 11, at 119.

40. Silberman, supra note 8, *passim.*

Chapter 9

1. Interview with Judge Wright, July, 1983.

2. Statement by President Kennedy on introducing Judge Wright to Mrs. Kennedy at a White House Reception in 1963. Quoted to the present author in an interview with Judge Wright, August, 1982.

3. Brennan, *Chief Judge J. Skelly Wright*, 7 Hastings Constitutional Law Quarterly 859 (1980).

4. Tuttle, *Chief Judge Skelly Wright: Some Words of Appreciation,* 7 Hastings Constitutional Law Quarterly 869 (1980).

5. Ibid., at 871.

6. Interview with Judge Wright, June, 1983.

7. Quoted in Bernick, *The Unusual Odyssey of J. Skelly Wright*, 7 Hastings Constitutional Law Quarterly 971 (1980).

8. Judge Wright vividly recalls writing that statement, but apparently the document has now been lost. Interview with Judge Wright, July, 1983.

9. Judge Wright's case files from his tenure as a district judge in New Orleans are now in the Manuscript Division of the Library of Congress. The statement was written on the back cover of a "slip opinion" in an entirely unrelated case.

10. Interview with Judge Wright, July, 1983.

11. Wright, *Professor Bickel, the Scholarly Tradition, and the Supreme Court*, 84 Harvard Law Review 769 (1971). Bickel well knew about the article and its telling shafts against his position. He was unhappy about it. Conversation with Alexander Bickel by present author, August, 1973.

12. Interview with Judge Wright, June, 1983. The managerial role of judges has

232   Notes

been discussed in Resnik, *Managerial Judges*, 96 Harvard Law Review 374 (1982) and Chayes, *The Role of the Judge in Public Law Litigation*, 89 Harvard Law Review 1281 (1976).

13. See Wright, *No Matter How Small*, 2 Human Rights 115 (1972).

14. G. White, Earl Warren: A Public Life 350 (1982).

15. H. Simon, Reason in Human Affairs (1983).

16. Letter from Judge Wright to present author, quoted with permission.

17. M. Shapiro, Courts: A Comparative and Political Analysis 34 (1980).

18. Fiss, *Objectivity and Interpretation*, 34 Stanford Law Review 939 (1982). For effective refutation, see Brest, *Interpretation and Interest*, 34 Stanford Law Review 765 (1982). See also Brest, *The Substance of Process*, 42 Ohio State Law Journal 131 (1981); Parker, *The Past of Constitutional Theory—And Its Future*, 42 Ohio State Law Journal 223 (1981); Miller, *Toward a Definition of "The" Constitution,* 8 University of Dayton Law Review 633 (1983).

19. Interview with Judge Wright by Professor J. Woodford Howard, Nov. 3, 1969 (copy of typescript of interview; used with permission).

20. Professor Aviam Soifer. The quotation comes from a letter from Professor Soifer to the present author, dated April 28, 1982; used with permission.

21. Professor Michael C. Harper. The quotation comes from a letter from Professor Harper to the present author, dated October 22, 1981; used with permission.

22. Letter from Professor Ray Forrester to present author, dated Feb. 3, 1982; used with permission.

23. Frank, *Judge Wright and the First Amendment*, 7 Hastings Constitutional Law Quarterly 879 (1980).

Bibliographic Essay

There are relatively few biographies of American judges; of them, almost all are of Supreme Court Justices. State court judges rarely are nationally known, and judges on lower federal courts are generally little known outside their home states. It is fair to say that J. Skelly Wright is, except for Supreme Court Justices, far and away the best known federal judge. Even so, little has been written about his career. This bibliographical essay collects all the assessments of the professional as opposed to the personal life of Judge Wright as they appear in the literature. In addition, references are made to other relevant publications.

Judge Wright's own judicial writings—he has participated in more than 1,100 cases—are to be found in the standard law reports—*Federal Supplement,* for his district court days, and *Federal Reporter,* for his Court of Appeals tenure. Both are published by the West Publishing Company, St. Paul, Minnesota. His nonjudicial writings are listed in A. Miller (ed.), *On Courts and Democracy: Selected Nonjudicial Writings of Judge J. Skelly Wright* (Westport: Greenwood Press, 1984). Nine of his more important articles are reprinted in that volume (some are listed below). An assessment of the nine articles may be found in Thomas C. Grey's introduction to the book, "Radical Democracy and Judicial Review: J. Skelly Wright's Approach to Public Law."

The following articles, all of which appear in volume 7 of the *Hastings Constitutional Law Quarterly* (1980) are either tributes to or evaluations of parts of Judge Wright's career; Roger K. Newman, "Introduction" (pp. 857-58); William J. Brennan, Jr., "Chief Judge J. Skelly Wright" (pp. 859-61); Arthur J. Goldberg, "A Tribute to Chief Judge J. Skelly Wright" (pp. 862-63); David L. Bazelon, "A Colleague's Tribute to Chief Judge J. Skelly Wright" (pp. 864-68); Elbert P. Tuttle, "Chief Judge Skelly Wright: Some Words of Appreciation" (pp. 869-72); Thomas C. Grey, "J. Skelly Wright" (873-78); John P. Frank, "Judge Wright and the First Amendment" (pp. 879-906); Martin Lyon Levine, " 'The Great Executive Hand of Criminal Justice': The Crime Problem and the Activist Judge" (pp. 907-70); and Michael S. Bernick, "The Unusual Odyssey of J. Skelly Wright" (pp. 971-99). In addition, see Arthur S. Miller & Jeffrey H. Bowman, "Judge J. Skelly Wright and the Administrative Process: Activism or Passivism—Or Both?" 18 *New England Law Review* 807 (1983). Fuller discussion of Judge Wright's first case as a lawyer before the Supreme Court may be found in Arthur S. Miller & Jeffrey H. Bowman,

" 'Slow Dance on the Killing Ground': The *Willie Francis* Case Revisited," 32 *DePaul Law Review* 1 (1982).

Jack Bass, *Unlikely Heroes* (New York: Simon and Schuster, 1981) has a chapter dealing with Judge Wright's difficulties in New Orleans when he was desegregating the public schools. See also J. W. Peltason, *Fifty-eight Lonely Men: Southern Federal Judges and School Desegregation* (New York: Harcourt, Brace & World, Inc., 1961; paperback ed., Urbana: University of Illinois Press, 1971); Morton Inger, *Politics and Reality in an American City: The New Orleans School Crisis of 1960* (New York: Center for Urban Education, 1969); Robert L. Crain, *The Politics of School Desegregation* (Chicago: Aldine Publishing Co., 1968); Frank T. Read & Lucy S. McGough, *Let Them Be Judged* (Metuchen, N.J.: Scarecrow Press, 1978); Leon Friedman (ed.), *Southern Justice* (New York: Pantheon Books, Inc., 1965). All of these books deal with various aspects of school desegregation in the South. And see Owen Fiss, *The Civil Rights Injunction* (Bloomington, Ind.: Indiana University Press, 1979), for a technical discussion of the use of the injunction as a legal remedy. Victor Navasky, *Kennedy Justice* (New York: Atheneum, 1971), gives an account of how the Kennedy administration dealt with racial matters.

Little has been written about Judge Wright's career as an appeals judge in Washington, D.C. Donald L. Horowitz, *The Courts and Social Policy* (Washington, D.C.: The Brookings Institution, 1977) has a chapter that criticizes Judge Wright's decision in *Hobson v. Hansen*. J. Woodford Howard, Jr., *Courts of Appeals in the Federal Judicial System: A Study of the Second, Fifth, and District of Columbia Circuits* (Princeton: Princeton University Press, 1981), offers a general analysis of the work of the three courts, but with only incidental mention of Judge Wright. Specific criticisms of and agreement with some of Judge Wright's decisions are to be found in back issues of the *New York Times* and the *Washington Post*. The New Orleans *Times-Picayune* carried numerous articles about Wright, both as a judge and as United States Attorney.

Of peripheral interest are Carl McGowan, *The Organization of Judicial Power in the United States* (Evanston: Northwestern University Press, 1969); Richard J. Richardson & Kenneth N. Vines, *The Politics of Federal Courts: Lower Courts in the United States* (Boston: Little, Brown & Co., 1970); Alexander M. Bickel, *The Supreme Court and the Idea of Progress* (New York: Harper & Row, 1970). The last book was severely criticized by Judge Wright in Wright, "Professor Bickel, the Scholarly Tradition, and the Supreme Court," 84 *Harvard Law Review* 769 (1971); Charles V. Hamilton, *The Bench and the Ballot: Southern Federal Judges and Black Voters* (New York: Oxford University Press, 1973); Harold W. Chase, *Federal Judges: The Appointing Process* (Minneapolis: University of Minnesota Press, 1972); Kenneth N. Vines, "Federal District Judges and Race Relations Cases in the South," 26 *Journal of Politics* 337 (1964); Abram Chayes, "The Role of the Judge in Public Law Litigation," 89 *Harvard Law Review* 1281 (1976); Judith N. Shklar, *Legalism* (1964); Judith Resnik, "Managerial Judges," 96 *Harvard Law Review* 374 (1982); Michael S. Moore, "The Semantics of Judging," 54 *Southern California Law Review* 151 (1981); and Peter Westen, "The Empty Idea of Equality," 95 *Harvard Law Review* 537 (1982).

Judge Wright's views on the role of the judiciary may be found in the following articles that he has written: "Professor Bickel, The Scholarly Tradition, and the Supreme Court," 84 *Harvard Law Review* 769 (1971); "Judicial Review and the

Equal Protection Clause," 15 *Harvard Civil Rights-Civil Liberties Law Review* 1 (1980); "Color-Blind Theories and Color-Conscious Remedies," 47 *University of Chicago Law Review* 213 (1980); "The Courts and the Rulemaking Process: The Limits of Judicial Review," 59 *Cornell Law Review* 375 (1974); "Money and the Pollution of Politics: Is the First Amendment an Obstacle to Political Equality?" 82 *Columbia Law Review* (1982); "The Role of the Supreme Court in a Democratic Society—Judicial Activism or Restraint," 54 *Cornell Law Review* 1 (1968); and "Politics and the Constitution: Is Money Speech?" 85 *Yale Law Journal* 1001 (1976).

The following publications bear upon some of the more generalized discussions in the biography: David Miller, *Social Justice* (Oxford: Oxford University Press, 1976); William A. Galston, *Justice and the Human Good* (Chicago: University of Chicago Press, 1980); Orlando Patterson, "The Black Community: Is There a Future?" in Seymour Martin Lipset (ed.), *The Third Century: America as a Post-Industrial Society* 279 (Chicago: University of Chicago Press, 1979); Frank N. Trager & Philip S. Kronenberg, *National Security and American Society: Theory, Process and Policy* (Lawrence, Kansas: University Press of Kansas, 1973); Marcus Raskin, "Democracy versus the National Security State," 40 *Law & Contemporary Problems* No. 3 (1976); Kenneth Culp Davis, *Administrative Law Treatise* (St. Paul: West Publishing Co., 1958); Stuart Scheingold, *The Politics of Rights: Lawyers, Public Policy, and Social Change* (New Haven: Yale University Press, 1974); Thomas Emerson, *Toward a General Theory of the First Amendment* (New York: Viking, 1966); Joel Feinberg, "Autonomy, Sovereignty, and Privacy: Moral Ideals in the Constitution?" 58 *Notre Dame Law Review* 445 (1983); Herbert Packer, "Two Models of the Criminal Process," 113 *University of Pennsylvania Law Review* 250 (1964); Charles Silberman, *Criminal Violence, Criminal Justice* (New York: Random House, 1978); Owen Fiss, "Objectivity and Interpretation," 34 *Stanford Law Review* 939 (1982); Paul Brest, "Interpretation and Interest," 34 *Stanford Law Review* 965 (1982); Arthur S. Miller & Ronald F. Howell, "The Myth of Neutrality in Constitutional Adjudication," 27 *University of Chicago Law Review* 661 (1960), reprinted in Arthur Selwyn Miller, *The Supreme Court: Myth and Reality,* c. 3 (Westport: Greenwood Press, 1978); Julius Stone, *Legal Systems and Lawyers' Reasonings* (Stanford: Stanford University Press, 1964); Frank Browning & John Gerassi, *The American Way of Crime* (New York: G. P. Putnam's Sons, 1980); J. Woodford Howard, Jr., "On the Fluidity of Judicial Choice," 62 *American Political Science Review* 43 (1968); Nathan Glazer, "Towards an Imperial Judiciary?" 41 *The Public Interest* 104 (1975); Frank M. Johnson, Jr., "The Constitution and the Federal District Judge," 54 *Texas Law Review* 903 (1976); Karl N. Llewellyn, *The Common Law Tradition: Deciding Appeals* (Boston: Little, Brown & Co., 1960); Glendon Schubert, *Judicial Policy-Making* (Chicago: Scott, Foresman, rev. ed., 1974); G. Edward White, *The American Judicial Tradition: Profiles of Leading American Judges* (New York: Oxford University Press, 1976); Felix Cohen, "Transcendental Nonsense and the Functional Approach," 35 *Columbia Law Review* 809 (1935); Richard Davies Parker, "The Past of Constitutional Theory—And Its Future," 42 *Ohio State Law Journal* 223 (1981); and Herbert A. Simon, *Reason in Human Affairs* (Stanford: Stanford University Press, 1983).

Finally, for technical discussions of some of Judge Wright's many decisions, consult the *Index to Legal Periodicals* under the names of the cases.

Index

About the Author

Arthur Selwyn Miller is Professor Emeritus of Law at George Washington University and Adjunct Professor of Law at Nova University Center for the Study of Law. He is the editor of *On Courts and Democracy: Selected Nonjudicial Writings of J. Skelly Wright* (Greenwood Press, 1984), a companion to this volume, and coeditor of *Nuclear Weapons and Law* (with Martin Feinrider, Greenwood Press, 1984). His previously published books include *Toward Increased Judicial Activism: The Political Role of the Supreme Court* (1982), *Democratic Dictatorship: The Emergent Constitution of Control* (1981), and *The Modern Corporate State: Private Governments and the American Constitution* (1976), all published by Greenwood Press, and many articles in legal, political science, and economics journals.